Mega Mergers and Acquisitions

Also by B. Rajesh Kumar

MERGERS & ACQUISITIONS: Text and Cases

GROWTH STRATEGIES OF INDIAN PHARMA

Mega Mergers and Acquisitions

Case Studies from Key Industries

B. Rajesh Kumar
Institute of Management Technology, Dubai, UAE

palgrave
macmillan

Softcover reprint of the hardcover 1st edition 2012 978-1-137-00589-2

First published 2012 by
PALGRAVE MACMILLAN

Palgrave Macmillan in the UK is an imprint of Macmillan Publishers Limited, registered in England, company number 785998, of Houndmills, Basingstoke, Hampshire RG21 6XS.

Palgrave Macmillan in the US is a division of St Martin's Press LLC, 175 Fifth Avenue, New York, NY 10010.

Palgrave Macmillan is the global academic imprint of the above companies and has companies and representatives throughout the world.

Palgrave® and Macmillan® are registered trademarks in the United States, the United Kingdom, Europe and other countries.

ISBN 978-1-349-43487-9 ISBN 978-1-137-00590-8 (eBook)
DOI 10.1057/9781137005908

This book is printed on paper suitable for recycling and made from fully managed and sustained forest sources. Logging, pulping and manufacturing processes are expected to conform to the environmental regulations of the country of origin.

A catalogue record for this book is available from the British Library.

A catalog record for this book is available from the Library of Congress.

10 9 8 7 6 5 4 3 2 1
21 20 19 18 17 16 15 14 13 12

To my beloved wife
Sreelatha

Contents

List of Tables

Preface

Mergers and acquisitions (M&As) have become inevitable phenomena in the modern corporate environment. Whether in times of boom or bust, M&As have emerged as a compelling strategy for growth that has been adopted by most of the world's largest companies. This casebook analyses the largest deals by value undertaken by companies in different sectors. Five of the biggest ever blockbuster deals took place during the period 2000–2008. Vodafone's acquisition of Mannesmann, valued at $202.8 billion, is, at the time of writing, the largest deal ever recorded. Other major deals include AOL/Time Warner, valued at $181.6 billion and Altria Shareholders' spin-off of Philip Morris, valued at $113 billion. There are also the buyout of ABN Amro and AT&T's merger with BellSouth, which were valued at $98.2 billion and $89.4 billion respectively.

The pharmaceutical industry (Chapter 1) experienced a high rate of M&A activity in the 1980s and 1990s. Most of the largest firms in the sector are the result of multiple mergers. The Pfizer/Warner Lambert deal valued at $87 billion is the largest. The key drivers for M&A in the sector have been the desire for greater scale, market share, enhanced geographical expansion and increased technological capabilities. Pharmaceutical firms face major challenges on account of the patent expiration of a large number of important drugs. The cost of development of new drugs has compelled firms to undertake M&A activity to achieve synergies in research and development.

The ongoing regulatory liberalization and privatization of the world telecommunications industry (Chapter 2) have brought about fierce competition in both the domestic and cross-border telecommunications services markets. Trends in the late 1990s indicate that strategic alliances among huge telecommunication enterprises have been replaced by M&A. Costly investment is also forcing companies to undertake M&A. One of the reasons for the surge in increased market concentration is the fall in mobile telephony revenues.

In the technology sector (Chapter 3), M&As have become a strategic tool for companies to acquire new products and technologies in order to maintain competitive advantage, growth rate and profitability. Acquisition of knowledge is the main value driver for M&As in the IT sector. The latest trends indicate that innovations in security, smart mobile technology, cloud computing and social networking have become important strategic drivers facilitating M&As in the global technology sectors. A major change factor that has become a strategic imperative for M&As in the technology market has been the blurring of the boundary between the software and hardware sectors.

In the media and entertainment sector (Chapter 4), the strategic shift toward digital media, strong corporate cash reserves and proliferation of private equity firms have all acted as key catalysts for deal activity.

In the electrical and electronics sectors (Chapter 5), majors like Siemens have had a history of acquisitions dating from the 1890s. Cisco Systems, the master acquirer, consistently earned above-average returns and gained strategic competitiveness through its acquisition strategy. During the period 1981–2011, General Electric Company made 791 acquisitions.

M&A activity in the energy sector (Chapter 6) is concentrated in the Exploration and Production (E&P) segment. Worldwide deepwater assets are the major focus of attraction for multinational and national oil companies. Consolidation of oil companies is the result of high production costs and weak oil prices.

The major drivers encouraging consolidation in the finance sector (Chapter 7) are advances in information technology, financial deregulation, globalization of financial markets and real markets, increasing shareholder pressure for financial performance and financial distress. M&As in the banking sector are primarily aimed at reaping the benefits of economies of scale. Synergies in finance sector M&As may arise from client-driven, geographic and product-driven linkages. Over the past two decades, many governments have removed legal and regulatory barriers to financial industry consolidation.

Consolidation in the metal sector (Chapter 8) has been necessitated by the need to reduce the cost of production of steel and supply steel at competitive prices. Major steel producers seek low-cost producers in new markets or aim to consolidate their position in existing markets.

The strategic drivers for mergers in the automobile sector (Chapter 9) were basically for economies of scale, growth and augmentation of product ranges. The trend is that automotive companies are investing in strategic deals that could broaden their geographic footprint and strengthen their technology portfolio.

In the consumer goods sector (Chapter 10), companies are using M&A as a strategy to expand global reach, enter new markets and consolidate the focus on their core brands. Acquisitions are also used to vertically integrate and optimize supply chain operations.

Finally, in the airline industry (Chapter 11), mergers happen in anticipation of or response to changes in dynamic economic conditions. The nature of international aviation has altered as international markets have been gradually deregulated. Deregulation of the industry has also led to the rise of low cost-airlines. Mergers are considered as an efficient response to deregulation.

Acknowledgments

I would like to thank all the people in the production and editorial staff at Palgrave Macmillan who guided this book through the publication process. My special thanks to Virginia Thorp, Senior Commissioning Editor at Palgrave Macmillan, for accepting my proposal. I thank Keri Dickens and the team at MPS for all their support in the publication of this book. I also acknowledge the numerous articles and papers that appeared in magazines, newspapers and web sites that I had referred while preparing the book. I acknowledge the permission given by Deloitte, Common cause to use their data in my book. I thank my family for all the support. My special gratitude to my wife for her understanding and support.

B. Rajesh Kumar

1
Mergers and Acquisitions in the Pharmaceutical Industry

Introduction

The pharmaceutical–biotechnology industry has become increasingly concentrated over the past two decades. In 1985 the ten largest firms accounted for about 20 percent of worldwide sales, whereas in 2002 the ten largest firms accounted for 48 percent of sales. Much of this consolidation is the result of mergers. The value of mergers and acquisitions (M&A) activity in this industry exceeded $500 billion during the period 1988–2000.

The pharmaceutical (pharma) industry experienced a high rate of M&A activity in the 1980s and 1990s. Most of the leading firms in 2003 are the result of one or more horizontal mergers—for example, GlaxoSmithKline's antecedents include Glaxo, Wellcome, Smith, Kline French and Beecham; Aventis is the cross-national consolidation of Hoechst (German), Rhône-Poulenc (French), Rorer, Marion, Merrill and Dow. Pfizer is the combination of Pfizer, Warner-Lambert and Pharmacia, which included Upjohn.

The 1980s signified a period of tremendous growth and profitability for the pharmaceutical industry. In the period 1980–1992, the pharmaceutical stock index registered a growth rate of 959 percent compared to the Standard & Poor's (S&P) increase of 386 percent. Tremendous growth was achieved in the sector through innovations that were driven from adoption of more rational and scientific approaches to drug discovery and also through a market structure that allowed annual price increases in the range of 8–12 percent. The pharmaceutical industry's first wave of consolidation took place in the late 1980s, with mergers such as Smith, Kline and Beecham, and Bristol-Myers and Squibb. These mergers resulted in increased scale and scope as a result of sales force efficiency. The primary synergies in these mergers were revenue-based due to increased physician and geographical coverage. Pharma companies also benefitted from reduced costs.

By the early 1990s the scenario had changed. The average stock price dropped drastically and average price increases dropped significantly. The factors that contributed to dramatic change in the growth and profit outlook for the pharmaceutical industry included enhanced buyer power, increased competition from generic and "me-too"[1] drugs, the rise of biotech as an alternative, increased government pressure, rising research costs and major patent expiration. Pharma firms had to evolve strategies to limit buyer power, improve research and development (R&D) productivity and control costs. Mergers and acquisitions became a compelling strategy to meet these challenges. Pharmaceutical firms vertically integrated by purchasing pharmacy benefit managers (PBMs)[2] to help counteract rising buyer power. By the early 1990s, 82 percent of pharmaceuticals in the United States were sold through PBMs, chain pharmacies or hospitals. As a consequence, the weighted average price discount to distributors grew from 4 percent in 1987 to 16 percent in 1992. Efforts were initiated to develop R&D capabilities through the acquisition of biotech firms.

Above all the 1990s were known as the era of horizontal mergers. Companies such as American Home Products (AHP) and American Cyanamid, Glaxo and Wellcome, Hoechst and MMD, Upjohn and Pharmacia undertook horizontal mergers and acquisition for value creation. These mergers were basically for cost synergies. Others such as Merck, Lilly and Zeneca vertically integrated during this merger wave of the 1990s. Half of the deals occurred in the period 1994–1996.

These mergers dramatically increased firm size. Approximately 50 pharmaceutical mergers had a value of over $1 billion and accounted for 70 percent of the merger value. Ten of the top 15 pharmaceutical deals were horizontal in nature. The announcement of the top 65 drug acquisitions created $18.8 billion of value for the combined bidder and target. The largest of these pharmaceutical deals was Glaxo's 1995 hostile acquisition of Burroughs Wellcome. In the period between 1980 and 1994, Glaxo's sales increased from €618 million to €5656 million. This growth was led by the best-selling prescription drug in history—Zantac, a peptic ulcer treatment—that was launched in 1981. For much of this period, Zantac accounted for over 40 percent of Glaxo's sales. Wellcome's sales, which increased from €1005 million to €2662 million between 1986 and 1994, primarily on account of its leading product Zovirax (a product for sores/shingles/genital herpes), which also comprised 40 percent of Wellcome's sales. This drug was also the fourth best-selling drug in the industry for much of the 1990s. The US patent on this drug expired in 1997. Glaxo and Wellcome faced the challenges of a changing industry environment and the decline of their major sources of growth. By combining two firms with similar problems, Glaxo Wellcome created over $2 billion in stock market value upon the announcement of the merger. These acquisitions created value by reducing cost and enhancing revenue.

Between 1985 and the 2007, 51 large companies in the industry consolidated into only ten organizations. Mergers and acquisitions between large pharmaceutical companies will continue because they are an effective method of cutting costs. They allow the combined company to reduce staff in administrative support functions such as human resources, legal, marketing staff and senior management, and in research staff for similar product lines. During the ten years ending December 31, 2009, a total of 1345 mergers and acquisitions of pharmaceutical assets and companies were announced, with disclosed prices totaling more than $694 billion, according to DealSearchOnline.com.

Reasons for mega mergers

The key drivers for mergers and acquisitions were the desire for greater scale, market share, enhanced geographical expansion and increased technological capabilities. The top ten leading players account for 45 percent of the global market but no single company has a market share greater than 10 percent. One of the reasons for a spate of mergers in global big pharma is the hunt for pipelines and synergies in R&D. Now major pharma companies go shopping to build up their drug pipelines. They are searching labs, universities and research-based companies worldwide for new and interesting molecules. The increasing cost of the cycle of development of New Chemical Entity and the competitive pipeline of blockbuster drugs forces companies to consider the alternative options before them.

The merger of multinational giants Glaxo Wellcome and SmithKline Beecham Plc reflects how important research becomes critical for the survival of pharma companies. The rationale for mergers like Glaxo-SmithKline Beecham, Pfizer, American Home Products and Ciba–Geigy Sandoz (Novartis) were based on the perception that R&D-based large multinational (MNC) companies are still subcritical in size when it comes to investment needs for new drugs.

Table 1.1 Largest mega mergers

Date	Acquirer	Target	Value ($ billions)
June 2000	Pfizer	Warner-Lambert	87
December 2000	Glaxo Wellcome	SmithKline Beecham	76
January 2009	Pfizer	Wyeth	68
July 2004	Sanofi-Synthélabo	Aventis	65.5
July 2002	Pfizer	Pharmacia	60
June 2009	Merck	Schering Plough	41.1
December 1998	Zeneca	Astra	37
January 1997	Ciba	Sandoz	30.1
December 1999	Monsanto	Pharmacia & Upjohn	26
December 1999	Hoechst	Rhône-Poulenc (Aventis)	21.5
December 2006	Bayer AG	Schering AG	21.5
November 1995	Pharmacia	Upjohn	15
January 1995	Glaxo	Wellcome	14
December 1998	Sanofi	Synthélabo	11
March 2001	Johnson & Johnson	ALZA	11
May 1997	Roche	Boehringer Mannheim	11
August 1994	American Home Products	American Cynamid	10
May 2001	Bristol-Myers Squibb	DuPont Pharmaceuticals	8
March 1989	Smith, Kline	Beecham	7.9
February 2010	Merck	Millipore	7
May 1994	Roche	Syntex	5.3
March 2010	Teva	Ratio Pharm	4.9

Source: Capgemini, Ernst & Young Analysis, company reports.

Mergers and acquisitions often lead to synergy in scale and operations. In the global context, it is worth mentioning the story of Teva, the Israel-based generics leader, which doubled its sales to $2 billion of which 42 percent of the growth came through acquisitions.

The late 1980s and early 1990s saw the genesis of megamergers. The Ciba–Sandoz merger of 1996 that created the agribusiness giant Novartis realized enormous cost savings of CHF1.5 billion in the first year alone of the merger. Soaring costs and the impact on the highly complex supply chain that supported the manufacturing business were cited as strategic reasons for cost reduction at the time of merger. The Glaxo/Wellcome combination also realized significant merger synergies in terms of cost savings of 10.8 percent and 16.8 percent reduction in combined expenses.

One of the most obvious reasons to merge or acquire is a shortfall in the R&D pipeline. This was the position Glaxo faced in 1995 when Zantac, the world's best-ever selling drug at the time was coming to the end of its lifespan. Following its timely acquisition of Wellcome, the company renewed its pipeline overnight to create a substantial and innovative asset, which included drugs like Seroxat. Astra and Zeneca achieved geographic expansion and increased critical mass with their merger in 2000.

In 2009, Pfizer entered into an agreement to buy Wyeth. One study has estimated that, for the period between 2002 and 2007, US patents expired on 35 drugs representing approximately $73 billion in revenues. When a patent expires, revenues generally decrease drastically owing to sales from competing generic products, which can be sold at lower prices. Sales for Prozac, for example, fell by approximately 22 percent in the first year alone after it came off patent.[3]

Industry consolidation

Pfizer Warner Lambert Pharmacia AB Agouron Upjohn Company Monsanto (Searle) Esperion Therapeutics, Inc. Viruron Pharmaceuticals ID Biomedical Corp.	**GlaxoSmithKline** SmithKline Beckman Beecham Group Glaxo Wellcome Diversified Pharmaceutical Services, Inc. Sterling Health Block Drug Co.
Abbott Knole G Thera Sense, Inc. OS Pharmaceuticals	**Merck** Sirna Serono Medco
Wyeth American Cyanamid (Lederle) American Home Products H. Robins Co. Genetics Institute, Inc.	**AstraZeneca** Astra AB Zeneca Group Plc MedImmune Cambridge Antibody Technology
Sanofi Aventis Rhône-Poulenc Rorer Marion Laboratories	**Novartis** Ciba-Geigy Sandoz Eon Labs

Merrell Dow Pharmaceuticals Hoechst Roussel Uclaf Synthélabo Sanofi Fisons	Hexal AG Chiron
Bristol-Myers Squibb Bristol-Myers Squibb DuPont Pharmaceuticals	**Eli Lilly** Eli Lilly ICOS Corp.

Motives for consolidation in the pharma industry

Revenue pressures

The major challenge that faced the pharmaceutical firms in the early 1990s was the forthcoming patent expiration of a large number of blockbuster drugs without clear indication of replacements. In 2013, nearly $137 billion worth of branded products are expected to be lost owing to the expiration of their market exclusivity.

Pfizer's revenues from Zoloft and Zithromax have plunged more than 70 percent since the patents on the two drugs expired in 2006 and 2005. The biggest blockbuster drug—Lipitor of Pfizer—became off patent in 2011. Many pharmaceutical companies had to rely on a small number of drugs for much of their revenues. It does not appear that the drugs in the development pipeline will generate revenues that could match up with the revenues of expiring patents. Mergers have led to the consolidation of the industry. In 2012 only ten firms control nearly 56 percent of the managed care market.

Many of the past century's blockbuster drugs were for widespread afflictions like hypertension, pain management, sexual dysfunction and depression, which were quickly adopted by millions of patients, generating revenues in the billions. In contrast many of the products currently being developed could treat fewer potential patients. By one estimate nearly 75 percent of the drugs currently in the pipeline across the industry are such specialty medications. Even if these new drugs receive regulatory approval, the revenue generated will be much less than many of their blockbuster predecessors. In most cases these medications have to compete with drugs that are already in use as well as off-patented ones.

Costs and risk of development of new drugs

The pharmaceutical industry is a highly risky business with long-term payoffs. In the United States, for example, the average time from discovery to Food and Drug Administration (FDA) approval is around 15 years. The odds of a compound making it through this process are around one in 10,000, while the cost of getting it through is around $200 million. To cover this cost and risk, the drug companies depend on a few blockbuster drugs. Even for a large firm, it is not uncommon for one drug to account for almost half of its revenue. Despite these challenges, pharmaceutical firms earned consistently high accounting profits and experienced significant growth rates throughout the 1970s and 1980s. The peculiar way in which drugs were purchased was one of the contributing factors for these high growth rates.

The cost of research process is increasing significantly as many of the drugs are focusing on complex and difficult targets. Moreover, unlike in the past, instead of clear commercial applications, today's R&D research is driven by scientific discoveries. Another observed fact is that the regulatory approval process has become more complex and costly. The plaintiff-favorable litigation environment also has an effect on the company's profitability. During the last decade more than 65,000 product liability lawsuits have been filed against prescription drug makers. Of the 2900 drugs currently undergoing research and development in the US, 312 are targeted toward heart diseases, 150 for diabetes and 109 for AIDS.

Consolidation and alliances will transform the pharmaceutical market as companies adapt to the changing conditions. The pharma sector registered548 deals valued at $51.5 billion in 2010, which represented a sharp decline of 68 percent in value terms with respect to previous year. The largest deal in 2009 was the acquisition of Wyeth by Pfizer for $67.9 billion. In 2010 the biggest deal was the acquisition of Ratiopharma by Teva Group. Global pharma players acquired domestic generic and manufacturing companies in the emerging markets, which accounted for 50 percent of M&A targets during the period 2008–2010. According to industry experts, pharma—biotech mergers will increase in the next ten years.

Growth of GlaxoSmithKline Beecham through M&A

GlaxoSmithKline Beecham (GSK) is one of the world's leading research-based pharmaceutical and healthcare companies. Headquartered in the UK, GSK has offices in over 100 countries and major research centers in the UK, USA, Belgium and China. GSK is one among the few pharma companies researching both medicines and vaccines for the World Health Organization's three priority diseases—HIV/AIDS, tuberculosis and malaria. The company produces medicines that treat major disease areas such as asthma, antiviral conditions, infections, mental health, diabetes, cardiovascular and digestive conditions. GSK is also a leader in important areas of vaccines and new treatments for cancer.

GSK employs over 96,500 people in over 100 countries. Around 13,000 people work in research teams to discover new medicines. GSK delivered 1.4 billion vaccine doses to 179 countries in 2010. The vaccines developed by GSK have been included in immunization campaigns in 182 countries worldwide. GSK is one of the world's biggest investors in R&D and is the biggest private sector funder of R&D in the UK. In 2010, the company spent £3.96 billion in R&D before major restructuring, or 14 percent of total sales.

The products offered by GSK can be categorized into:

Prescription medicines: These include treatments for a wide range of conditions such as infections, depression, skin conditions, asthma, heart and circulatory disease and cancer. This portfolio consists of approximately 100 drugs.

Vaccines: GSK markets over 30 vaccines worldwide to treat potentially life-threatening or crippling illnesses such as hepatitis A, hepatitis B, diphtheria, tetanus, whooping cough, measles, mumps, rubella, polio, typhoid, influenza and bacterial meningitis. The majority of the vaccine R&D activities are conducted at GlaxoSmithKline Biologicals in Rixensart, Belgium.

Consumer health: This includes dental health products, over-the-counter medicines and nutritional drinks. Many of the brands, such as Sensodyne, Panadol, Aquafresh, Lucozade and Nicorette/Niquitin, are familiar around the world.

M&A growth history

Period	Event
1850–1899	In 1880, Burroughs Wellcome & Amp Company is established in London In 1891, Smith, Kline acquires French, Richards and Company, providing greater brands of portfolio.

1938–1949	In 1938, Beecham acquires Macleans Ltd and Eno's Proprietaries Ltd. Macleans toothpaste and Lucozade energy-replacement drink are added to Beecham's product line. In 1939, Beecham acquires County Perfumery Co. Ltd, manufacturers of Brylcreem, a men's hair application. In 1947, Glaxo Laboratories Ltd absorbs the Joseph Nathan Company and becomes the parent company. In 1949, Beecham Group Ltd acquires C. L. Bencard Ltd, a company specializing in allergy vaccines. It is a first step toward ethical products for the Beecham company.
1950–1999	In 1958, Glaxo acquires Allen &Hanburys Ltd. In 1959, The Wellcome Foundation acquires Cooper, McDougall and Robertson Ltd, an animal health company founded in 1843. In the mid-1960s, Smith Kline and French acquires RIT (Recherche et Industrie Thérapeutiques), a vaccines business. In 1969, Smith, Kline and French enters the clinical laboratories business through the purchase of seven laboratories in the US and one in Canada. In 1978, through the acquisition of Meyer Laboratories, Inc., Glaxo's business in the US is started, to become Glaxo, Inc. from 1980. In 1982, Smith, Kline acquires Allergan, an eye and skincare business, and merges with Beckman Instruments, Inc., a company specializing in diagnostics and measurement instruments and supplies. The company is renamed SmithKline Beckman. In 1986, Beecham acquires the US firm Norcliff Thayer, adding Tums antacid tablets and Oxy skin care to its portfolio. In 1988, SmithKline BioScience Laboratories acquires one of its largest competitors, International Clinical Laboratories, Inc., increasing the company's size by half. In 1989, SmithKline Beckman and The Beecham Group Plc merge, to form SmithKline Beecham Plc.

	In 1994, SmithKline Beecham purchases Diversified Pharmaceutical Services, Inc., a pharmaceutical benefits manager. Sterling Health also is acquired, making SmithKline Beecham the third-largest over-the-counter medicines company in the world. In 1995, Glaxo and Wellcome merge to form Glaxo Wellcome. Glaxo Wellcome acquires California-based Affymax, a leader in the field of combinatorial chemistry.
2000–2010	In 2000, GlaxoSmithKline is formed through the merger of Glaxo Wellcome and SmithKline Beecham. In 2007, GSK acquires Domantis, a leader in developing antibody therapies, Praesis Pharmaceuticals, a biopharmaceuticals company, and Reliant Pharmaceuticals, a producer of cardiovascular medicines. In 2008, GSK acquires Sirtris Pharmaceuticals, Inc., a world leader in sirtuin research and development. GSK also acquires the leading dry-mouth brand, Biotene. In 2009, GSK becomes a leader in skincare with the acquisition of Stiefel. In 2010, GSK drives Latin America growth strategy with acquisition of Laboratorios Phoenix.

The basic strategy of GSK[4] is centered on:

1) **Growing a diversified global business**: GSK is focusing on diversifying the business to create a more balanced product portfolio and move away from a reliance on traditional Western markets. Sales generated from these markets and products have decreased from 40 percent in 2007 to 25 percent in 2010. The company hopes to reduce the adverse impact of patent expirations on the group. The company expects to generate future sales growth by strengthening the core pharmaceuticals business and supplementing it with increased investment in growth areas such as emerging markets, vaccines, dermatology and consumer healthcare.
2) **Delivering more products of value**: With the aim of sustaining an industry-leading pipeline of products that deliver value for healthcare providers, the company has been focusing on improving rates of

Table 1.2 Key performance indicators of GSK

	2006	2007	2008	2009	2010
Turnover (£bn)	23.2	22.7	24.4	28.4	28.4
Free cash flow (£mn)	2623	3857	4679	5254	4486
EPS (pence)	95.5	99.1	104.7	121.2	53.9

return and delivering the best science in its R&D organization. GSK has one of the largest development pipelines in the industry, with approximately 30 late-stage molecules. The vast majority of these programs address unmet medical need and, importantly, nearly two-thirds are new chemical entities or new vaccines.

3) **A simplified operation model**: The focus is to improve the operating model to reduce complexities, improve efficiencies and reduce cost. Through the global restructuring program, GSK has removed £1.7 billion of cost since 2008 and is on track to deliver its target of £2.2 billion of annual savings by 2012.

The SmithKline/Beecham merger

In 1830, John K. Smith opened a drugstore in Philadelphia, and his younger brother, George, joined him in 1841 to form John K. Smith & Co. In 1865, Mahlon Kline joined the company. In 1875 Mahlon K. Smith and Company, was renamed Smith, Kline and Company.

In 1891, Smith, Kline and Company acquired French, Richards and Company, which provided the company with a greater portfolio of consumer brands. In 1929 Smith, Kline and French Company was renamed Smith, Kline and French Laboratories, and the company put more focus on research in order to sustain its business. In 1968, the company acquired Recherche et Industries Thérapeutiques in Belgium and changed its name to SmithKline-RIT.

In 1982, Smith, Kline acquired Allergan, an eye and skincare business, and merged with Beckman Instruments, Inc., a company specializing in diagnostics and measurement instruments and supplies. After the merger the company was renamed SmithKline Beckman.

Beecham was a British pharmaceutical company. It was once a constituent of the FTSE 100 Index. Beecham was the family business of Thomas Beecham (1820–1907), a chemist. Under Thomas' son, Sir Joseph Beecham, the business expanded, but remained a patent medicine company and engaged in little research. In 1943, it decided to focus more on improving its research and built Beecham Research Laboratories. In 1945, the company was named Beecham Group Ltd.

In the 1950s and 1960s, Beecham, in tandem with Bristol-Myers, developed penicillin derivatives. The group focused on pharmaceutical development. In 1953, it bought C. L. Bencard, which specialized in allergy vaccines. In 1972, Beecham launched Amoxil (amoxicillin), which became one of the most widely prescribed antibiotics. In 1986, the Beecham Group sold its numerous soft drink brands, including Tango, Top Deck, Corona and Quosh, as well as the UK franchises for Pepsi and 7 Up, to Britvic. The same year, Beecham acquired Norcliff Thayer, the makers of Tums, Oxy and Avail.

Merger highlights

In 1989, The Beecham Group Plc and SmithKline Beckman merged to form SmithKline Beecham Plc. This merger was termed a "merger of equals" since both companies had equal capitalization of £3.5 billion.

The merger of SmithKline with Beecham was basically to maintain their position as a world leader in the production of pharmaceuticals and consumer products. SmithKline was unable to restore the income from its core drug, Tagamet, in spite of an aggressive sales force in the US. Beecham, a consumer goods company, achieved success in its early research attempt on antibiotics, but had no competencies to become a major pharmaceutical player. Their merger resulted in an organization with an international marketing presence. The merger was aimed at combining the resources of the two companies to increase research and development capability and strengthen global marketing.

The consumer healthcare division formed after the merger manufactures well-known products such as Tums, Sominex and Aqua Fresh Toothpaste. In the year of merger SmithKline Beecham became the second-largest drug company in the world. On the basis of 1988 results, SmithKline Beecham had revenues of $6.7 billion, behind Merck & Company. The company ranked second in worldwide prescription drug sales and non-prescription or over-the-counter medicines, and fourth in the smaller market for animal drugs and medicines.

As a part of the merger, SmithKline sold off Allergen, Inc., an eye-care subsidiary. SmithKline also distributed to existing shareholders its 84 percent stake in Beckman Instruments, Inc., a scientific-instrument business. Beecham also sold off its cosmetics operations, including its Yardley, Margaret Astor and Lancaster lines, which in 1988 had sales of roughly $700 million.

From a financial angle, the deal was complex owing to tax considerations. The deal was designed to give shareholders of both SmithKline and Beecham equal values, dividends and voting rights.

For each share of common stock in SmithKline, holders received five common shares in SmithKline Beecham and one preferred share, allowing the shareholder to receive a special cash dividend of $5.50. In addition, each SmithKline shareholder received 0.5 share of Allergen and 0.18 share of Beckman Instruments.

For each share of Beecham common stock, holders received 0.8784 share of SmithKline Beecham plus $1.75, or $2.96, in unsecured loan stock, which was a cash-equivalent security often used as a form of payout in British merger deals. After the merger announcement, the value of both Beecham and SmithKline shares gyrated heavily in stock market trading. Some analysts opined that the merger deal undervalued Beecham.

Strategic motives for the merger

As a second-tier pharmaceutical maker, Beecham could not afford to spend heavily to develop and test a wide range of promising new drugs. Its R&D budget was less than one-third the size of Merck's. But on account of this merger, the R&D budget of the combined company was comparable to Merck's budget. Beecham was expected to benefit from access to SmithKline's sales force in the US and Japan, the world's two biggest drug markets.

SmithKline also faced formidable challenges. It was witnessing its fortunes waning along with the slow growth and decline of its anti-ulcer drug, Tagamet. Tagamet lost its ranking as the best-selling drug to Glaxo Plc's Zantac, a rival anti-ulcer drug with sales of $2 billion a year. Despite annual research and development spending of more than $350 million, SmithKline has not been able to develop new drugs to make up for Tagamet, and its diversification efforts have been lackluster. It was a matter of concern as it was certain that Tagamet's sales and profits would further plunge on account of competition from low-cost generic substitutes as the drug was expected to lose patent status by 1992 in Europe and in 1994 in US.

The Glaxo/Wellcome merger

Glaxo was founded in Bunnythorpe, New Zealand in 1904. Originally Glaxo was a baby food manufacturer processing local milk into a baby food by the same name. Glaxo became Glaxo Laboratories, and opened new units in London in 1935.Glaxo Laboratories bought two companies, Joseph Nathan and Allen & Hanburys, in 1947 and 1958 respectively.

In 1961 Glaxo Group Ltd was formed, with Glaxo Laboratories Ltd becoming its UK subsidiary. In 1971, Glaxo Holdings Ltd was established as the parent company.

Glaxo Laboratories Ltd produced about 80 percent of Britain's penicillin doses during World War II. After the company bought Meyer Laboratories in 1978, it started to play an important role in the US market. In 1981, the anti-ulcerant drug Zantac was launched, which became the best-selling prescription drug in history. Glaxo displayed its marketing prowess by beating out Tagamet in the peptic ulcer market, even though its product Zantac was developed six years after Tagamet. "Me-too" drugs were not supposed to be blockbusters. Glaxo also was active in biotech joint ventures, licenses and acquisitions. The most dramatic of these was Glaxo's 1995 acquisition of Affymax, the leader in combinatorial chemistry, for over $500 million.

In 1880, Burroughs Wellcome & Company was founded in London by American pharmacists Henry Wellcome and Silas Burroughs. The Wellcome Tropical Research Laboratories opened in 1902. In 1959, the Wellcome Company bought Cooper, McDougall & Robertson, Inc., to become more active in animal health. Henry Wellcome gave Wellcome a firm foundation in research, global outlook and marketing.

On Henry Wellcome's death in 1936 the Wellcome Trust, a charitable foundation for the advancement of research established under his will, became sole owner of The Wellcome Foundation. Wellcome became a public company in 1986 when Wellcome Trust sold 25 percent of its ownership to the public. It sold another 35 percent in 1992.

The company pioneered medical research, as well as developed well-known home remedies like Calpol. An academic-quality research tradition helped Wellcome to achieve the premier position in antivirals. Wellcome also became a leader in tropical disease treatment.

Merger highlights

Glaxo Wellcome was created in March 1995, when Glaxo took over Wellcome for £9 billion, in what was then the biggest merger in UK corporate history. The merger was completed in just seven weeks after the formal announcement.

The process started off on January 20, 1995, with Glaxo announcing its intent to acquire Wellcome. A shocked Wellcome management quickly rejected the offer and began seeking a white knight. It failed to do so basically because of the pledge by Wellcome Trust to sell its 40 percent to Glaxo. On March 7, 1995, Wellcome agreed to the merger.

The new pharmaceutical and fine chemicals group operated in 60 countries with 58,000 employees and had annual sales worth £9.3 billion. This merger was also significant in the context that it brought together two completely different cultures from opposite sides of the Atlantic.

Both the Federal Trade Commission (FTC) of the US and the European Commission cleared the creation of the world's largest prescription drug maker, with more than $13.7 billion of annual sales. Under an agreement with the FTC, Glaxo had to divest itself of rights to 311C90, a Wellcome compound for treating migraine that was in late-stage clinical trials.

Glaxo Wellcome, Inc.'s primary business was to market prescription products to physicians and healthcare providers. One of the top three pharmaceutical firms in the world, Glaxo Wellcome, Inc. held about 4 percent of the worldwide prescription pharmaceutical market. The US market represented approximately 40 percent of worldwide sales while the UK produced about 7 percent for the UK-based company. Migraine medicine was a primary growth area for Glaxo. The company was the first to manufacture and market triptans, a new class of prescription migraine medicine.

Glaxo Wellcome created over $2 billion in stock market value upon the announcement of the merger. Glaxo paid a 40 percent premium (or $3.8 billion) for Wellcome. Three days later, Glaxo announced the acquisition of Affymax, a leader in combinatorial chemistry, for $592 million. Event study analysis of the merger reveals that Glaxo paid a 40.7 percent premium for Wellcome, increasing Wellcome shareholder value by $3.8 billion.[5]

Motives for the acquisition

Glaxo's sales increased from €618 million to €5656 million between 1980 and 1994. This growth was led by the best-selling prescription drug, Zantac, which accounted for over 40 percent of Glaxo's sales. Wellcome's sales increased from €1005 million to €2662 million between 1986 and 1994. Its leading product, Zovirax (a treatment for genital herpes and shingles first sold in 1982), also accounted for over 40 percent of Wellcome's sales and was the fourth best-selling drug in the industry for much of the 1990s.

Glaxo and Wellcome faced the challenges of a changing industry environment and the decline of their major sources of growth since the US patents on both these drugs were expected to expire in 1997. Glaxo and Wellcome's phenomenal successes with Zantac and Zovirax, respectively, turned out to be a double-edged sword. Glaxo and Wellcome were employing the classic defenses of these products, including improved formulation, litigation to delay early entry and moving to over-the-counter (OTC) status before expiration (although Zovirax was denied FDA approval for OTC). Despite these efforts, analysts estimated that both products would lose two-thirds or more of sales by the year 2000. Generic drug firms were ready to move as soon as the Zantac and Zovirax patents expired.

By the end of 1996, three firms had production facilities with tentative FDA approval ready to produce a generic Zantac. Valtrex, Wellcome's improved formulation of Zovirax, already faced competition from a similar SmithKline Beecham drug, Famvir.

Multiple sources of competition for new unique successful drugs developed by Glaxo, like the migraine drug Imitrex, were just on the horizon (including one developed by Wellcome). While Wellcome retained its premier position in antivirals, competition in this area was increasing. The US government continued to put pressure on Wellcome to keep prices down and the French government has complained about the high price of Imitrex. Hospitals, HMOs and PBMs have been successful in obtaining rebates on Wellcome and Glaxo products even before patent expiration and the onset of new competition.

The cost of doing research continued to rise. Zantac and Zovirax were generating enough money to cover these costs and still build up cash reserves, but time was running out. Glaxo struggled to find a replacement for its blockbuster, whose patent has expired in the US, and for Zovirax, Wellcome's anti-herpes drug, which has already become available without a prescription.

Glaxo had high hopes for its anti-flu drug, Relenza, and was disappointed when the UK's National Institute for Clinical Excellence (NICE) told doctors not to routinely prescribe the drug on the National Health Service.

Glaxo's CEO attributed this merger to two aspects—the squeeze on healthcare costs caused by recession, whereby drug companies became easy targets for governments to cut costs, and the expected decline in revenues on account of off patents. It is often stated that Glaxo's acquisition of Wellcome produced only short-term savings but no long-term growth.

The Glaxo/SmithKline merger

On January 17, 2000, Glaxo Wellcome and SmithKline Beecham announced their $76 billion proposed merger, which gave the combined company a global market share of 7.3 percent and an R&D budget of $4 billion. The merger, termed as the "merger of equals," created the world's largest pharmaceutical company, with combined sales of approximately $24.9 billion. On July 31, 2000, the merger was approved by the shareholders of Glaxo Wellcome and SmithKline. The board of directors was drawn equally from the existing Glaxo Wellcome and SmithKline Beecham boards. GSK has its primary listing on the London Stock Exchange and is a constituent of the FTSE 100 Index. It has a secondary listing on the New York Stock Exchange.

Features of the combined group

- Enhanced R&D capability combining both companies' expertise and technology. The key benefit of the merger for SmithKline Beecham was that the combined company's increased pharmaceutical revenues provided greater funds for pharmaceutical R&D. The combined company had the highest R&D budget in the industry.
- One of the most extensive development pipelines in the pharmaceutical industry, with a total of 30 new chemical entities (NCEs) and 19 vaccines in clinical development (phase II/III), of which 13 NCEs and ten vaccines were in late-stage development (phase III).
- A market leader in four of the five largest therapeutic categories in the pharmaceutical industry: anti-infectives, CNS, respiratory, alimentary and metabolic.
- A leading position in the vaccines market and a strong position in consumer healthcare and over-the-counter medicines.
- An industry-leading sales and marketing force of approximately 40,000 employees globally.
- It was estimated that up to 15,000 jobs losses would occur worldwide and about 5000 job losses in the UK alone.
- A truly global organization with wide geographic spread and strong presence in the important US market.

Medium of exchange

Under the Scheme of Arrangement, Glaxo Wellcome shareholders and SmithKline Beecham shareholders received shares in a new holding company, Glaxo SmithKline. Glaxo Wellcome shareholders received approximately 58.75 percent of the issued ordinary share capital of Glaxo SmithKline and SmithKline Beecham shareholders received approximately 41.25 percent of the issued ordinary share capital of Glaxo SmithKline.

Under the arrangement shareholders of Glaxo Wellcome Plc and SmithKline Beecham Plc received shares in GlaxoSmithKline as follows:

For each Glaxo Wellcome share—one GlaxoSmithKline share.
For each SmithKline Beecham share—0.4552 GlaxoSmithKline shares.

Regulatory constraints

Initially the Federal Trade Commission (FTC) alleged that the merger of Glaxo Wellcome and SmithKline Beecham would create a monopoly in the manufacture of certain products, and with the elimination of competition, post-merger prices would be likely to increase for some products resulting in unfavorable prices for the consumer. Later on the approval was given.

Advantages of the merger

Economies of scale in the pharmaceutical sector: Based on September 1999 moving annual total (MAT) market estimates of pharmaceutical industry sales, GlaxoSmithKline had been ranked the largest pharmaceutical company in the world. Based on combined 1998 pharmaceutical sales, GlaxoSmithKline would have derived approximately 45 percent of revenues from the United States, approximately 33 percent from Europe and approximately 22 percent from the rest of the world. As a result of the merger GlaxoSmithKline became the world's biggest producer of prescription drugs and had a market share of more than 7 percent.

Avoidance of increased R&D costs: Rising R&D costs have meant that drug companies have been unable to pursue research projects alone and have had to utilize the expertise and resources of other drug companies in order to survive in a cutthroat market. R&D investment was rising, with an increasing proportion to sales from $20 billion in the 1990s to $35 billion in 1999.

Enhanced R&D capability: GlaxoSmithKline was described as the 'most powerful force in British science' after the UK government, with research and development spending at more than £2 billion a year accounting for almost 50 percent of such expenditure in the industry.

The merger was aimed to help GlaxoSmithKline become the most productive research organization in the pharmaceutical industry by means of creating more drug targets and reducing time to market through the integration of technologies. At the time of the merger, GlaxoSmithKline was expected to have one of the most extensive development pipelines in the pharmaceutical industry, with a total of 30 NCEs and 19 vaccines in various clinical development stages. Patent expiry can reduce innovator sale up to 80 percent, hence it was argued that merging research laboratories and product pipelines would result in added knowledge from which potential blockbuster drugs could emerge.

Improved marketing communication: GlaxoSmithKline Beecham, with one of the largest sales force and marketing resources in the global pharmaceutical industry, was expected to enhance its influence with physicians and opinion leaders in the healthcare industry.

SmithKline Beecham's strong consumer healthcare and OTC medicine businesses were expected to provide value to GlaxoSmithKline with enhanced expertise in consumer-oriented marketing strategies, which could benefit sales of prescription pharmaceutical products.

Enlarged complementary portfolio: In terms of portfolio-fit strategies, Glaxo Wellcome and SmithKline Beecham had two core areas in common: anti-infectives and CNS. The merger was aimed at enhancing the strength of the combined company in these markets and creating synergies between the two company's sales and R&D infrastructure. As SmithKline Beecham's anti-infectives portfolio was focused on antibacterial, while Glaxo Wellcome's was focused on antivirals, few product divestments were required.

Significant cost savings were also expected through the strengthening of cancer and gastrointestinal portfolios. Moreover Glaxo Wellcome's respiratory therapeutic area combined with SmithKline Beecham's strength in vaccines and arthritis was expected to broaden the portfolio with little reliance on any one therapy area. Significant potential for cost synergies also existed between Glaxo Wellcome and SmithKline Beecham's R&D pipelines, both being focused on anti-infectives, CNS and cardiovascular products. In addition to having a broad portfolio of products, GlaxoSmithKline became a leader in four of the five largest therapeutic areas, which together represented approximately 50 percent of the global pharmaceutical market. This was complemented by a leading position in vaccines.

Synergies and cost savings: The merger was expected to generate substantial operational synergies, and the two companies estimated that annual pre-tax cost savings of £1.0 billion were achievable from the third anniversary of completion of the merger. It was expected that £250 million of these savings would be derived from combining the two R&D organizations and would be reinvested in R&D. The other cost savings of £750 million were expected to come from reducing the overlap in administration, selling and marketing and manufacturing facilities.

Geographic strategy: Glaxo Wellcome had a strong global presence, with only 44.7 percent of total sales derived from the US in 1998. SmithKline Beecham was more US-focused, with US revenues making up 51 percent of total sales in 1998. The merger between Glaxo Wellcome and SmithKline Beecham was aimed at significantly increasing both companies' global strength. In US the merged company had one of the largest sales forces in the industry. Thus the merger benefitted both the companies in increasing geographic strength.

The American Home Products/Cyanamid deal

American Home Products

AHP is one of the largest healthcare concerns in US. The company also has food and household product divisions. The company originated with the merger of several companies in related businesses. It focused on the strategy of licensing rather than building its own in-house capabilities for drug discovery and commercialization.

By the end of the 1930s, American Home Products had acquired firms in six major businesses, which included drug preparations. Early in the postwar era, AHP moved out of chemicals but continued to expand its other lines, both by internal investment and acquisition. In pharmaceuticals, it concentrated on enlarging its OTC business by exploiting its advertising skills.

By 1979 it had developed a broader line of new prescription drugs. By this time prescription drugs accounted for 39 percent of total sales and 55 percent of net income. As the company expanded its high-technology line, it divested itself of its cosmetics and toilet preparations.

In the early 1980s, AHP decided to enlarge its higher-value-added healthcare business by attaching medical equipment to its portfolio and by divesting itself of the lower-margin non-healthcare divisions.

AHP acquired John Wyeth & Brother, Inc. in 1931, Ayerst Laboratories in 1943, Sherwood Medical in 1982, and American Cyanamid in 1994. In 2002, American Home Products completed the transformation of itself into a strictly pharmaceutical company named Wyeth.

In 1986, AHP bought Chesebrough-Pond's hospital-supply products division for $260 million to reinforce its earlier acquisition of Sherwood. In 1987 came the company's purchase of Bristol-Myers's animal healthcare division for $62 million and the acquisition of VLI, the producer of a contraceptive sponge, for $74 million.

Each of these product lines was administered through a separate division integrating product development and marketing, but without significant research capability.

In 1988, the company acquired A. H. Robbins, which was involved in OTC business, making it second in sales after Johnson & Johnson. The acquisition strengthened AHP's new animal health unit and established prescription drug line.

Though over the decade the company had built capabilities in production and marketing, still it had yet to develop in-house capabilities in R&D and commercialization of new biotechnology. This lack of technical capabilities led to two major acquisitions in the twentieth century. In 1989, AHP acquired, for $666 million, 60 percent of the equity of Genetics Institute. This same lack of technical capabilities on the part of AHP appeared to have accounted for the larger acquisition of American Cyanamid in 1994.

American Cyanamid

American Cyanamid was a large, diversified American chemical manufacturer founded by Frank Washburn in 1907. Lederle Laboratories was Cyanamid's pharmaceutical division, which made products like Centrum, Stresstabs, vitamins and the Orimune Sabin oral polio vaccine.

American Cyanamid was the only major American chemical company to enter the prescription drug business on a significant scale during the antibiotic revolution of the 1940s. It expanded steadily and so successfully in prescription drugs that in 1992 it spun off its remaining chemical business to its stockholders. With the 1992 announcement that it would sell Cytec to its shareholders, Cyanamid virtually finished its transformation from a chemical to a drug and agricultural products company.

In addition, the American Cyanamid purchase included Immunex, one of the very few biotech startups that had surpassed $100 million in revenues. In this way the acquisition of American Cyanamid provided American Home Products with a technical learning base in the innovative technologies of the 1970s and 1980s that it could hardly have built with its own internal resources.

In the 1980s, American Cyanamid moved from diversification into divestment of unprofitable product lines. In the mid-1980s, American Cyanamid shifted increasingly into pharmaceuticals via purchases and joint ventures. It bought 49.9 percent of Langford Labs, a Canadian company specializing in veterinary biologicals, and signed an agreement to jointly develop and market veterinary products with Enzon.

It bought Acufex Microsurgical, a medical equipment manufacturer, for $19 million, Storz Instrument for $100 million, and then, in mid-1986, formed a medical devices division.

Deal highlights

AHP's $9 billion hostile takeover of American Cyanamid (Cyanamid) was the largest merger-and-acquisition transaction in 1994, and made AHP the fourth largest pharmaceutical firm in the US. The merger brought together the makers of such products as Advil, Anacin, Robitussin and the Norplant contraceptive.

At the time of AHP's offer, Cyanamid had already begun to restructure by selling its consumer products businesses, spinning off its chemicals division and entering into asset swap negotiations with SmithKline Beecham. AHP entered to block the asset swap deal. AHP had twice sweetened its buyout offer to Cyanamid shareholders, which resulted in a $1010 share cash offer approved by directors of both companies. The offer was about $600 million more than AHP's initial bid of $95 a share and about 60 percent more than Cyanamid share trading level in August 1994.

Cyanamid management reportedly tried unsuccessfully to find a white knight or a friendly buyer to thwart the takeover attempt by AHP.

The acquisition was initially financed through the sale by AHP and certain of its subsidiaries of short-term privately placed notes and through the company's general corporate funds. AHP had in place a $7.0 billion, 364-day bank credit facility and a $3.0 billion, five-year bank credit facility. These credit facilities were available to support AHP's privately placed notes.

The M&A strategy of Novartis

The history of Novartis traces back to three companies: Geigy, whose origin goes back to the middle of the eighteenth century; Ciba, founded in 1859; and Sandoz, established in 1886. In 1970 Ciba and Geigy merged to form Ciba-Geigy. In 1996, Sandoz and Ciba-Geigy merged to form Novartis.

Novartis is the world's third largest pharmaceutical company in terms of revenues. It is a world leader in innovative pharmaceuticals, generics, vaccines, diagnostic tools and consumer health products.

In addition, the group's healthcare portfolio is complemented by 77 percent ownership of Alcon, Inc., which discovers and develops innovative eye care products. The growth strategy of Novartis is focused on three pillars of core priorities—extending the lead in innovation; accelerating growth across all divisions; and enhancing productivity through efficiency initiatives. Novartis achieved net sales of $50.6 billion in 2010, while net income amounted to $10.0 billion. Novartis invested $9.1 billion in R&D in 2010.

Headquartered in Basel, Switzerland, Novartis employed 119,418 employees in 2010 and has operations spanning 140 countries. The Pharmaceuticals Division is the largest contributor among the four divisions of Novartis.

The product portfolio of the Pharmaceuticals Division includes more than 60 key marketed products, many of which are leaders in their respective therapeutic areas. In addition, the division's portfolio of development projects includes 147 potential new products.

Novartis continues to lead the industry in innovation, with 13 key product approvals and 16 major filings in pharmaceuticals in 2010, including the breakthrough multiple sclerosis therapy, Gilenya, which has been launched in the US.

The Ciba–Geigymerger

Ciba–Geigy was the largest chemical company in Switzerland. But since the country offers only a limited market and lacks many essential raw materials, Swiss chemical companies have been forced to enter foreign markets. By 1960 both Ciba and Geigy were diversified manufacturers, competing directly in pharmaceuticals, dyes, plastics, textile auxiliaries, and agricultural and specialty chemicals. Each year Geigy's sales grew stronger, and in 1967 the company overtook Ciba.

The idea to merge was first raised when the two companies jointly established a factory at Toms River, New Jersey. With increasingly difficult conditions in export markets—particularly in the United States—officials of the two companies began to explore the benefits of combining their textile and pharmaceutical research—Geigy's strength in agricultural chemicals complemented Ciba's leading position in synthetic resins and petrochemicals.

Ciba and Geigy were both in excellent financial condition. However, some of the same market conditions that had led them to form Basle AG in 1918 were once again prevalent. Competition against German companies in export markets had intensified. But it was as a defense against emerging petrochemical industries in oil-rich Persian Gulf states that the merger was most attractive.

The largest obstacle to the merger between Ciba and Geigy was US antitrust legislation. Antitrust sentiment in the United States was so strong that federal prosecutors vowed to block the merger in Switzerland if it threatened to restrain American trade in any way. In order to win approval in the US, Ciba agreed to sell its American dye works to Crompton and Knowles, and Geigy consented to turn over its American pharmaceutical holdings to Revlon. In spite of challenges, the merger was approved.

Mechanically, the merger consisted of a takeover of Ciba by Geigy. This was done to minimize tax penalties amounting to CHF55 million. The Ciba–Geigy merger proved to be synergistic. The more profitable but less diversified Geigy has benefitted from Ciba's research capabilities. Ciba, on the other hand, has profited from Geigy's more modern approach to marketing and management. The company's worldwide sales in 1978 were CHF17.5 billion, 30 percent of which came from US operations. Despite a 14 percent drop in profits between 1978 and 1980, Ciba–Geigy has maintained strong annual sales growth since 1981; profits as a percentage of sales were 8.1 percent in 1985.

Ciba–Geigy became one of the five largest chemical companies in the world. In 1994 Ciba acquired baby food company Gerber.

Sandoz—growth profile

The chemical company Kern and Sandoz was founded in Basel, Switzerland in 1886. It first produced dyes called alizarin blue and auramine. In 1895, the company made its first pharmaceutical substance, antipyrine, a fever-controlling agent. In 1917, the pharmaceutical division was created. In 1918, Ciba, Sandoz and Geigy created a pooling agreement, which was abandoned in 1950. In 1929, the company laid the foundations for modern calcium therapy by introducing calcium Sandoz. In 1939, the company entered into agribusiness. In 1963, the company acquired the biotechnology firm Bohemia Gmbh. In 1967, Sandoz merged with Wanders Ltd, which marked the beginning of a diversification into the dietetics business.

Ciba–Geigy and Sandoz merger to form Novartis

The Novartis mega-merger, formally completed on January 1, 1997, was at that time the world's largest merger, with a market value of $80 billion. As a result of merger Novartis became the second largest corporation in Europe, and second largest pharmaceutical company in the world. The merger of Ciba and Sandoz had a lasting effect on the pharmaceutical industry, especially in Europe.

It set the stage for a new wave of mega-mergers, which was reflected through several huge deals with European involvement, such as Astra/Zeneca, Hoechst/Rhône-Poulenc and Glaxo/SmithKline. Both the firms were headquartered in Switzerland and had lot of complementarities. The merger was executed as a "merger of equals" through an exchange of equity, so that no takeover premiums had to be paid. The executive board of management and the board of directors were split equally between former Ciba and Sandoz representatives.

On December 17, 1996, the US Federal Trade Commission (FTC) granted provisional approval to an agreement with Ciba–Geigy and Sandoz for the creation of Novartis with core businesses in healthcare, agribusinesses and nutrition.

Part of the agreement between Ciba–Geigy and Sandoz was that the former's industrial chemicals business would be spun off as a separate business, leading to the formation of Ciba Specialty Chemicals Plc in 1997. Ciba Specialty Chemicals contributed CHF7.9 billion in sales revenues, which amounted to 38 percent of the group total. Ciba Specialty held number one position in pigments and additives while in textile dyes it was at number two. In 2008, the Ciba board of directors agreed to a €3.4 billion takeover offer from BASF, the world's largest chemicals company. Ciba Specialty Chemicals was renamed BASF Schweiz AG in March 2010.

The construction chemicals business of Sandoz was also spun off during this time period.

Healthcare was both Ciba's and Sandoz's most important business unit, in terms of both strategy and sales. It also has top priority within Novartis.

Analysts believed that merger synergy would result from the complementary nature of the two companies' product areas. It was stated that Ciba had a compelling reason for its merger with Sandoz as two of its most promising drugs for strokes, Selfotel and anti-blood-clotting drug Hirudin, faced problems in clinical trials.

Novartis expected to have strong positions in seven therapeutic areas. Most of the group's top ten products were expected to achieve double-digit growth. They included Voltaren, Ciba's arthritis and rheumatism treatment, which achieved sales of CHF1.5 billion in 1995, and Sandimmun/Neoral, which notched up CHF1.4 billion.

Ciba and Sandoz expected that the merger would release CHF1.8 billion in synergy benefits over three years. Around 10 percent of the combined workforce or 13,000 people were expected to lose their jobs on account of the merger.

The merger was conducted through an exchange of shares. Sandoz shareholders received 55 percent of the new company's shares and Ciba shareholders 45 percent.

Strategic perspective of the merger

At the time of consolidation, Novartis had 4.4 percent of the global market, just behind the 4.7 percent of GlaxoSmithKline Beecham. After the merger, Novartis' business mix constituted 59 percent healthcare, 27 percent agribusiness and 14 percent nutrition. After the merger, Novartis became the second largest drug company after Glaxo Wellcome with annual sales of $22 billion and market capitalization of about $80 billion.

In 1996, the largest pharma company was holding less than 5 percent of the world market share. This corporate merger brought together two long-standing neighbors and created the largest life sciences group in the world. Before the merger the two companies were already major players in world markets, ranking tenth and 14th respectively in terms of pharmaceutical sales and with strong positions in other sectors.

After the merger Novartis became the 12th largest company in the world and the third largest in Europe. According to analysts, this merger allowed both the companies to leapfrog the competition in the context of scarce resources to sustain competitive advantage.

Ciba and Sandoz predicted cost savings of at least CHF1.8 billion within three years, by streamlining production and internal structures: half of these savings were expected to be realized within the first 18 months of Novartis' formation. The companies also hoped to reap the benefit of broader product portfolios and better asset utilization.

The companies spent CHF2 billion on restructuring costs. This included setting up a CHF100 million fund to finance retraining schemes and startup businesses, particularly in biotechnology.

Pharmaceuticals became the largest single sector for Novartis, with 94 products. The company had the generic versions of 88 of the top 100 patented drugs. Novartis became the top crop protection company in the world with 85 percent higher sales than its nearest rival, AgrEvo. Novartis' seeds division now ranked second in the world behind Pioneer. The nutrition business from Sandoz continued to be the second largest company in the US behind Ross.

After the merger the strategic focus of Novartis had been the transformation from a diverse group including agribusiness to a highly focused leading healthcare company. Novartis continued its acquisition spree with the purchase of Hexal and Eon Labs, creating a world leader in generics under the brand name Sandoz as well as the acquisition of Chiron Vaccines in 2006, thereby taking Novartis to the forefront of vaccines and diagnostics.

Both merger partners agreed on a focusing strategy to strengthen strategic core businesses and to push innovation as reflected in the merger agreement. The firm's annual research budget amounted to CHF3 billion. The bulk part of the corporate research budget was accounted for by the Pharmaceuticals Division. In 1996, Novartis became worldwide leader in terms of pharma R&D budget (CHF2.3 billion), followed by Glaxo (CHF2.2 billion), Roche (CHF 2.1 billion) and Pfizer (CHF1.9 billion).

The merged company focused on developing biotechnology and genetic engineering as cross-divisional research areas. Biotechnology was used as a means to generate synergies between pharma, agribusiness and animal health. The maintenance and expansion of research networks was given high strategic importance. One-third of research resources was committed to external alliances and cooperation.

Major acquisitions of Novartis

2002

- Acquires Lek, a generic company, which became an important center for additional research and manufacturing activities.

2003

- Novartis acquires the adult medical nutrition business of Mead Johnson and Company, a subsidiary of Bristol-Myers Squibb.

2004

- The company acquires two generic business companies: Danish firm Durasacan A/S from AstraZeneca, and Sabex Holding Ltd of Canada.

2005

- Acquires Hexel AG a leading generics company based in Germany and Eon Labs, an American generics company; this makes Novartis a world leader in generic pharmaceuticals.
- Novartis acquires the North American OTC brand portfolio of Bristol-Myers Squibb.

2009

- Sandoz completes the acquisition of EBEWE Pharma, which provides a platform for future growth of differentiated generic business such as cancer medicines.

2010

Novartis proposes to complete the purchase of a majority stake in Alcon, followed by an all-share direct merger of Alcon into Novartis. The addition of eye care will strengthen the Novartis healthcare portfolio.

Sandoz announces the acquisition of Oriel Therapeutics.

2011

- Novartis announces agreement to acquire Genoptix, Inc. in an all-cash tender offer at $25.00 per share. Genoptix's laboratory service offerings would provide a strategic fit with the portfolio of the Molecular Diagnostics unit.

Growth strategy of Pfizer through M&A

Pfizer is the global pharmaceutical company, ranking number one in world sales. The company is based in New York City and has its research headquarters in Groton, Connecticut. During the 1980s and 1990s Pfizer underwent a period of growth sustained by the discovery and marketing of Zoloft, Lipitor, Norvasc, Zithromax, Aricept, Diflucan and Viagra. In the last decade, Pfizer had grown by mergers, including those with Warner Lambert (2000), Pharmacia (2003) and Wyeth (2009).

Pfizer ranked first in the medicine and healthcare industry according to global sales in 2010. Pfizer had the greatest number of blockbuster products in 2009 with 14, which includes five inherited through the acquisition of Wyeth.

Pfizer has nine diverse healthcare businesses: Primary Care, Specialty Care, Oncology, Emerging Markets, Established Products, Consumer Healthcare, Nutrition, Animal Health and Capsugel. Pfizer has created

Table 1.3 Financial highlights of Novartis ($ billion)

	2009	2010
Net sales	44.26	50.63
Operating income	9.98	11.53
Net income	8.45	9.97
EPS (US$)	3.70	4.28
Free cash flow	9.45	12.35

Source: Novartis website.

Table 1.4 Financial highlights of Pfizer ($ million)

	2008	2009	2010
Revenues	48,296	50,009	67,809
R&D expenses	7945	7845	9413
Net income	8104	8635	8257

Source: Pfizer Website.

two distinct research organizations: the Pharma Therapeutics Research and Development Group focuses on the discovery of small molecules and related modalities; and the BioTherapeutics Research and Development Group focuses on large-molecule research, including vaccines. In 2010, products like Lipitor, Enbrel, Lyrica, Prevnar/Prevenar 13 and Celebrex each delivered at least $2 billion in revenues.

Pfizer's M&A milestones

Year	Milestones
1953–1971	**1953** Pfizer acquires J. B. Roerig and Company, specialists in nutritional supplements. Pfizer partners with Japan's Taito to manufacture and distribute antibiotics Pfizer acquires full ownership of Taito in 1983. **1971** Pfizer acquires Mack Illertissen, a prosperous manufacturer of pharmaceutical, chemical and consumer products oriented to the needs of the German marketplace.
2000+	**2000** Pfizer and Warner-Lambert merge to form the new Pfizer, creating the world's fastest-growing major pharmaceutical company. **2003** On April 16, 2003 Pfizer, Inc. and Pharmacia Corporation combine operations. **2009** On October 15, 2009, Pfizer acquires Wyeth, creating a company with a broad range of products and therapies.

Origins of Upjohn

In 1886, W. E. Upjohn, M. D. established The Upjohn Pill and Granule Company of Kalamazoo, Michigan (USA). The company continued its growth throughout the nineteenth century, eventually evolving into an innovative, international company. In 1903, the company shortened its name to The Upjohn Company. The actual impetus for the company's success occurred during World War II when Upjohn, like many other drug companies, developed a broad line of antibiotics, including penicillin and streptomycin. By 1958, Upjohn was the sixth largest manufacturer of antibiotics. Upjohn's portfolio included Halcion sleeping tablets, Rogaine baldness treatment and an anti-impotence drug called Caverject.

By 1989, the patents on many of Upjohn's major products began to expire. In the early 1990s, Upjohn's problems compounded to a greater extent. Halcion, one of its product mainstays, lost 45 percent of its sales following concerns about its side effects. Patent expirations on other important products like Xanax paved the way for competition among lower-priced generic brands. The company's new products like Vantin were not expected to offset the revenue losses of the patent expirations in the long term. By November 1992, Upjohn showed the lowest multiple of all pharmaceutical stocks.

Origins of Pharmacia

The roots of Pharmacia Corporation date back over 150 years to 1837, when a leading Italian pharmacist, Carlo Erba, started his own company, which later became Farmitalia Carlo Erba. This company later united with Kabi Pharmacia, which began in 1951. These two companies, along with Pharmacia Aktiebolaget, formed the three main points of origin for Pharmacia AB, which was established in Sweden in 1911. In 1990, Pharmacia merged with two Swedish food and drug companies, Procordia and Provenda.

By 1993, the company had grown to third largest among pharmaceutical companies worldwide, with sales that year of more than $3 billion. Pharmacia was a niche specialized group focusing on drugs for growth hormones, cataract surgery and smoking. On account of its niche sales, Pharmacia sold mainly to its hospitals, thereby decreasing its marketing costs compared to other companies that relied on large sales staff.

The Pharmacia/Upjohn merger

In 1995, Pharmacia and Upjohn merged through a tax-free stock swap. The merger was valued at close to $6 billion. Pharmacia & Upjohn became a global provider of human healthcare products, animal health products, diagnostics and specialty products. The combined group became one of the world's largest pharmaceuticals companies, with a turnover of about SKr50 billion (£4.5 billion). The merged group also became one of the most debt-free companies in the industry. The combined entity became the ninth largest drug maker worldwide with annual sales of $7 billion. The combined corporate headquarters was based in London and had listings on the Stock Exchange in London, New York and Stockholm.

Since 1996 four of the top drugs of Upjohn, generating sales of $1 billion, had lost US patent protection. Rogaine was refused a license by the American Food and Drug Administration and stroke-related drug Freedox had its trials halted after reports of safety problems.

In the 1990s, larger companies captured more resources than smaller ones. By 1995, Pharmacia's position had dropped to that of ninth largest pharmaceutical company in the world. The company at the time of introduction of a new drug for the treatment of glaucoma realized that it needed a partner with capabilities for mass marketing in the US. The merger of Pharmacia and Upjohn created a global company with business activities in Europe, United States and Asia.

Volvo, one of the main promoters of Pharmacia, had been keen to sell its stake in Pharmacia as part of a disposal program of non-core businesses. Volvo exchanged its 27.5 percent stake in Pharmacia for a 13.8 percent holding in the enlarged group. Shareholders of Upjohn received 1.45 shares of the new company, while Pharmacia shareholders received one share of the new company, which had 504 million shares outstanding.

In terms of cost synergy both the companies estimated cost savings of around SKr3.5 billion (£312m). But in 1996 the combined company witnessed a fall in stock prices as well as operating performance. During 1997, the company's biotechnology supply subsidiary Pharmacia Biotech merged with Amersham Life Science. The merger also created cultural problems as the management of the company consisted of British, Italian, American and Swedish executives speaking different languages.

Pharmacia and Upjohn had comparable market values, and the merger was touted as a "merger of equals." Before the merger, Upjohn had been the world's 19th largest pharmaceutical company and Pharmacia the 18th largest.

At the time of the merger, Upjohn was weak in terms of R&D compared to its competitors in the industry. Its patents on several drugs, including Xanax, had expired. With no profitable drugs in the pipeline, the company was seeking a European partner. For Pharmacia, finding and merging with a complementary partner within the same industry was a necessity for its survival. The most interesting target was direct competitors or one company very closely related to its line of business. Upjohn was a huge company that was strong in the US, but it did not have access to world markets. Upjohn needed capabilities outside the US to maximize the value of the product it had. The merger allowed Pharmacia to utilize Upjohn's distribution network in the US while allowing Upjohn to take advantage of Pharmacia's distribution network in Europe.

The combined Pharmacia & Upjohn, Inc. developed and marketed a variety of pharmaceutical and health-related products, including those for infectious and metabolic diseases, central nervous system disorders, cancer and health concerns. The company developed and sold vaccines and pharmaceuticals for pets, livestock and other food animals. The company was also involved in selling specialty products for hospitals as well as diagnostics and nutritional supplements.

Formation of Pharmacia

In December 1999, Monsanto and Pharmacia & Upjohn agreed to merge. The combination created the 11th largest pharmaceutical firm in the world, with $10 billion in prescription drug sales. The combined company had total sales of $17 billion, including agribusiness units and other products. The merger was completed in April 2000. The company had top-selling drugs to treat ailments including arthritis, glaucoma, colorectal cancer and insomnia. Monsanto's Celebrex arthritis treatment, introduced in 1999, had already topped $1.4 billion in sales, while Pharmacia's Xalatan was the world's best-selling prescription medication for glaucoma.

Under the terms of the agreement, each Pharmacia share was exchanged for 1.19 shares of the combined company, while each Monsanto share was worth one share. Monsanto shareholders owned 51 percent of the combined company. Pharmacia and Monsanto each had ten seats on the new board of directors.

Following the merger, Pharmacia continued Searle's agreement with Pfizer to co-promote Celebrex, which was originally co-developed by Searle and Pfizer. In August 2002, Pharmacia completed the spin-off of its agricultural subsidiary, Monsanto Company.

Monsanto, troubled by a depressed stock price and mounting opposition to its controversial genetically modified crops, had decided to split off its agribusiness unit or be acquired by a larger company. Monsanto also had a huge debt load following spending of $8.5 billion in agricultural input acquisitions. The combined company had a research budget of $2 billion, and a broader sales force to push each other's drugs. Monsanto's Searle division, which sold the popular arthritis treatment Celebrex, was to be used to bolster the launch of Pharmacia's new antibiotic called Zyvox.

Monsanto and Pharmacia expected to achieve annual cost savings of more than $600 million within three years of the merger. The merger resulted in a market capitalization of $50 billion.

Along with Monsanto's Searle unit came Celebrex, one of a new class of Cox-2 anti-arthritis drugs and Pharmacia's first true blockbuster. With 2001 sales of more than $3 billion, Celebrex put Pharmacia in the industry's big league, alongside peers such as Pfizer, Wyeth, Eli Lilly and Merck.

History of Warner-Lambert

Like Pfizer, Warner-Lambert traces its history back to the mid-nineteenth century. In 1856, William R. Warner launched his own drug store in Philadelphia, Pennsylvania. He invented a tablet-coating process to encase harsh-tasting medicines in sugar shells. He then focused solely on drug manufacturing under the name William R. Warner & Co. Meanwhile, in the American Midwest, Jordan Wheat Lambert launched Lambert Pharmaceutical Company in St Louis. Lambert's main product was Listerine antiseptic, and it was marketed only to medical professionals. Another St Louis-based company, Pfeiffer Chemical, bought William R. Warner in 1908, kept the Warner name, and expanded the company through acquisition.

In 1955, Warner Company and Lambert combined to form Warner-Lambert Pharmaceutical Company. The company grew through acquisition. In 1962, the company bought American Chicle Company, a New York City-based company that was among the world's largest producers of gums and mints. In 1965, Warner-Lambert purchased a small cough tablet company in the UK and expanded the brand known as Halls Mentholyptus to global stature.

The year 1970 was a turning point for the growth of Warner-Lambert, acquiring Parke-Davis, once the largest drug manufacturer. Parke-Davis had pioneered the standardization of medications and built the first modern pharmaceutical laboratory. In the first half of twentieth century, Parke-Davis introduced a number of breakthrough products including the first bacterial vaccine, a pure form of adrenaline and dilantin called Phenytoin, the first widely available treatment for epilepsy and seizure.

In the 1980s, Warner-Lambert refocused on three main businesses: prescription pharmaceuticals, consumer healthcare products, and gums and mints. In 1993, Warner-Lambert acquired Wilkinson Sword, combining it with Schick to create the world's second largest wet-shave business.

The breakthrough for the company in terms of expansion came in 1996 when Warner-Lambert entered into a co-marketing agreement with Pfizer on Lipitor (atorvastatin calcium), a new entry into the statin class of lipid-lowering agents. Discovered by Parke-Davis Research and introduced in 1997, Lipitor is the largest-selling pharmaceutical of any kind worldwide. In 1999, Warner-Lambert acquired Agouron, based in La Jolla, California. Agouron is a leader in protein-based drug design and marketer of the protease inhibitor Viracept (nelfinavirmesylate).

The Pfizer/Warner-Lambert, Inc. merger

The battle began when Warner-Lambert and AHP announced in November 1999 their plans to merge, thus creating the world's largest pharmaceutical company. Pfizer sought to block this move the next day by announcing an unsolicited $80 billion stock offer for Warner, the largest hostile takeover attempt in the history of the pharmaceutical business. Warner fought and threatened to end the companies' co-marketing agreement for Lipitor, adding that Pfizer's unsolicited bid might violate a standstill agreement in the deal.

Tensions began to wane, and the companies came to an agreement. The merger agreement between Warner and AHP, which received a $1.8 billion break-up fee, was terminated. AHP subsequently spun off its non-pharma businesses and rebranded itself as Wyeth—now part of Pfizer.

In the year 2000, the union created the largest drug company in the US and the second largest worldwide behind Switzerland's Novartis when ranked by sales. AHP, a loser in the merger battle, got $1.8 billion. With Warner-Lambert, Pfizer gained product lines ranging from Parke-Davis branded pharmaceuticals to Listerine mouthwash to Schick and Wilkinson Sword wet-shave products.

Pfizer exchanged 2.75 of its shares for each Warner-Lambert share, valuing the deal at $90 billion using the Pfizer closing price of $35.75. The new exchange ratio was10 percent higher than the 2.5 shares Pfizer originally offered, and considerably higher than the 1.49 shares AHP offered. Pfizer's shareholders owned about 61 percent of the new company on a fully diluted basis, and Warner-Lambert shareholders owned 39 percent of the combined company. The combined company had annual revenues of about $28 billion, including $21 billion in prescription pharmaceutical sales, and a market capitalization of over $230 billion. The research and development budget totaled $4.7 billion and profit amounted to about $4.9 billion.

Motives for the merger

Pfizer had secured the full ownership of rapidly growing Lipitor (a drug previously co-promoted by Pfizer and Warner-Lambert), co-promotion rights for the hit arthritis drug Celebrex and solid growth from several portfolio drugs. At the time of merger, Lipitor's sales were expected to exceed $5 billion worldwide.

Cost synergies

Pfizer also expected cost savings of $1.6 billion. Savings of $200 million were forecast for the end of 2001 and $1.6 billion at the end of 2002. The savings were expected to come from cutting manufacturing costs and overlaps in administrative and support service in research and development, selling, general and administrative expenses.

Additional synergies were expected from the combination of product portfolios in key therapeutic categories, such as cardiovascular, central nervous system, infectious disease and diabetics. The growth was forecast to accelerate as the combined company had seven drugs each with over $1 billion in sales. The growth would be fueled by continued strong pharmaceutical sales growth, led by super-blockbuster cholesterol drug Lipitor. The company was also expected to have a strong new six-product line with launches of drugs.

The Pfizer/Pharmacia merger

In July 2002, Pfizer, Inc. announced the acquisition of Pharmacia Corporation, which created the largest pharmaceutical company in the world, with a projected $48 billion in annual revenue and a research budget of more than $7 billion. The merger forged one of the world's fastest-growing and most valuable companies.

Pfizer, Inc. and Pharmacia Corporation had to divest pharmaceutical products in nine separate product markets to different third parties to settle FTC charges of anti-competitive effects. Under the terms of the deal, Pharmacia had to spin off its remaining 84 percent ownership of Monsanto Co. to its current shareholders.

After the spinoff, Pharmacia shareholders received 1.4 shares of Pfizer stock for each share of Pharmacia, valuing Pharmacia stock at $45.08 per share, representing a 36 percent premium. Pfizer shareholders owned about 77 percent of the company, with Pharmacia shareholders owning around 23 percent. Pfizer announced that it would save $2.5 billion in total cost as a result of the merger. These cost savings were basically in the form of reduced labor costs from downsizing as well as the complete closure of one or more local operations.

The deal came amid unprecedented pressure on pharmaceutical companies as the industry struggled with its research laboratories, and faced rising competition from generics makers and intense pressure on prices from governments and private buyers. As a result, drug companies were threatened with declining revenues.

In addition to the blockbuster Celebrex, the merger joined Pfizer's dominant cardiovascular franchise—including the cholesterol drug Lipitor and the blood pressure pill Norvasc, as well as its Zithromax antibiotic and its epilepsy medicine Neurontin—with such popular Pharmacia drugs as Xalatan for glaucoma and the cancer drug Camptosar. As a result of the merger, Pfizer's global share of total pharmaceutical sales rose from 8 to 11 percent when the deal was completed.

Industry experts had long speculated about a deal between Pfizer and Pharmacia because of the good strategic fit. The two companies had had a partnership since 1998 to market Celebrex, the world's leading arthritis medicine and the seventh best-selling global drug overall, and have continued that arrangement with Bextra, a second-generation medicine launched in the US.

Through the merger, Pfizer acquired a relatively strong drug company with four drugs that each had $1 billion-plus sales. Pfizer already had eight drugs at those sales levels and an even dozen blockbusters. Moreover, Pharmacia's major drugs did not face any patent threats for years, although its cancer drug Camptosar was due for patent expiration in 2008.

Pfizer had been looking to expand into the lucrative market for cancer drugs, a strength of Pharmacia's, and also picked up ophthalmology, where Pharmacia's glaucoma treatment Xalatan was already on the verge of $1 billion in annual sales.

Wyeth—history

Wyeth is a global pharmaceutical research and manufacturing company. It develops and markets traditional pharmaceuticals, vaccines and biotechnology products that serve both human and animal healthcare. It has strong product lines in both prescription medications and in consumer health products, including over-the-counter (OTC) medications and nutritional supplements. Wyeth markets its products in more than 140 countries, and has manufacturing facilities on five continents.

Table 1.5 Premerger highlights of Pfizer/Pharmacia

	Pfizer	**Pharmacia**
2001 Revenue	\$32.30 billion	\$13.80 billion
2001 Net income	\$7.78 billion	\$1.50 billion
2001 R&D expenses	\$4.80 billion	\$2.30 billion
Major products	Lipitor (cholesterol), Norvasc (hypertension), Zoloft (depression), Viracept (HIV/AIDS), Viagra (sexual dysfunction), Zyrtec (allergy)	Celebrex (arthritis), Xalatan (glaucoma), Detrol (urinary incontinence), Bextra (arthritis)

During the 1990s, Wyeth—which at the time was called American Home Products (AHP)—began selling off the wide-ranging businesses it had acquired over the years, retaining a focus on medicine and pharmaceuticals. In 2002, the company changed its name from American Home Products to Wyeth.

Pfizer's acquisition of Wyeth

On January 25, 2009, the board of Pfizer, the world's largest drug maker, agreed to acquire Wyeth for \$68 billion. Wyeth became a wholly owned subsidiary of Pfizer, Inc.

Four banks (Goldman Sachs, J. P. Morgan Chase, Citigroup and Bank of America) had agreed to lend Pfizer \$22.5 billion to pay for the deal. Pfizer, which had roughly \$26 billion in cash, financed the remainder through a combination of cash and stock.

Pfizer expected to save \$4 billion annually by combining with Wyeth. Pfizer faces a run of 14 patent expirations through 2014, which would add up to lost revenue of about \$35 billion as those drugs give way to cheap generics.

Under the terms of the transaction, each outstanding share of Wyeth common stock had been converted into the right to receive \$33 in cash (without interest) and 0.985 of a share of Pfizer common stock.

The major issue with Pfizer has been its inability to bring to market new blockbuster drugs, which would replace the revenues that the company would lose as a large portion of its drugs lose their patents around 2011–2012. One of the primary reasons for the \$68 billion purchase of Wyeth was to gain access to its promising lineup of vaccines and biotechnology medicines at a time when Pfizer was facing the late 2011 loss of patent protection on its \$12 billion-a-year cholesterol fighter Lipitor, the world's biggest-selling medicine.

Despite spending between $7.2 and $8.1 billion annually on R&D over recent years, Pfizer had not come out with any blockbuster drugs to replace the revenues it would forfeit from its major drugs when they lose their patents. Some analysts estimated that Pfizer would lose 50 to 70 percent of its revenues by 2015 if it did not bring new drugs to the market.

Through Wyeth's acquisition, Pfizer would achieve an extra $23 billion in sales from Wyeth's portfolio of drugs. Wyeth's revenues are more diversified and, unlike Pfizer, the company does not rely on a single drug for a large portion of sales.

Wyeth had one of the best new product pipelines in the pharmaceuticals industry, with over 60 new products in development. Some of the most important new drug launches include Tygacil, Torisel, Lybrel and Pristiq. Wyeth had three drugs approved in 2008—antidepressant Pristiq, Relistor for constipation caused by narcotic painkillers, and the hemophilia drug Xyntha.

After reviewing the combined drug development portfolios of Pfizer and Wyeth, the company decided to trim 600 existing projects to about 500, with some 70 percent of those remaining focused on six key therapeutic areas—oncology, pain, inflammation, Alzheimer's disease, psychoses and diabetes. Pfizer would no longer seek US approval to sell pain drug Lyrica as an add-on treatment for anxiety.

Pfizer has also boosted its vaccines and biotechnology projects through its acquisition of Wyeth, with six vaccines and 27 biotech drugs now in development, up from one vaccine and 16 biologics.

Formation of AstraZeneca

AstraZeneca

AstraZeneca is a global, innovation-driven, integrated biopharmaceutical company. The company discovers, develops, manufactures and markets prescription medicines for six important areas of healthcare, which include some of the world's most serious illnesses: cancer, cardiovascular, gastrointestinal, infection, neuroscience, and respiratory and inflammation. AstraZeneca is active in over 100 countries, with a growing presence in emerging markets including China, Brazil, Mexico and Russia.

Astra AB

Founded in 1913 and headquartered in Södertälje, Sweden, Astra was an international pharmaceutical group engaged in the research, development, manufacture and marketing of pharmaceutical products, primarily for four main product groups: gastrointestinal, cardiovascular, respiratory and pain control. Astra marketed a range of other pharmaceutical products, including anti-infective products, and also operated Astra Tech, a medical devices group.

Zeneca Group Plc

On June 1, 1993, Imperial Chemical Industries (ICI, founded in 1926) demerged three of its businesses (Pharmaceuticals, Agrochemicals and Specialties) to form a separate company, Zeneca. Headquartered in London, Zeneca was a major international bioscience group engaged in the research, development, manufacture and marketing of pharmaceuticals (focusing on cancer, cardiovascular, central nervous system, respiratory and anesthesia), agricultural chemicals and specialty chemicals, and the provision of disease-specific healthcare services. Its businesses were research and technology intensive, with extensive international development and marketing skills, and a strong common science base.

Merger highlights

On December 9, 1998, UK-based Zeneca and Astra of Sweden announced their merger to form AstraZeneca, the fourth largest drug company in the world, with a value of $41 billion. The merger was one of the largest-ever European mergers at that time. The merger process was completed on April 6, 1999. Both Astra and Zeneca had similar science-based cultures and a shared vision of the pharmaceutical industry. The merger led to cost savings of $1.1 billion and the loss of 6000 jobs worldwide. The deal took AstraZeneca to second place in Europe, ahead of the two biggest UK pharmaceutical companies, Glaxo and SmithKline Beecham.

Many analysts opined that Astra and Zeneca were a perfect fit in terms of highly complementary product portfolios as well as sales and

Table 1.6 Financial highlights of AstraZeneca ($ million)

	2006	2007	2008	2009	2010
Revenue	26,475	29,559	31,601	32,804	33,269
Operating profit	8216	8094	9144	11,543	11,494
Net profit	6063	5627	6130	7544	8081
EPS	$3.86	$3.74	$4.20	$5.19	$5.60
Operating profit as % of Revenue	31%	27.4%	28.9%	35.2%	34.5%
Total assets	29,932	47,988	46,950	54,920	56,127

Source: Company website.

marketing organizations. The merger linked the makers of two of the world's best-known drugs in Astra's blockbuster ulcer pill Losec and Zeneca's cancer treatment Tamoxifen. Zeneca bid for all Astra shares, with Astra shareholders receiving 0.5045 shares in the new concern AstraZeneca for each Astra A-series or B-series share. Under the terms of the deal, Zeneca shareholders received 53.5 percent of the new company and Astra shareholders 46.5 percent of the new company. Astra had to overcome resistance from its biggest shareholder, the Wallenberg family, who owned 12 percent of the company.

Strategic reasons for the merger

The merger aimed to improve the combined companies' ability to deliver long-term growth and enduring shareholder value. The driving force behind the merger was the tremendous step-up in global sales and marketing power. As a result of merger, AstraZeneca was ranked third in the world for prescription drug sales, holding the number two slot in Europe and seventh position in the US market. The combined entity had widespread coverage in key therapy areas such as cardiovascular and respiratory diseases. There was a major presence in primary care, particularly in gastrointestinal, cardiovascular and respiratory medicine. There was greater scope for strengthening the pipeline through drug discovery and development.

Astra's dependence on a few products, the patents of which were about to expire, was one of the reasons for a merger pursuit. Losec, which generated most of Astra's turnover, was about to lose its protection from patents, and no strong replacements existed in Astra's research. But historically Astra had defended its major products successfully when losing its patent rights. Zeneca's research and development portfolio were much smaller than Astra's portfolio. The advantages of a merged Astra in relation to R&D mainly rested on the large costs in R&D activities, which would create economies of scale.

An important driving force behind a merger was the possibility of quick access to new research areas. Zeneca, for example, was a leader in the cancer area. In spite of possessing best-selling hypertension drug Zestril (Zeneca) and ulcer drug Prilosec (Astra), they had to find partners to compete with giants like Glaxo Wellcome and Merck.

The merger of Hoechst and Rhône-Poulenc to form Aventis

The Hoechst Group was an international network of innovative and customer-oriented companies, which were among the top three suppliers in the pharmaceutical, agricultural and industrial chemical centers of Europe, the Americas and Asia. From its roots as a dyestuffs producer, the company grew to become one of Germany's top three chemical firms.

In the 1970s, the firm diversified into the pharmaceutical sector. In the 1970s, Hoechst had almost gained control of the entire diuretic market, and was a leader in oral medication for diabetics.

In the 1990s, the company evolved strategies to use joint ventures and acquisitions for growth. The company acquired three European powder coatings operations, a German fibers producer and a controlling stake in an American manufacturer of generic drugs. In a 1995 bid to re-establish itself as a leading player in the drug business, the company acquired American pharmaceutical company Marion Merrell Dow for $7.1 billion to form Hoechst Marion Roussel, or HMR. The merger moved Hoechst into third place in the continuously consolidating pharmaceutical industry.

During the period 1988–2011, Hoechst AG has made 26 acquisitions while taking stakes in 18 companies. At the time of the merger with Rhône-Poulenc, Hoechst had seven primary businesses. These were Hoechst Marion Roussel (HMR), AgrEvo, HR Vet, Dade Behring, Centeon, Celanese (with several smaller chemical companies) and Messer. HMR, the pharmaceutical group, developed drugs in a range of therapeutic areas. AgrEvo, a joint venture with Schering, produced and sold crop protection agents and pest control products. The Dade Behring and Centeon joint ventures focused on blood plasma protein and diagnostics respectively. Celanese and Messer produced chemicals, acetate products and industrial gases.

Rhône-Poulenc SA ranked among the world's ten largest chemical companies, with interests in agricultural chemicals; human and veterinary pharmaceuticals; fibers and polymers; specialty chemicals; and organic and inorganic intermediates. Rhône-Poulenc's business was dramatically internationalized through myriad acquisitions in the late 1980s and early 1990s. By the end of 1993, the company had operations in 140 countries, and almost 80 percent of its income came from outside France.

Two smaller chemical firms, Progil and Péchiney Saint Gobain, were acquired in 1969. By 1969, Rhône-Poulenc had become the largest chemical company in France. This series of M&A activities helped to establish a corporate identity that remained intact throughout the mid-1970s. By the end of 1983, Rhône-Poulenc was making a profit for the first time since 1979. The company's most significant expansion occurred in its farm chemicals area, with the acquisition of all related interests of the Union Carbide Corporation in 1986.

From 1986 to 1992, Rhône-Poulenc spent more than $7 billion on acquisitions and sold at least 80 subsidiaries. Major acquisitions included Canada's Connaught Laboratories, the UK's RTZ Chemicals and US's GAF and Rorer Group. By 1992, 75 percent of Rhône-Poulenc's business was outside France, and it operated in 140 countries. Compared with other world agrochemical leaders, Rhône-Poulenc Agro (RPA) was characterized by a focus on its core business: crop protection.

As a major player in biotechnology and agrochemicals, Rhône-Poulenc described itself as a "life sciences company" with two main business focuses. The company had developed a human health focus, built around Pasteur Merieux Connaught, Rhône-Poulenc Rorer and Centeon (a joint venture with Hoechst). Its other business focus was in plant and animal health, which included three main companies—Rhône-Poulenc Agro, Rhône-Poulenc Animal Nutrition and Merial (a 50/50 joint venture with Merck).

Merger highlights

Hoechst was merged with Rhône-Poulenc SA to form Aventis in 1999. The merger identified three preliminary steps: a share repurchase by Hoechst, a special dividend payment for Hoechst shareholders, and a divestiture of Celanese that included Hoechst specialty chemical assets and €1 billion in consolidated net debt. The special dividend served as an added incentive for shareholders to tender and compensate Hoechst shareholders for tax credits that were to be issued after the completion of the exchange. The Celanese divestiture further increased Aventis' focus on life sciences. Hoechst also decided to sell its HR vet business, since it did not fit into the other animal nutrition businesses of Aventis.

During the exchange, which took place in October 1999, Rhône-Poulenc acquired 90 percent of Hoechst. Hoechst shareholders received one Rhône-Poulenc share for every 1.333 Hoechst shares they held. Rhône-Poulenc also agreed to acquire the holdings of Gallus GmbH, a subsidiary of Kuwait Petroleum Company that held about 25 percent of Hoechst shares. The exchange ratio was based on the ratio of the market valuations, each company's outstanding share numbers and the number of desired Aventis shares. The exchange was conditional on Rhône-Poulenc purchasing at least 90 percent of Hoechst.

The merged Aventis focused on two industry sectors—pharmaceuticals and agricultural products. The pharma division was headquartered in Frankfurt, Germany and the crop science division in Lyon, France. The pharma division consisted of Aventis Pharma, Centeon, Aventis Vaccines, Pasteur Merieux and Dade Behring. The crop science division contained Aventis Crop Science, Aventis Animal Nutrition and Merial. The pharmaceutical sector accounted for approximately 73 percent of Aventis sales.

Post-merger, Aventis Pharma became one of the largest pharmaceutical companies in the world, with sales of €2.3 billion in 1999. The merger reinvigorated the combined companies' strategic products and filled gaps in their respective pipelines. Products such as the antihistamine Allegra (fexofenadine), cancer-fighter Taxotere (docetaxel), anticoagulant Lovenox (enoxaparin), and a drug for postmenopausal osteoporosis called Actonel attracted more revenues. Post-merger Aventis had placed greater focus on global products, boosted spending on R&D, and quickly expanded its US marketing and sales organization. The company concentrated on development of cardiovascular, oncology, anti-infective, central nervous system and diabetes drugs, and vaccines, as well as its initiatives in gene therapy and metabolic disorders.

Strategic rationale for the merger

The Hoechst and Rhône-Poulenc management cited the geographic fit between the companies, their complementary product mixes and shared entrepreneurial vision as factors that led to the creation of the world's largest life science company. The merger was aimed at creation of global scale, enhanced innovation potential, strong product portfolio, expanded global sales and marketing forces and improved cost position through better manufacturing, administration and research and development.

The projected gains included annual gross margin improvements of between 0.5 and 1 percent and net margin improvements of 1.5–2.0 percent from 1999 and 2002. The company also anticipated about €1.2 billion per year in direct cost savings and synergies.

Mergers by the Sanofi Group

Historical perspective—Sanofi Group

The history of Sanofi Group began in 1973, when the French state-owned Elf Aquitaine oil company consolidated a number of cosmetic, healthcare and animal nutrition firms into a corporate subsidiary, the Sanofi Group. In 1979, all of its pharmaceutical activities were regrouped under a single organization. Between 1978 and 1982 Sanofi's international sales improved by 275 percent. By gaining access to two of the world's most important markets, the United States and Japan, Sanofi's overseas activities generated nearly half of the company's consolidated revenues.

In 1983, Choay, a pharmaceutical company specializing in the area of venous thrombosis, was acquired by Sanofi, which as a result gained access to a new line of important pharmaceuticals. By 1984 Elf Aquitaine's increasing biotechnological activities compelled the state-owned oil group to reorganize its company structure. Most of Elf Aquitaine's activities in this area, from healthcare to agricultural products, were transferred to Sanofi's control. Sanofi merged with Rousselot, a gelatin protein and glue producer, in which Elf Aquitaine formerly held a majority interest. Through the action of this merger, Elf Aquitaine's stake in Sanofi increased to 62 percent.

Additional foreign acquisitions included a Brazilian subsidiary of Revlon, as well as a 50 percent interest in a South Korean company. Through a series of acquisitions, Sanofi gained expertise in the area of biotechnological processes in food additives, dairy products and large crop seed sectors. In the 1990s, the company initiated steps to create international presence in the rapidly growing drug industry. In 1991, it entered into a strategic partnership with American drug company Sterling Winthrop, itself a subsidiary of Kodak. This alliance helped Sanofi to gain entry into the lucrative North American drug market. In 1996, Sanofi acquired the Bock Pharmacal Company, doubling its US sales and marketing force. In 1999, Sanofi merged with rival French pharmaceutical company Synthélabo. The deal allowed Sanofi to sell off its other businesses and focus on pharmaceuticals. Over the course of the 1990s, the shareholding of Elf in Sanofi fell from 61 percent in 1990 to 52 percent in 1994 and finally to 35.1 percent in 1999, with the Synthélabo merger.

Key milestones

1973: Sanofi Group is formed as a subsidiary of Elf Aquitaine.
1981: Sanofi forms joint subsidiary with American Home Products.
1983: Sanofi opens biotechnology center in Labège, France.
1991: Sanofi enters strategic alliance with Sterling Winthrop.
1999: Sanofi merges with Synthélabo to form the Sanofi-Synthélabo Group.
2004: Sanofi-Synthélabo Group merges with Aventis.

The Sanofi/Synthélabomerger

Synthélabo was created in 1970. It was purchased in 1973 by L'Oréal, the world's cosmetic leader. In 1999, France's second and third-biggest drug companies, Sanofi and Synthélabo, merged to create a new industry powerhouse with sales of FF35 billion ($6.2 billion) and market value of FF166 billion ($29.5 billion). Sanofi-Synthélabo became the sixth largest pharmaceutical company in Europe. The merger also propelled the combined entity to a position in the world's top 20 drug companies.

The shareholders in the two companies exchanged their current holdings at a ratio of 13 Sanofi shares to ten Synthélabo shares. The oil giant Elf Aquitaine, which controlled Sanofi, held 35.1 percent and L'Oréal, which controlled Synthélabo, held 19.4 percent of the capital in the new group. Elf held 45 percent of the voting rights while L'Oréal held about 25 percent of the voting rights.

Sanofi and Synthélabo had strong complementarity in the therapeutic areas of central nervous system, cardiovascular, oncology and internal medicine. The two companies' combined pro-forma research and development spending for 1998 had been close to FF6 billion. The deal excluded Sanofi's beauty products division. After merging with Synthélabo in 1999 the company sold off its cosmetics business and began focusing exclusively on pharmaceuticals.

The Sanofi-Synthélabo/Aventis merger

In 2004, Sanofi-Synthélabo made a hostile takeover bid worth €47.8 billion ($65.5 billion) for Aventis. Initially, Aventis rejected the bid because it felt that the bid offered was low based on share valuation. The three-month takeover battle concluded when Sanofi-Synthélabo launched a friendly bid of €54.5 billion in place of the previously rejected hostile bid. The French government also put pressure on Sanofi-Synthélabo to raise its bid for Aventis after it became known that Novartis, the Swiss pharma company, was also in the fray for acquisition.

The new company, christened Sanofi-Aventis, became the third largest pharmaceutical company in the world and ranked number one in Europe. Sanofi-Synthélabo now controlled Aventis with 95.47 percent of the share capital. The new group had a scientific research budget of €4.2 billion. Sanofi expected that the €52 billion stock-and-cash takeover would yield synergies of €1.6 billion by 2006, with 10 percent of the synergies in 2004, 50 percent in 2005 and the rest in 2006.

The companies had a good therapeutic fit. The merged companies expected considerable synergies for its pipeline. Sanofi-Synthélabo had several potential blockbusters, including ciclenoside, an inhaled corticosteroid. Aventis had more anti-infectives in development than Sanofi-Synthélabo. However, the two companies were equally matched in the number of alimentary/metabolic, anti-cancer and cardiovascular drugs under development.

Growth of Sanofi-Aventis

Sanofi-Aventis grew into a diversified global healthcare company engaged in the research, development, manufacture and marketing of healthcare products. The businesses include pharmaceuticals, comprising prescription drugs, consumer healthcare and generics, vaccines and animal health. The company is a world leader in vaccines. It employs 100,000 people in 100 countries. In 2010, net sales amounted to €30.4 billion.

Sanofi-Aventis' pharmaceuticals business notably focuses on diabetes, oncology and other flagship products in thrombosis and cardiovascular areas. Sanofi-Aventis has core strength in the field of healthcare with six growth platforms: emerging markets; human vaccines; consumer health; diabetics treatment; innovative products; and animal health. One of Sanofi's strategic priorities is to advance its R&D model to boost creativity. In 2010, Sanofi-Aventis finalized 37 operations including nine acquisitions. In 2010, the company laid off 1700 US employees following restructuring triggered by generic competition. The company dropped the -Aventis suffix of its name on May 6, 2011 after receiving approval at its AGM.

The company focuses on three principles in order to deliver long-term sustainable growth: increasing innovation in R&D; seizing external growth opportunities; and adapting group structures for future challenges.

Sanofi Pasteur, the fully integrated vaccines business of Sanofi-Aventis, is the world leader in the vaccines industry, offering a large range of vaccines covering 20 different infectious diseases. In 2009, it acquired Indian company Shantha Biotechnics.

Merial, a wholly owned subsidiary of Sanofi-Aventis since September 18, 2009, is one of the world's leading animal health companies involved in the research, development, manufacture and delivery of innovative pharmaceuticals and vaccines used by veterinarians, farmers and pet owners.

The Merck/Schering Plough merger

Merck Ltd

Merck is a global healthcare company that delivers innovative health solutions through its prescription medicines, vaccines, biologic therapies, animal health and consumer care products, which it markets directly and through its joint ventures. The company's operations are principally managed on a products basis and are comprised of four operating segments—the Pharmaceutical, Animal Health, Consumer Care and Alliances segments—and one reportable segment, which is the Pharmaceutical segment. The Pharmaceutical segment includes human health pharmaceutical and vaccine products marketed either directly by the company or through joint ventures.

In 2000s, Merck built on its R&D abilities by entering into strategic targeted alliances and acquisitions. It acquired Sirna Therapeutics, Inc., a San Francisco-based biotechnology company that has been at the forefront of efforts to create chemically modified RNAi-based therapeutics. RNAi technology can be used to develop medicines that can literally turn off a targeted gene in a human cell, potentially rendering inoperative a gene responsible for triggering a specific disease. Merck also acquired two other leading biotech companies, Abmaxis, Inc. and GlycoFi, Inc., to find new treatments in therapeutic areas. In 2007 alone, Merck developed 55 significant new partnerships, and it entered into nearly 250 partnerships during the period 2003–2007.

Schering-Plough Corporation

Schering-Plough Corporation was a US-based pharmaceutical company founded in 1851 by Ernst Christian as Schering AG in Germany. In 1971, the Schering Corporation merged with Plough to form Schering-Plough. Schering-Plough manufactured several pharmaceutical drugs, the most well known of which were the allergy drugs Claritin and Clarinex, anti-cholesterol drug Vytorin and brain tumor drug Temodar. In 2007, Schering paid $14.4 billion for Organon, a biotechnology company that had several novel drugs, including a fertility treatment. In 2007, Schering-Plough acquired Organon Biosciences for approximately €11 billion in cash and bolstered its animal health business.

Merger highlights

On November 3, 2009, Merck & Co., Inc. ("Old Merck") and Schering-Plough Corporation ("Schering-Plough") merged. In the merger, Schering-Plough acquired all of the shares of Old Merck, which became a wholly-owned subsidiary of Schering-Plough and was renamed Merck Sharp & Dohme Corp. Schering-Plough continued as the surviving public company and was renamed Merck & Co., Inc. ("New Merck" or the "Company"). However, for accounting purposes only, the merger was treated as an acquisition with Old Merck considered the accounting acquirer.

Schering-Plough shareholders received 0.5767 of a share of New Merck common stock and $10.50 in cash for each share of Schering-Plough. For Merck shareholders, existing Merck share certificates automatically represented an equal number of shares in the New Merck after completion of the merger. Merck used $9.8 billion of its own cash for the purchase plus $8.5 billion in short-term financing. The cash-and-stock deal of value $41.1 billion made Merck a dominant player in cholesterol, respiratory and infectious disease drugs, and boosted its pipeline for new biologics, which are drugs made from living cells. As a part of the acquisition of Schering-Plough, Merck agreed to sell its half stake in Merial pet care business for $4 billion to partner Sanofi-Aventis.

The New Merck had five primary divisions: global human health; animal health; consumer healthcare; Merck research laboratories; and Merck manufacturing. Animal health and consumer healthcare operated as separate business units.

Merger motives

Merck's best-selling drugs, like former blockbuster bone drug Fosamax, had gone generic. The merger gave Merck access to successful Schering products with much longer patents, such as the prescription allergy spray Nasonex. Merck could also capitalize on Schering's investments in promising biotechnology drugs. Both Merck and Schering-Plough were strong science-based companies. The merger of Merck and Schering-Plough expanded the company's product offerings in a range of areas including heart and respiratory health, infectious diseases, sun care and women's health. The companies had overlapping portfolios for cardiovascular, respiratory and antiviral drugs and experimental drugs. Schering-Plough added animal health products and a consumer division to Merck's profile, while bolstering its women's health area, led by Merck's cervical cancer vaccine, Gardasil.

As a result of the merger, Merck was able to extend Merck's global reach. Schering provided Merck with popular consumer brands like Coppertone and Dr Scholl. About 70 percent of Schering revenue came from outside the United States.

Merck was expected to reap huge cost savings from the Schering-Plough merger by cutting 15 percent of the companies' combined workforce. The merger was expected to create annual cost savings of $3.5 billion beyond 2011 and double the number of its drugs in late-stage development to 18. Merck and Schering-Plough, with their combined resources, were better able to compete with Pfizer.

In February 2010, the Company completed the acquisition of Avecia Biologics Limited ("Avecia") for a total purchase price of approximately $190 million. Avecia is a contract manufacturing organization with specific expertise in microbial-derived biologics.

In December 2010, the Company acquired all of the outstanding stock of SmartCells, a private company developing a glucose-responsive insulin formulation for the treatment of diabetes mellitus for $138 million. During 2010, the Company made progress driving revenue growth for key products and expanding its global reach including within emerging markets. Sales increased to $46 billion in 2010, driven largely by incremental revenue resulting from the inclusion of a full year of results for Schering-Plough products.

Bayer HealthCare M&A

Bayer HealthCare combines the global activities of its Animal Health, Pharmaceuticals, Consumer Care and Medical Care divisions. Bayer HealthCare's success story in the pharmaceuticals business goes back more than 120 years. The first product marketed by the "Pharmaceutical Department" of Bayer was the antipyretic Phenacetin in 1888. Schering AG, the company acquired by Bayer in 2006, had already entered hormone research by the 1920s.

Bayer HealthCare Pharmaceuticals is today the highest-selling pharmaceuticals company in Germany and holds a worldwide leading position in its main therapeutic areas. The focus of growth is on specialty pharmaceuticals and the opportunities for growth in the field of general medicine. Bayer HealthCare markets products in more than 100 countries. Bayer Schering Pharma is a world market leader in the fields of fertility control and menopause management in women and certain specialized therapeutics such as multiple sclerosis, renal cell carcinoma or diagnostic imaging.

Merger milestones

Year	Milestones
1978	Bayer acquires Miles Lab, Inc., giving it a significant position in US pharma.
1986	Bayer reacquires from Sterling Drugs the right to use the Bayer trademark in the US.

1989	Bayer acquires Cooper Technicon, New York to become one of the world's largest suppliers of diagnostic systems and reagents of clinical chemistry.
1994	Bayer acquires the North American self-medication business of Sterling Winthrop.
2004	Bayer acquires Roche's OTC business. Bayer becomes one of the world's top three suppliers of non-prescription medicines.
2006	Bayer announces public takeover offer for Schering AG. The Berlin-based pharmaceuticals is officially renamed Bayer Schering AG.
2007	Bayer sells the diagnostics division of Bayer Healthcare to Siemens AG for €4.2 billion.

Schering AG

Schering AG was a research-centered German pharmaceutical company founded in 1851 by Ernst Christian Friedrich Schering. In North America, Schering operated mainly under the Berlex Laboratories brand. At the time of the merger with Bayer, the company employed more than 26,000 people in 140 subsidiaries worldwide. Schering AG focused on the business areas of gynecology, andrology, multiple sclerosis, oncology and contrast agents. Schering's best-known products are probably its brands of combined oral contraceptive pills. Other key products included the interferon-beta brand and the paramagnetic contrast agent Magnevist.

The Bayer AG/Schering AG merger

Bayer AG completed its €17 billion ($21.6 billion) takeover of German rival Schering AG, creating the country's largest drug maker, in July 2006. Bayer controlled 92.4 percent of outstanding Schering shares. The acquisition of Schering was the largest takeover in Bayer's history and created a healthcare group with sales of more than €15 billion a year. Under the name Bayer Schering Pharma AG, Germany, the joint pharmaceutical company aimed to become one of the largest players on the world market. Schering bought with it an extensive range of products in the fields of gynecology and andrology, diagnostic imaging, oncology and specialized therapeutics, which ideally complemented Bayer's existing portfolio. Analysts believed that the deal was an attempt by Bayer to forge a German pharmaceutical powerhouse and restore the country as a vibrant center for drug discovery and manufacturing.

The deal gave Bayer access to Schering's lineup of best-selling multiple sclerosis treatments as well as Yasmin, a birth control product. Schering was the world market leader in hormonal contraceptives for women. Schering helped bolster Bayer's healthcare unit with the multiple sclerosis treatment Betaseron and the world's biggest stable of birth-control pills. Growth at the enlarged company was envisaged as being led by new products and demand for cancer drugs such as Bayer's Nexavar. Bayer also had farm chemicals and material science units. The company expected to gain almost half of its revenue from healthcare products. Schering was active in Specialized Therapeutics, a division with a relatively small number of products. Bayer had struggled in drugs since the recall of its anti-cholesterol treatment Baycol over safety concerns in 2001.

Before the merger, Bayer's annual revenues accounted for less than 40 percent of annual revenues. With the acquisition of Schering, healthcare became the largest part of Bayer, with projected sales of $18 billion a year.

Two weeks before the offer Merck attempted a hostile takeover bid for Schering to create a new German super-pharma company. Bayer's offer of $21.6 billion topped a $17.9 billion offer by Merck.

Schering was the world leader in oral contraceptives and also specialized in cancer drugs, while Bayer had focused its pharmaceutical research on cancer and cardiovascular drugs. The only overlap had been in oncology. The company expected €700 million in annual savings from the merger by 2009. The merger synergy was basically expected in marketing of cancer drugs. Schering had established a sales force for its portfolio of cancer drugs, which Bayer could exploit.

Bayer was famous for inventing aspirin and for its prescription medication such as Cipro and Levitra, which was used to treat erectile dysfunction.

The unified company was listed among the top ten pharmaceutical companies in the world. The new strategy focused on the development of medicines for use in hospitals and treatments for cancer and hematological diseases. The company also continued to make products for gynecology, diagnostic imaging and general disorders. The strategic aim was to increase the share of innovative medications for specialized therapy up to 70 percent of total sales. In the world market of specialized medications, Bayer Schering Pharma held sixth place after Roche/Genentech, Amgen, Johnson & Johnson, Novo Nordisk and Baxter.

Table 1.7 Financial highlights of Bayer HealthCare (€ million)

	2009	2010
Sales	15,988	16,913
Employees (number)	55,700	55,800
R&D	1847	2066
EBIT	2640	1861
Gross cash flow	3153	2948

M&A by Bristol-Myers Squibb (BMS)

Bristol-Myers Squibb (BMS) is a global biopharma company that focuses on the discovery and development of innovative medicines. The long history of Bristol-Myers started in 1887 when William Bristol and John Myers bought the former Clinton Pharmaceuticals. After World War II, Bristol-Myers became more diversified over four decades, buying up companies such as Mead Johnson, Clairol, Drackett and Zimmer.

Most of the company's sales come from products in the therapeutic areas of cardiovascular, immunoscience, metabolics, neuroscience, oncology and virology. BMS has about 20 manufacturing plants worldwide and about ten R&D centers in five countries, and sells products globally. The US accounts for more than half of sales. The company's R&D strategy is based on three pillars of a continuous focus on innovative portfolio, an integrated business model and continuous improvement. Based on the trend that 25 percent of major drugs in the future are likely to be biologics, about one-third of the company's research compounds in development are biologics. The company focuses on co-development and co-commercialization deals for several pipeline products to mitigate risks and optimize pipeline value. In early 2007, Bristol-Myers Squibb entered into co-development and co-commercialization agreements with AstraZeneca and Pfizer for investigational compounds discovered by Bristol-Myers Squibb.

The core strategy of a "string of pearls" aims to accelerate the discovery and development of new therapies with innovative alliances, partnerships and acquisitions. Since the acquisition of Adnexus Therapeutics in October 2007, the company has successfully completed 11 "pearl" transactions encompassing many of the key disease areas, including cancer, cardiovascular disease, immunology, neuroscience, rheumatoid arthritis and virology. Currently for BMS, more than 40 percent of the pipeline and 50 percent of revenue come from alliances with other companies.

The largest "pearl" transaction to date has been the acquisition of Medarex, Inc. in August 2009 for $2.3 billion. With this acquisition the company significantly expanded the oncology pipeline and biologics capabilities and obtained full rights to ipilimumab, an investigational immunotherapy for metastatic melanoma.

The company entered into or restructured collaboration agreements with various companies during 2010, including Eli Lilly and Company (Lilly), Allergan, Inc., Exelixis, Inc. and Oncolys BioPharma, Inc.

M&A milestones

Year	Milestones
1943	Bristol-Myers buys Cheplin Laboratories—a Syracuse, New York, manufacturer of acidophilus milk—and breaks ground for a new penicillin plant.
1967	Bristol-Myers acquires Mead Johnson & Company, a leader in science-based infant and children's nutrition.
1989	Bristol-Myers merges with Squibb, creating a global leader in the healthcare industry.
2001	The company announces the purchase of DuPont Pharmaceuticals Company for $7.8 billion, with the intention of further strengthening Bristol-Myers Squibb's medicines business.
2007	Bristol-Myers Squibb acquires Adnexus Therapeutics.
2008	Bristol-Myers Squibb purchases Kosan Biosciences, a cancer therapeutics company based in California, for approximately $190 million. This acquisition enhances the company's pipeline with compounds in two important classes of anti-cancer agents.
2009	Bristol-Myers Squibb acquires Medarex, Inc., a biotech company and a partner since 2005. This acquisition was the largest "string of pearls" transaction to date, and significantly expanded the company.
2010	In October, Bristol-Myers Squibb acquired ZymoGenetics, securing an existing product, RECOTHROM® (recombinant), as well as pipeline assets in hepatitis C, cancer and other therapeutic areas.

2011	In September, Bristol-Myers Squibb acquires Amira Pharmaceuticals, a small-molecule pharmaceutical company focused on the discovery and early development of new drugs to treat inflammatory and fibrotic diseases.

The Bristol-Myers/Squibb merger

The merger between Bristol-Myers and Squibb Corporation took place in 1989. Bristol-Myers was founded in 1887 and Squibb Corporation in 1858. The merger created Bristol-Myers Squibb Company, which was then the world's second-largest pharmaceutical enterprise. The merger, which was valued at $11.5 billion, was a stock swap merger on the basis of closing price of the shares. At the time of merger, Bristol-Myers Squibb's annual revenues totaled $8.6 billion, second only to Merck & Company. As per the merger agreement, Bristol-Myers exchanged 2.4 of its common shares for each share of Squibb. In all, Bristol-Myers issued 242 million shares. To prevent a hostile takeover, Squibb granted Bristol-Myers the right to buy about 20 percent of Squibb's outstanding stock for $123.90 a share.

The combination was meant to boost the competitive strength of the combined entity in pharmaceuticals, healthcare, consumer products and nutrition. Squibb had been looking to expand its product line because it was heavily dependent on one drug—Capoten. The merger blended Squibb's near-lock on the hypertension drug market with Bristol-Myers' consumer products, over-the-counter drugs and cancer-fighting prescription drugs.

At the time of merger, Bristol-Myers and Squibb had a combined sales force of more than 4000 people.

The merger resulted in great synergy in over 60 products and netting $50 million in worldwide sales within five years. Bristol-Myers Squibb

Table 1.8 Financial highlights of BMS ($ million)

	2006	2007	2008	2009	2010
Net sales	13,863	15,617	17,715	18,808	19,484
Operating cash flow	1450	2523	4776	5602	6071
Net earnings	787	1296	2697	3239	3102
Total assets	25,271	25,867	29,486	31,008	31,076
Debt	7248	4381	6585	6130	5328

owns 20 plants around the world as well as ten science centers. It has committed $4 billion toward R&D expenses.

Bristol-Myers Squibb's DuPont acquisition

BMS acquired DuPont Pharmaceuticals for $7.8 billion in 2001. DuPont's Pharma business included pharmaceuticals, medical imaging and radio pharmacies. The acquisition was basically undertaken to provide a greater focus on its medicine business, particularly in the area of virology and cardiovascular diseases. With the DuPont acquisition, Bristol-Myers Squibb added Sustiva® (efavirenz) to its HIV portfolio and also gained products such as Coumadin® (warfarin sodium), the US leading prescribed anticoagulant. BMS also gained a productive R&D pipeline that contained a number of early compounds with potential to be blockbusters. The pipeline consisted of compounds in five therapeutic areas—virology, cardiovascular diseases, inflammatory diseases, cancer and disorders of the central nervous system.

Other major acquisitions by BMS

In 2010, BMS acquired ZymoGenetics, which focuses on developing and commercializing therapeutic protein-based products for the treatment of diseases. The total cost for the acquisition was $10 million. The acquisition of Medarex positioned BMS for long-term leadership in biologics and gave the company full rights to a promising phase III compound for the treatment of cancer. Medarex's technology platform, people and pipeline provided a strong complement to BMS's biological strategy, specifically in immune oncology areas. In 2009, the acquisition of Kosan Biosciences enhanced BMS's pipeline with compounds in two important classes of anti-cancer agents. BMS had also acquired Adnexus Therapeutics, the developer of new class of biologics called adnectins. The acquisition helped advance BMS's biologics strategy across multiple therapeutic areas. Adnexus was the first acquisition in the company's "string of pearls" strategy.

Acquisitions by Johnson & Johnson

Johnson & Johnson (J&J) is the world's sixth largest consumer health company. It is the largest and most diverse medical devices and diagnostics company globally. The company is also the world's fifth largest biologics company and eighth largest pharmaceutical company. The J&J family of companies has more than 250 operating companies in

60 countries, employing approximately 116,000 people. The company is headquartered in New Brunswick, New Jersey.

In 1886, Johnson & Johnson was established in New Jersey. In 1888, J&J pioneered the first commercial aid kids. J&J acquired McNeil Laboratories in the US and Cilaq Chemie AG in Europe, giving the company a foothold in the growing field of pharmaceutical medicines. In 2002, J&J acquired Tibotec Virco BVBA to help address the vast unmet needs of patients with HIV/AIDS and other infectious diseases such as tuberculosis. In 2006, J&J acquired Pfizer Consumer Healthcare, which added heritage consumer brands such as Listerine antiseptic. In 2010, J&J celebrated 125 years of transforming the concept of care for patients, consumers and communities around the world.

In 2009, Johnson & Johnson announced the completion of its previously publicized acquisition of Mentor Corporation (NYSE: MNT), a leading supplier of medical products for the global esthetic market. Mentor operates as a standalone business unit reporting through Ethicon, Inc., a J&J company and a leading provider of suture, mesh and other products for a wide range of surgical procedures.

Additional References

1. William R. Pursche, "Mergers and Acquisitions: Pharmaceuticals—The Consolidation isn't Over," *McKinsey Quarterly*, No. 2, 1996.
2. Patricia M. Danzon, Andrew Epstein and Sean Nicholson, *Mergers and Acquisitions in the Pharmaceutical and Biotech Industries*, Wharton School, University of Pennsylvania, Working Paper.
3. David J. Ravenscraft and William F. Long, "The Paths to Creating Value in Pharmaceutical Mergers," http://www.nber.org/chapters/c8653; http://www.nber.org/books/kapl00-1
4. http://www.biojobblog.com/uploads/file/apiandgenerics.pdf
5. www.frost.com › Home › Our Services › CIF › Insights.
6. Michael Stanier, David Bugen and Brian K. William, "The Continuing Evolution of the Pharmaceutical Industry: Career Challenges and Opportunities," *Fiduciary Network*, Regent Atlantic Capital LLC, 2007.
7. IMAP, *Pharma and Biotech Industry Global Report 2011*.
8. http://www.rsc.org/chemistryworld/News/2009/March/13030903.asp
9. http://www.imaa-institute.org/docs/Mergers%20&%20Acquisitions%20Report_Ph
10. http://www.fiercepharma.com/signup?sourceform=Viral-Tynt-FiercePharma-FiercePharma
11. http://www.who.int/pmnch/media/press_materials/pr/2011/report-panel2.pdf
12. Pharma 2020, "Marketing the Future—Which Path Will You Take?" *PWC Pharma 2020 series*, February 2009.

13. http://www.unido.org/fileadmin/user_media/UNIDO_Worldwide/Africa_Programme/CAMI/RoundTable_Pharma.pdf
14. European Pharmaceutical Industry, "Delivering Sales Excellence in Turbulent Times," https://www.rolandberger.com/media/pdf/rb_press/RB_study-Sales_excellence_20060606.pdf
15. http://www.eaepc.org/parallel_distribution/myth.php?n=2#challenges
16. GSK website—www.gsk.com
17. www.nytimes.com/1989/.../smithkline-beecham-to-merge.html (accessed June 15, 2011).
18. http://www.nytimes.com/1995/03/17/business/international-briefs-glaxo-wellcome-merger-receives-ftc-approval.html (accessed June 16, 2011).
19. M&A Monitor Ltd, "UK 2002," http://www.m-a-monitor.com/xam-bin/m?mah01894
20. http://www.wsws.org/articles/2000/jan2000/glax-j22.shtml
21. http://www.pharmaceuticalonline.com/article.mvc/Glaxo-Wellcome-and-SmithKline-Beecham-Merge-a-0001
22. http://www.digitaltermpapers.com/a11904.html (accessed May 15, 2011).
23. http://hbswk.hbs.edu/item/4769.html
24. http://articles.latimes.com/1994-08-18/business/fi-28562_1_american-home-products
25. http://www.fundinguniverse.com/company-histories/American-Cyanamid-Company-History.html
26. Sascha Schmidt and Edwin Ruhli, "Prior Strategy Process as a Key to Understanding Mega Mergers: The Novartis Case," *European Management Journal*, Vol. 20, No. 3, pp. 223–234, June 2002, http://www.latec.uff.br/mestrado/sg_qualidade/Artigos%20Turma%20-%20segunda/science22.pdf
27. http://www.entrepreneur.com/tradejournals/article/18702231.html (accessed May 15, 2011).
28. http://www.independent.co.uk/news/business/cibageigy-and-sandoz-to-merge-into-pounds-40bn-giant-1340926.html
29. www.novartis.com
30. http://www.answers.com/topic/ciba-geigy#ixzz1S4rKJqYA
31. http://www.fundinguniverse.com/company-histories/Pharmacia-amp;-Upjohn-Inc-Company-History.html
32. http://www.biotech-info.net/monsanto_pharmacia.html
33. http://www.independent.co.uk/news/business/pharmacia-and-upjohn-merge-1597299.html
34. http://www.independent.co.uk/news/business/news/monsanto-in-50-billion-merger-740767.html
35. http://www.proessay.com/argumentative-essay-topics-and-conroversial-essay/pharmaceutical-industry/riding-the-pharma-roller-coaster.html
36. *Pharmaceutical Market Trends 2010–2014*, Urch Publishing, October 2010.
37. www.Pfizer.com
38. http://www.crystalra.com/media/The%20Street.com%20-%20Pfizer%20Warner%20Lambert%20-%2002-07-00.pdf
39. Carolyn Koo, "Pfizer, Warner-Lambert ink Merger Deal," TheStreet.com/NYTimes.com, February 7, 2000.
40. http://www.fool.com/news/2000/pfe000621.htm

41. "Pfizer vs. Warner-Lambert—Biggest Battles in Biopharma," *FiercePharma*, http://www.fiercepharma.com/special-reports/biggest-battles-biopharma/pfizer-vs-warner-lambert-biggest-battles-biopharma#ixzz1PdmhUHOj
42. http://www.fiercepharma.com/special-reports/biggest-battles-biopharma/pfizer-vs-warner-lambert-biggest-battles-biopharma
43. http://news.bbc.co.uk/2/hi/business/633782.stm
44. http://www.chelationtherapyonline.com/technical/p39.htm
45. http://www.nytimes.com/2009/01/26/business/26drug.html
46. http://seekingalpha.com/article/116484-pfizer-s-acquisition-of-wyeth-could-be-short-boon-to-shareholders
47. http://www.reuters.com/article/2010/01/27/pfizer-pipeline-idUSN2718349820100127
48. http://www.astrazeneca.com/About-Us/History/Merger-partners-in-brief
49. news.bbc.co.uk/2/hi/business/231213.stm
50. Bo Hellgren and Jan Lowstedt, "The Reproduction of Efficiency Theory: The Construction of the AstraZeneca in the Public Discourse," *International Journal of Business*, Vol. 6, No. 5, May 2011.
51. http://www.fundinguniverse.com/company-histories/Rhocirc;nePoulenc-SA-Company-History.html
52. http://www.fundinguniverse.com/company-histories/Hoechst/Company-History.html
53. http://www.icis.com/Articles/1998/12/07/72356/plans-come-to-fruition-as-hoechst-and-r-p-merge-in-life-sciences.html
54. http://www.agbioforum.org/v4n1/v4n1a05-assouline.htm
55. http://www.arturobris.com/index_files/aventis.pdf
56. http://business.highbeam.com/137364/article-1G1-68162421/aventis-last-richard-markham-ceo-aventis-pharma
57. http://www.thepharmaletter.com/file/18652/hoechst-rhone-poulenc-merge-to-create-aventis.html
58. www.sanofi.com
59. http://money.cnn.com/1998/12/03/europe/sanofi/
60. http://www.answers.com/topic/the-sanofi-synth-labo-group#ixzz1TP5LBDN3
61. http://www.answers.com/topic/the-sanofi-synth-labo-group#ixzz1TP9sMBh0
62. www.loreal-finance.com/.../sanofi-and-synthelabo-to-merge
63. http://www.answers.com/topic/the-sanofi-synth-labo-group#ixzz1TP5gHBYw
64. http://www.outsourcing-pharma.com/Preclinical-Research/Sanofi-Aventis-merger-completes
65. www.merck.com
66. http://www.nytimes.com/2009/03/10/business/10drug.html?pagewanted=2
67. http://www.reuters.com/article/2009/11/03/us-merck-scheringplough-idUSTRE5A23YZ20091103
68. http://www.usatoday.com/money/industries/health/2009-03-09-pharmaceutical-merge_N.htm
69. www.bayer.com
70. http://www.bayerpharma.com/en/company/history/index.php
71. http://www.bayer.com/en/innovative-products-from-schering.aspx
72. http://www.nytimes.com/2006/03/24/business/worldbusiness/24iht-web.0324bayer.html
73. http://www.inpharm.com/news/schering-backs-merger-bayer

74. http://www.telegraph.co.uk/finance/2941133/Bayer-acquires-Schering-in-17bn-deal.html
75. Yekaterina Dranitsynahttp://www.sptimes.ru/index.php?action_id=2&story_id=2139
76. http://articles.latimes.com/1989-07-28/business/fi-295_1_bristol-myers-squibb
77. www.bms.com
78. http://www.lexpert.ca/Magazine/deal.aspx?id=87
79. http://www.mesotheliomatreatment.net/bristol-myers-squibb
80. www.kosan.com
81. http://www.jnj.com

2
Mergers and Acquisitions in the Telecommunications Industry

Introduction

The telecommunications (telecom) industry is one of the most profitable and rapidly developing industries in the world, and is regarded as an indispensable component of the worldwide utility and services sector. The mobile industry generates around $900 billion of annual revenue and accounts for around 1.5 percent of world GDP. There are currently 5.6 billion mobile customers, which is equivalent to around 80 percent of the world population. Approximately 75 percent of mobile customers are in emerging markets such as India and China. Globally, the goal of bringing the benefits of competition, including lower prices, higher quality and greater innovation to telecommunications consumers has resulted in the removal of many barriers to entry into telecommunications markets. As a result, firms in the sector find it strategically desirable to enter new markets by merging, acquiring or forming an alliance with a firm that already has a presence in that market. Telecommunications operators are facing the challenges of growth, convergence, business transformation, technological change and regulatory pressures.

M&A in the telecom sector—trends and strategic reasons

The M&A wave peaked twice during the "noughties" decade. The first wave observed during the technology bubble of 1999–2000 was basically related to building of scale. Regional consolidation phases in the US mobile market and European broadband sectors led to the second wave of deal-making activity during 2005–2007. Then the financial crisis led to a slowdown of M&A activity. Post-2008, large European operators have increased their exposure to emerging markets, with Africa outperforming developing Asia as a target market as a footprint for growth.

The recent flurry of activity could help reverse the trend in M&A deals. The year 2010 witnessed four major telecom deals: the $27 billion acquisition of Mexico's Carso Global Telecom by America Movil SAB; the $25 billion acquisition of US-based GDF Suez International by International Power Plc; the $22 billion purchase of the US telecom company Qwest Communications International by Century Link; and the $20.6 billion deal for certain telecom assets of Egyptian-based Weather Investments by VimpelCom.

In March 2011, AT&T stuck a $39 billion deal to buy Deutsche Telekom AG's T-Mobile USA. The cash-and-stock deal gave AT&T, the current second-ranked US mobile carrier, an estimated 43 percent market share of customers in the United States, up from its previous 32 percent share.

In the US, for decades AT&T, or "Ma Bell" as it was fondly termed, delivered every piece of the telecom service value chain. In the 1900s people subscribing to multiple telephone services purchased a separate telephone from each company in order to make calls. Following the breakup of AT&T in 1984, the industry witnessed an intense accelerated horizontal diversification. Many new players entered the telecommunications arena, offering new options for telephone service in a tightly focused niche market.

Numerous M&A took place in the 1990s, primarily in the United States and Europe. The M&A trend in the world telecommunications market was caused by three significant events as well as by the ongoing regulatory liberalization and privatization of the industry. The three significant events that contributed to the M&A wave are: (1) the revision of the American Telecommunications Act in 1996, (2) a WTO agreement in 1997, and (3) the integration of the European Union in 1998. These changes have brought about fierce competition, which led to decreases in profit in both the domestic and cross-border telecommunications service markets.

One of the main objectives of the new US Act was to enhance competition in the local telephone service market by allowing long-distance telephone service providers to enter the local market and vice versa. In the US after the revision of the Telecommunications Act, mega mergers such as those of WorldCom and MCI, and SBC and Ameritech took place. WorldCom and MCI merged to compete with AT&T in the long-distance market. SBC and Ameritech merged to geographically extend SBC's operations to the western part of the country. In the shake-up, the American telecommunication market was led by AT&T, WorldCom MCI, Sprint and two or three RBOC (Regional Bell Operating Company) groups. The AT&T takeover of BellSouth in 2006 created the largest operator in the US by customer in landline, broadband and mobile phone markets.

The liberalization of the world's telecommunications market is also related to deregulation and free competition in the European Union (EU). Before the liberalization of the telecommunications market, most of the EU member states monopolized their markets with the aid of government controls. After the formation of EU in 1998, an M&A wave in telecom spread across the Europe. Two government enterprises, namely Telia of Sweden and Telenor of Norway, merged. Telecom Italia was acquired through a hostile takeover by Olivetti (Italy) after the breakdown of M&A negotiations between Telecom Italia and Deutsche Telecom. After Deutsche Telecom's (Germany) failure to acquire Telecom Italia, One2One of the UK was acquired by Deutsche Telecom. The merger between Mannesmann of Germany and Orange of the UK marked the beginning of the subsequent market penetration of the German telecom giant. The union of Vodafone AirTouch of the UK and Mannesmann was approved after Mannesmann divested its stake of ownership in Orange.

As a result of these series of M&A, Germany, the UK and France became the dominant powers in the EU telecommunications industry. By 2009, the number of market players in these significant markets was reduced by consolidation. During this period, Sunrise was acquired by Orange Switzerland; a joint venture was formed between mobile phone subsidiaries of France Telecom and Deutsche Telekom; and the mobile telephony activities of Holland's KPN were taken over by Mobistar.

In Asia, M&A activity in the telecom sector was first witnessed in Japan and Hong Kong. For example, DDI, KDD and IDO merged in 2000 to better serve the Japanese telecommunications market, which had grown considerably following deregulation and technological developments. Singapore Telecom announced the acquisition of Hong Kong Telecom in 2000 to take a major role in the Asian market.

The trends in the late 1990s indicate that strategic alliances between huge telecommunication enterprises have been replaced by M&As. In general, a strategic alliance in the telecom industry was helpful when direct investments were difficult owing to government regulations. With worldwide deregulation, however, a strategic alliance is no longer the best solution for a telecom firm. Another underlying fact that emerged was that after a significant portion of the entry barriers between regions and/or countries was eliminated, it was much more difficult for small and local telecom firms to enjoy profitability, even in niche markets, without joining the mega-carriers. Thirdly, the loosening of regional and national barriers in the market, and ongoing integration of fixed and mobile networks, forced telecom firms to become integrated service providers who offered not only telephony services but also data communication services such as the Internet. Finally, cross-border M&As became prevalent when telecom service firms without a global network could not continue to meet users' needs, including international data communication services.

Costly investments are also forcing companies to undertake M&As. One of the reasons for the surge in increased market concentration is the fall in mobile telephony revenues. In the context of growing demand and use of smartphones, mobile Internet services provide an attractive new growth area; it requires huge investments for capacity expansion. Substantial investment is also needed in new fixed networks (Next Generation Networks, NGN). Such complex investment decisions exert consolidation pressures on smaller firms in the sector

It has been observed that mergers between national rivals have accounted for a higher percentage of M&A volume in recent years. Major players are attracted toward emerging markets where customer growth is continuing at an above-average rate. For example, in 2009, Senegalese mobile company Sonatel was acquired by France Telecom.

Most European mobile markets are mature and static, with a handful of operators typically competing for each other's customers. With cell phone penetration rates exceeding 100 percent, there is limited scope for growth in these markets.

The recent trend analysis suggests that the bigger deals are seen as coming in Africa and the Middle East, where mobile phone penetration remains low. The regional operators Bharti Airtel and Reliance Communications of India, Etisalat of Abu Dhabi, Qtel of Qatar, Zain and Orascom have all built their groups through acquisitions.

The favorable financial environment is also acting as a catalyst for increased M&A activity in the sector. Many telecom firms have low levels of debt and can access very favorable terms on bond markets. Incentives for the consolidation trend are particularly favorable in the two big markets of the US and Germany.

In 2001, the cable giant Comcast completed the acquisition of AT&T Broadband, valued at $72 billion, including the debt of AT&T Broadband. The acquisition created a new giant, AT&T Comcast, which had $19 billion in annual revenues and 22.8 million subscribers clustered in major markets. As a result of the union, AT&T Comcast accelerated

Table 2.1 World's largest telecom M&A deals

Year	Deal	Amount in $ billions
1997	WorldCom/MCI	42.8
1998	Bell Atlantic/GTE	65.5
1998	SBC/Ameritech	70.4
1999	Vodafone AirTouch/Mannesmann	202.8
1999	Vodafone/AirTouch	65.88
1999	Qwest/US West	58.8
2000	France Telecom/Orange	39.7
2000	Shareholders/Nortel Network spinoff	60
2004	Sprint/Nextel	46.5
2004	Cingular Wireless/AT&T Wireless Services	47.1
2006	AT&T/BellSouth	89.4
2011	AT&T/T-Mobile	39

Source: Various sources.

Table 2.2 Other big deals in telecom

Year	Acquirer	Target	Price in $ billions
2001	Comcast	AT&T Broadband	72
2007	OTTP	BCE	48.5
2005	Telefonica	O2	31.66
2005	Comcast/Time Warner	Adelphia	17.61

its deployment of competitive local phone services via its cable lines. The new combination had a total of 22.8 million subscribers controlling 29 percent of the market, which was nearly twice as many customers as its nearest competitor, AOL Time Warner, Inc.

In July 2007, Ontario Teachers' Pension Plan (OTPP) took over the Canadian telecommunication giant BCE, Inc. (Bell Canada) in a deal worth $48.5 billion. In 2009, OTTP sold off much of its stake in Canadian Bell. In 2005, Telefonica acquired the UK mobile operator O2 for $31.66 billion. The acquisition enhanced scale for Telefonica by facilitating entry into two of Europe's largest markets, Germany and the UK.

In 2005, Comcast and Time Warner bought Adelphia for $17.6 billion. Adelphia had filed for bankruptcy in 2002. Time Warner had a net gain of about 3.5 million basic cable subscribers through the deal. Time Warner paid $9.2 billion in cash for the Adelphia assets in addition to issuing the stake in its cable units, as well as paying $2 billion to Comcast for a stake it had held in Time Warner Cable. Comcast acquired a net gain of 1.8 million additional subscribers as a result of the acquisition.

Types of consolidation

Basically consolidations in the telecom sector can be categorized into three types:

A) Cross-market consolidation

The cross-market form of consolidation involves cross-market mega-deals in which major telecom operator groups acquire controlling stakes in other groups that have a presence in multiple markets. Operators will pursue scale through cross-border mergers and acquisitions, entering new markets via large transactions. They also will bolster their competitive advantage through transactions in markets where they already operate.

For example, through the acquisition of Zain's African operations in 2010, Bharti extended footprint across a range of emerging African markets. In the process Bharti became a key regional player and allowed the operator group to export its low-cost operating model from India to markets abroad. VimpleCom announced its $6.5 billion merger with Wind Telecom (formerly Weather Investments), which controls Orascom Telecom. The combination forms a new global operator with operations in 20 countries, creating the world's sixth-largest telecom group.

Vodafone's acquisition of Vodacom is an example of a small regional African player that opted to merge with a larger operator. In one move the transaction provided Vodacom with the benefits of being part of a large global group, and enabled Vodafone to establish a presence in multiple African markets adjacent to its existing footprint. Vodafone had also acquired Essar's stake in Hutchison in India.

B) In-market consolidation

This type of consolidation involves merging operations within the same market. In other words, operators will seek to acquire current competitors. In-market consolidation enables operators to increase their subscriber base and garner higher market share. This type of consolidation also benefits operators to gain spectrum, expand network coverage and improve service quality along with a better cost structure by optimizing network and IT infrastructure.

Examples include the merger of T Mobile and Orange in 2009. At the time of the merger, no single UK operator had a greater market share than 27 percent. The merger created the UK's largest operator with a combined market share of 37 percent. The merger also resulted in synergies including expanded network coverage, quality and improved customer service. AT&T's acquisition of the Deutsche Telekom subsidiary in 2011 catapulted AT&T into being the largest mobile operator, ahead of Verizon in terms of subscribers. The acquisition provided AT&T with complementary network assets and improved network quality. The acquisition was also aimed at facilitating the significant expansion of the robust 4G LTE platform to approximately 95 percent of the US population.

C) Consolidation of ownership for control

Basically operators seek ownership consolidation for greater control of operations. Increased control helps the promoters make effective decisions on strategic, financial and operational issues. Ownership control also helps in the process of value and synergy creation in aspects such as new product introduction, implementation of technology and procurement cost optimization programs.

Examples include Etisalat increasing its stake from 50 to 70 percent in 2007 and then fully acquiring Atlantique in 2010. Qtel consolidated its ownership of Indostat in 2008 by increasing its stake from 40.8 to 65 percent. Vodafone has adopted a policy of divesting investments over which it does not have full control.

The merger of WorldCom and MCI

WorldCom

WorldCom began as a reseller of long-distance services in 1983, before emerging as the fourth largest long-distance provider and a full-service telecommunications powerhouse in the mid-1990s. WorldCom was formerly known as LDDS, and later relabeled LDDS WorldCom. Consolidation and acquisitions were the principal factors that enabled LDDS to accomplish rapid growth in the late 1980s. It acquired long-distance companies at a total cost of about $35 million and expanded its reach to various regions in the US.

WorldCom's growth was aided by a series of major acquisitions, including Resurgens Communications Group, Inc. and Metromedia Communications Corporation (1993); IDB Communications Group, Inc. (1994); WilTel Network Services (1995); MFS Communications Company, Inc. and UUNET Technologies, Inc. (1996); and Brooks Fiber Properties, Inc., CompuServe Corporation's data network, and America Online, Inc.'s network services subsidiary, which were all acquired in 1998.

Table 2.3 Major deals by LDDS

Year	Deals
1987	Telesphere Network, Inc., Com-Link 21
1988	Telephone Management Corporation
1989	Inter-Comm Telephone, Inc., ClayDesta Communications, Microtel, Inc., Galesi Telecommunications

Source: Company Reports.

WorldCom became a significant player in the telecommunications industry through the successful completion of 65 acquisitions. Between 1991 and 1997, WorldCom spent almost $60 billion in the acquisition of many of these companies and accumulated $41 billion in debt. Two of these acquisitions were particularly significant. The MFS Communications acquisition enabled WorldCom to obtain UUNet, a major supplier of Internet services to business, and MCI Communications gave WorldCom one of the largest providers of business and consumer telephone services.

MCI Communications

MCI Communications, founded in 1968, was well known as the company that led the charge in introducing competition in the telecommunications industry and precipitated the breakup of AT&T's Bell System. Following the breakup, MCI quickly became a multibillion-dollar global enterprise. By 1995 MCI had entered the cellular phone market by acquiring for $210 million Nationwide Cellular Service, Inc., which was the largest independent reseller of cellular services. MCI expanded Nationwide through additional contracts to resell service and was able to offer service to 75 percent of the US population by early 1996. In other words, MCI quickly gained significant presence in the fast-growing telecom sector without investing billions of dollars for developing a wireless infrastructure.

The MCI/WorldCom merger

On November 10, 1997, WorldCom and MCI Communication announced their $37 billion merger to form MCI WorldCom, making it the largest merger in US history at that time. The $37 billion deal included $7 billion in cash paid by WorldCom to acquire British Telecommunication's 20 percent stake in MCI. The combined MCI WorldCom, Inc. had 22 million customers, 25 percent of the long-distance market in the United States, some 933,000 miles of fiber for long-distance services, local network facilities in 100 US markets, 508,000 fiber miles for local service, and an international presence in more than 200 countries. European regulators forced MCI to divest all of its Internet assets, and it sold them to Cable & Wireless PLC for about $1.6 billion in cash. However, MCI WorldCom was able to keep WorldCom's UUNET Internet operation. Many analysts believed that WorldCom had purchased MCI at a highly inflated price.

MCI WorldCom, Inc. became one of the largest telecommunications companies in the world. The company's operations are organized around three divisions: MCI WorldCom, for US telecommunications; UUNET WorldCom, for Internet and technology services; and WorldCom International. The MCI WorldCom division is the second largest long-distance company in the US (after AT&T), with a 45,000-mile nation-wide fiber optic network, which provides local phone services in more than 100 markets and offers data, Internet and other communications services. UUNET WorldCom maintains a highly reliable backbone network that provides local access to the Internet from more than 1000 locations in the United States, Canada, Europe and the Asia-Pacific region, in addition to a wide range of other Internet services.

On October 5, 1999 Sprint Corporation and MCI WorldCom announced a $129 billion merger agreement that would have put MCI WorldCom ahead of AT&T as the largest communications company in the US. The deal, however, did not go through because of pressure from the US Department of Justice and the European Union on concerns of creating a monopoly.

By the end of 2003, the company was embroiled in accounting fraud to the tune of $11 billion, the figure put on the illegal inflation of the company's total assets. WorldCom filed for Chapter 11 bankruptcy protection in the largest such filing in US history at that time. On April 14, 2003, WorldCom MCI changed its name to MCI. Analysts have opined that dozens of acquisitions were never consolidated into a single, seamless enterprise. As a result of the accounting maneuvers, each new acquisition allowed the company to report higher per share profits, even when its core businesses were losing ground. The alleged fraud involved improperly inflating the company's earnings by more than $3.8 billion to help keep the stock price high.

Verizon acquires MCI

Verizon is a global leader in delivering innovative communications, information and entertainment. The company offers voice, data and video products and services over intelligent wireless, broadband and global IP networks. In 2005, Verizon acquired MCI for $7.6 billion, consisting of $4.8 billion in equity and $488 million in cash. The deal consisted of paying MCI shareholders 0.4062 shares of Verizon common stock for each common share of MCI plus $1.50 in cash per share. The acquisition was based on the logical extension of Verizon's strategy to serve growth markets and offer broadband technologies. MCI's 10,000 enterprise customers were the primary target of the deal.

The merger of Bell Atlantic and GTE to form Verizon Communications

Verizon Communications

This US-based telecommunications and broadband company was formed as a result of the Bell Atlantic/GTE merger. Headquartered in New York City, the company has one of the most reliable wireless networks, with 106.3 million total connections. Its enterprise/mid-market business customers included 96 percent of the Fortune 1000 companies. The company has primarily two divisions. The Global wholesale business serves CLEC, wireless, long-distance and other service providers. The company makes some 143.7 million customers connections every day, which includes wireless, wire line and broadband. The company provided employment to 195,900 employees in 2010.

Verizon had the largest and most reliable 3G broadband network covering more than 290 million people. The company had launched 4G LTE technology in 38 markets and 175 in 2010 and 2011 respectively, covering more than 185 million people. Internationally, the company has operations or joint ventures in both wire line and wireless services in 40 countries and is part owner of many of the world's fiber optic links, including a major link connecting Asia and Europe.

Bell Atlantic

In January 1982, the US Department of Justice ended a 13-year antitrust suit[1] against the world's largest corporation, the American Telephone

Table 2.4 Financial highlights of Verizon Communications ($ million)

	2006	2007	2008	2009	2010
Operating revenue	88,144	93,469	97,354	107,808	106,565
Operating profit	27,918	29,955	31,449	30,559	31,050
Net income	6239	5652	12583	10358	2549

and Telegraph Company (AT&T). AT&T divested itself of 22 local operating companies, which were divided among seven regional holding companies (RHCs).

With this act, Bell Atlantic was freed of AT&T in 1983. The company served the northern Atlantic states and oversaw seven telephone subsidiaries. Bell Atlantic made several major acquisitions in its first year of operation. In October and December 1984, Bell Atlantic purchased Telecommunications Specialist, Inc. (TSI), an interconnect firm, and Tri Continental Leasing Corporation (Tri Con), a computer and telecommunications equipment provider. Other Bell Atlantic acquisitions of 1990 included Northern Telecom's regional PBX operations and Simborg Systems Corporation.

In 1988, Bell Atlantic announced the introduction of four new information services: an electronic message storage system; a telephone answering service; a voice mail service; and a videotext gateway service, through which databases and customers communicated.

In 1997, Bell Atlantic merged with another Bell Regional Operating Company, NYNEX, based in New York City. By early 1998, the new Bell Atlantic had 39.7 million domestic access lines, 5.4 million domestic wireless customers, 6.3 million global wireless customers, and services in 21 countries worldwide. The company was also the world's largest publisher of both print and electronic directories, with over 80 million distributed annually.

GTE Corporation

GTE had its origin back in 1918. GTE Corporation was ranked as the world's third-largest publicly owned telecom company in 1996. With over 20 million telephone access lines in 40 states, the communications conglomerate was America's leading provider of local telephone services.

Its $6.6 billion acquisition of Contel Corporation in 1990 nearly doubled GTE's Mobilnet cellular operations, making it the second-largest provider of cellular telephone services in the United States, with over two million customers. The merger strengthened GTE's assets in two of its three major areas of operations: telephone service and telecommunications products. The Contel merger created the largest telephone company in the Western Hemisphere, with just under 18.5 million residential and business lines installed at the time of acquisition. Of this total, 16 million were in the US, making the combination the fourth-largest domestic carrier behind Bell Atlantic, BellSouth and Ameritech.

GTE's strategy for the mid- to late 1990s focused on technological enhancement of wire line and wireless systems, expansion of data services, global expansion and diversification into video services. On July 27, 1998, Bell Atlantic and GTE Corporation announced a definitive agreement for an all-stock merger.

Merger highlights

The merger between Bell Atlantic and GTE was the latest in a string of mergers in the telecommunications industry following the passage of the 1996 Telecommunication Act, which allowed what were formerly the regional Bell companies to enter the long-distance market, and permitted the long-distance companies to begin providing local telephone services. The combined company, Verizon Communications, with headquarters in New York, became the second largest telecom company, just behind AT&T Corp. It became the largest US wireless company, with more than 260,000 employees. The deal came a day after AT&T Corp. agreed to merge its overseas operations with British Telecom, in a $10 billion joint venture.

Terms of the merger

Under the terms of the agreement, GTE shareholders received 1.22 shares of Bell Atlantic common stock for each share of GTE common stock that they owned. The merger was valued at $64.7 billion at the time of closing the deal after approval based on stock market values. Bell Atlantic shareholders continued to own their existing shares after the merger. In mid-May 1999, the majority of the shareholders of Bell Atlantic and GTE voted to support the merger. At Bell Atlantic, 64 percent of shareholders were in favor, while at GTE nearly 97 percent of shareholders were in favor. Verizon's board of directors had equal numbers of directors designated by Bell Atlantic and GTE.

The completion of the merger came after many approvals. The 27 state regulatory commissions, the Federal Communications Commission (FCC) and the Justice Department had approved the proposal. The FCC attached 25 conditions to its approval of the merger, conditions that were designed to open local markets to competition, foster out-of-region competition and improve residential telephone service. The conditions included a requirement that the new company restrict ownership in GTE's Internet assets, Genuity, Inc., to 9.5 percent. GTE spun off roughly 90 percent stake in Genuity, Inc.

In 1999, Bell Atlantic and Vodafone AirTouch Plc entered into a wireless joint venture called Verizon wireless. Verizon became the majority owner of Verizon Wireless.

Synergistic advantages of the merger

The merger was termed as a "merger of equals". The merger created a powerhouse that was capable of providing a wide range of services including long-distance, local and wireless services as well as Internet access.

As the result of merger, Verizon became the number two US telecom company behind AT&T Corporation. Verizon Wireless reached 90 percent of the US population and 96 percent of the 100 largest wireless markets in the country.

The merger combined Bell Atlantic's East Coast local franchise and GTE's national presence in the local market. The transaction was made to fuse GTE's national footprint, long-distance expertise and extensive data communications capabilities with Bell Atlantic's advanced network, which had been catering to its considerable data-intensive market.

The combined group had 63 million access lines in the US, making it the nation's largest local exchange carrier, even after the merger of SBC Communications and Ameritech in October 1999. Verizon had 25 million wireless customers nationwide. The new company Verizon also became the largest cellular service provider in the US, with 10.6 million customers, and a major provider of data communications and Internet services. Bell Atlantic estimated that the merger would generate significant capital convergence, producing higher capital efficiency and higher cash flow and margin growth.

Analysts estimated that by the third year after completion of the merger, annual revenue synergies of approximately $2000 million would result primarily from improved market penetration for value-added services and faster development of data and long-distance businesses. The merger was also expected to create annual capital synergies of approximately US$500 million through volume purchasing and elimination of certain capital costs associated with building a data network in Bell Atlantic's existing operating territory.

Restructuring AT&T—making a full circle

Origins of AT&T

The original AT&T Corp., formerly known as the American Telephone and Telegraph Corporation, is as old as the telephone itself. In 1876, Alexander Graham Bell invented the telephone. Along with Gardiner Hubbard and Thomas Sanders, Bell laid the foundation of the company that became AT&T—a brand that has become synonymous with the best, most reliable telephone service in the world. AT&T was incorporated in 1885 as a wholly owned subsidiary of American Bell, chartered to build and operate the original long-distance telephone network. In 1899, AT&T acquired the assets of American Bell and became the parent company of the Bell System. Over the years AT&T's Bell System provided what was by all accounts the best telephone system anywhere.

For much of its history, AT&T and its Bell System functioned as a legally sanctioned, regulated monopoly. However, the changes in telecommunications during the 1970s eventually led to an antitrust suit by the US government against AT&T. The suit began in 1974 and was settled in January 1982, when AT&T agreed to divest itself of the wholly owned Bell operating companies that provided local exchange services. AT&T was required to divest itself of 22 local telephone-operating companies. The key issue of the divestiture was to demonopolize the telecommunications industry and ensure equal access to the local exchange facilities by all long-distance carriers.

In the 1980s, AT&T again focused on restructuring its business operations. Acquisitions made by the company during the decade resulted in few synergies between the company's communications and manufacturing businesses. Hence, in 1995, AT&T restructured itself into three separate publicly traded companies: a systems and equipment company (Lucent Technologies), a computer company (NCR) and a communications services company (AT&T). This was the largest voluntary breakup in American corporate history.

The SBC/Ameritech merger

SBC

Originally one of the seven regional holding companies formed after the breakup of American Telephone & Telegraph Corporation's (AT&T) Bell System in 1983, SBC Communications, Inc. (formerly known as Southwestern Bell Corp.) had emerged in the 1990s as a national provider of local telephone services.

Twelve years later, the Telecommunications Act of 1996 triggered dramatic changes in the competitive landscape. SBC Communications, Inc. established itself as a global communications provider by acquiring Pacific Telesis Group (1997), Southern New England Telecommunications (1998) and Ameritech Corp. (1999). In 2005, SBC Communications, Inc. acquired AT&T Corp. itself, creating the new AT&T.

With the acquisition of BellSouth in 2006, and the consolidated ownership of Cingular Wireless and YP.com, AT&T is positioned to lead the

Table 2.5 Financial highlights of SBC Communications ($ million)

	2000	2001	2002	2003	2004
Revenues	50,881	45,381	42,821	40,498	40,787
Operating income	10,303	10,296	8438	6284	5901
Net income	7800	7008	5653	8505	5887
Total assets	98,735	96,416	95,170	100,233	108,844

industry in one of its most significant transformations since the invention of the telephone more than 130 years ago.[2]

Ameritech

Ameritech Corporation was one of the largest telecommunications companies in the United States. Ameritech's Bell Group, the holding company, which provided exchange telecommunications and local and long-distance exchange access service for business and residential customers in the Midwest, was made up of Illinois Bell, Indiana Bell, Michigan Bell, Ohio Bell and Wisconsin Bell. Ameritech Services and Ameritech Information Systems comprised the remaining operational sectors. As a whole, the corporation was structured into separate business units, which included consumer phone services, long-distance phone services, small-business services, advertising and cellular services.

Ameritech was one of the seven Regional Bell Operating Companies created following the breakup of the Bell System. Ameritech, along with its six sibling regional holding companies (RHCs), shared $147 billion in assets. By 1987 Ameritech had started focusing on fiber-optic and digital technologies. In March 1988, the fully owned subsidiary Ameritech Applied Technologies, Inc. was formed with the goal of integrating and updating RHC computers to one standardized system.

In January 1993, Ameritech officially retired the Bell brands and marketed itself using only the Ameritech name across all five states in its territory. Ameritech also owned Ameritech Cellular, a wireless company that operated cellular networks in many of the other cities of these states.

In 1999, Ameritech was acquired by SBC Communications, which subsequently acquired AT&T Corporation in 2006, becoming the present-day AT&T Inc.

Merger highlights

In the year 1999, SBC and Ameritech formed a company worth $146 billion that competed against incumbent local telecommunications

Table 2.6 Financial highlights of Ameritech ($ million)

	1995	1996	1997
Revenues	13.4	14.9	15.9
Net income	2.00	2.1	2.3
EPS (cents)	0.71	0.91	2.14

companies, local exchange carriers, long-distance companies and global service providers. The merger could be termed as a "logical and necessary response" to dramatic advances in technology and fundamental shifts in regulation that had opened major markets throughout the world, particularly in the context that a single carrier can now compete for all of a customer's needs locally, nationally and globally.

Under the terms of deal, Ameritech shareholders received a fixed exchange ratio of 1.316 SBC shares for each share of Ameritech. The combined company was called SBC. The existing shareholders of SBC owned approximately 56 percent of the company and the Ameritech shareholders the remaining 44 percent. By acquiring Ameritech, SBC gained access to 30 new local US markets outside its existing 13 state regions and gained a potential customer base of 180 million people. The combined company had the opportunity to enter international markets. Together SBC and Ameritech had operations in 19 countries in Europe, Asia, Africa, North America and South America. The combined entity was able to offer a mix of local, long-distance and Internet services.

As a part of the regulatory compliance of Federal and State regulators, SBC and Ameritech agreed to several conditions to ensure adequate competition. The merged company had to offer local phone service in 30 markets outside of its home territory within 30 months of the merger or pay a $1.1 billion penalty. Ameritech's cellular assets had to be sold off to GTE.

As the first post-Ameritech merger initiative, SBC announced plans to offer broadband services to approximately 80 percent of SBC's United States wire line customers over the next three years. SBC invested an estimated $6 billion in fiber, electronics and other technology in this broadband initiative.

The SBC/AT&T merger

In 2006, SBC bought AT&T and became the largest telecommunications company in the world. The merger was a pivotal element in the history of telecommunications markets. The merger was termed as a "mother and child reunion". Twenty-one years after Federal regulators forced the old AT&T to split up, Ma Bell had come full circle.

SBC Communications, a so-called "Baby Bell", acquired venerable "Ma Bell" AT&T, signifying the reunion of the two companies after the court had mandated the breakup decades before. SBC was one of the most ambitious of the Baby Bells and had about 50 million local telephone customers at the time of the merger. Following Federal decisions AT&T was unable to get back into the local market and connect up its local services with its long-distance services. The merger was approved by the FCC and the US Department of Justice, and the new company was allowed to keep the AT&T name.

Terms of the merger

Under the terms of agreement, the shareholders of AT&T received total consideration valued at $19.71 per share or approximately $16 billion. AT&T shareholders received 0.77942 shares of SBC common stock for each common share of AT&T. At the time of closing the deal, AT&T paid its shareholders a special dividend of $1.30 per share.

Significance of the merger

The combination of SBC and AT&T set the stage for the future of integrated communications and entertainment as a reality for consumers and businesses. The union of the two companies bought the local, global and wireless network resources under one entity and provided the expertise to set the standard for delivering meaningful innovations. The transaction combined AT&T's global systems capabilities, business and government customers and fast-growing Internet protocol (IP)-based business with SBC's local exchange, broadband and wireless solutions. It was expected that the merger would renew America's leadership in communications technology, enabling the combined entity to become a stronger US-based global competitor capable of delivering advanced network technologies.

SBC and AT&T had complementary world-class assets and industry-leading capabilities. AT&T bought to the combined company the world's most advanced communications network to meet the sophisticated data communication needs of large businesses with multiple locations. Beyond network capabilities, AT&T had complementary assets that allowed SBC to bring a full range of innovative voice and data services to customers around the world. These included a broad, high-end enterprise customer base, proven sales expertise in complex communications solutions, and an advanced product portfolio including a broad range of IP-based services. In addition, AT&T had the world's premier communications research organization: AT&T Labs had more than 5600 patents, issued or pending, worldwide at the time of the merger.

Synergies of the merger

SBC and AT&T expected the proposed transaction would yield a present value of more than $15 billion in synergies, net of the cost to achieve them. Synergies were expected from reduced costs over and above the expected cost improvements from the companies' ongoing productivity initiatives. Nearly half of the total net synergies were expected to come from network operations and IT; approximately 25 percent were expected from the combined business services organizations, on account of sales and support functions; and about 10 to 15 percent of the synergies were expected from eliminating duplicate corporate functions. SBC forecast that initially the acquisition would slow its revenue growth rate. AT&T's sales declined 11.6 percent in 2004. At the same time new revenue opportunities existed in expanded wireless sales in the enterprise space of small business and residential customers. The company believed that the merger would help in saving redundant sales, network and customer care costs to a tune of $1.5 billion a year.

The Cingular Wireless/AT&T Wireless Services merger

Cingular's history can be traced back to Advanced Mobile Phone Service, Inc., a subsidiary of AT&T, which was created in 1978 to provide nationwide cellular services in the USA. However, as a part of the Bell System divestiture in 1984, Cingular became one of the Regional Bell Operating Companies. Cingular Wireless was founded as a joint venture (60:40) of SBC Communications and BellSouth. The joint venture created the US's second largest carrier.

In 2004, Cingular Wireless and AT&T Wireless completed their $41 billion merger, creating the US's biggest wireless carrier in terms of subscribers. Cingular had purchased AT&T Wireless Services, Inc. after the bidding war with Britain's Vodafone Plc, which offered $38 billion.

As Cingular was jointly owned by Baby Bells SBC Communications and BellSouth Corp., SBC and BellSouth contributed $25 billion and $16 billion for AT&T Wireless.

Cingular had to divest itself of wireless customers and other assets in 13 US markets in order to gain Justice Department approval for the merger.

Cingular, which was the USA's number two cellular service provider, paid about a 27 percent premium to shareholders of AT&T Wireless.

Both Cingular and AT&T Wireless had networks that run on the global system for mobile communications (GSM) standard, the same standard that most networks in Europe operate.

The deal made the newly combined company, known as Cingular Wireless, the largest wireless carrier, ahead of Verizon Wireless, with about 46 million subscribers, comprising AT&T Wireless's 22 million subscribers and Cingular's 24 million. It also had licenses to operate wireless service in 49 of the 50 US states, and served the top 100 US metropolitan areas. The combined company offered network resources to customers free of roaming charges. Customers were able to make calls on six continents and in more than 100 countries. As a result of the merger the companies were expected to save costs of $1 billion.

At the time of the merger, the two companies had separate networks: the historic AT&T Blue Network and the Cingular Orange Network. Both networks contained a mix of both TDMA and GSM facilities. Approximately 50,000 cell sites had to be melded together. From a technical standpoint, the "blue" and "orange" networks were considered different networks until integration was completed in 2005.

The AT&T/BellSouth merger

Corporate history of BellSouth

BellSouth was formed in 1983 as part of the court-ordered breakup of the American Telephone and Telegraph Company (AT&T). AT&T had often used BellSouth as its testing ground for new technologies, which gave BellSouth a lead in high-technology services, such as using telephone lines to monitor gas meters.

BellSouth Corporation was one of the world's largest communications companies, serving close to 34 million customers in the United States and in 18 other countries, with a particularly large market in Latin America. The company provided local telecommunications as well as wireless local and long-distance service, long-distance access, cable and digital television, Internet access and other electronic commerce.

In 1986, BellSouth increased its presence in the lucrative cellular telephone market when it bought 15 percent of Mobile Communications Corp. of America for $107.5 million. The following year BellSouth Enterprises bought almost all the assets of Universal Communications Systems, Inc. for $79.1 million. BellSouth also bought out L. M. Berry & Co., a large independent yellow page publisher in 1986. By 1988, BellSouth was the fastest-growing regional holding company with an impressive use of new technologies and services and the addition of 600,000 new telephone lines to the network every year. In 1989, BellSouth bought 60 percent of Air Call Communications for $34.5 million. Until 1992, regulations stemming from the AT&T breakup had kept BellSouth and other Baby Bells from expanding into a broader range of information services.

Merger highlights

The AT&T and BellSouth $87 billion merger created the largest phone company in the United States, and left two major players in the US market—AT&T and Verizon. The merger was in tune with the regulatory reforms that led brick by brick to the old AT&T being put back together. The merger reunited large parts of AT&T's former domain by folding BellSouth's nine-state territories into AT&T's existing operations spanning the US Midwest, Southwest and West Coast. The merger gave AT&T complete control of Cingular Wireless, the country's largest mobile telephone provider, at a time when wireless was the newest frontier for expanding Internet access. The merger helped unite the Cingular, BellSouth and AT&T networks into a single fully integrated wireless and wire line Internet Protocol network offering a full range of advanced solutions. The merger facilitated the combined entity to speed the convergence of new and improved video services, which facilitated the industry's shift to the next-generation IP-based technologies.

Since AT&T and BellSouth are not actual competitors in the local, long-distance and video markets, and because BellSouth was not a significant competitor with AT&T in the enterprise market, the merger did not reduce competition in any of those markets.

The AT&T/BellSouth merger reflected the irrelevance of antitrust (anti-competitive) policies in a rapidly changing global environment.

AT&T and BellSouth offered conventional telephone service in different regions of the country. AT&T operated in the Southwest, Far West and the Midwest. BellSouth provided telephone service in the Southeast. Both companies were losing subscriber lines rather rapidly as consumers switched to cellular phones or 'Voice over Internet Protocol" (VoIP) provided by the cable companies or independent providers, such as Vonage. The new broadband (DSL) Internet services offered by AT&T and BellSouth had not been sufficient to offset the revenue losses from traditional telephone services. Combining these two companies provided useful synergies in their battle to compete with the cable television companies.

Analysts were of the opinion that moving away from three brands to one single brand, AT&T, would enhance efficiency in terms of advertising and support. With a market capitalization of $225 billion at the time of merger announcement, the new AT&T was positioned far ahead of its leading competitor Verizon. The combined company had 58 million cell phone customers, 67.5 million phone lines and 11.5 million broadband users. The company reported revenues of $115 billion in 2005.

Synergies of the merger

It was estimated that cost-savings opportunities in advertising and brand support were substantial. The company estimated cost savings of $500 million annually, starting in 2008. The total synergies expected were estimated to be over $2 billion in 2008. The net present value of these synergies was $18 billion. The major part of these synergies was expected to be from non-labor savings. By 2009, two-thirds of the total cost synergies came from sizable opportunities in network and sales operations, IT and procurement.

Terms of the merger

The acquisition was structured in a way that holders of BellSouth received 1.325 shares of AT&T for each BellSouth share, or roughly $37.09 per share. The deal was good for BellSouth shareholders as they received a meaningful premium of AT&T stock for each share they held. On the basis of the day of merger announcement, the equity portion was valued at $67.1 billion. The total enterprise value was estimated at $89.4 billion, which also accounted for BellSouth's debt, which included the proportional debt of $22 billion at Cingular.

Merger conditions

The US Federal Communications Commission approved the deal on the basis of a number of concessions made by AT&T, the most important of these being a network neutrality provision for two years after the merger. The neutrality provision entitled AT&T not to discriminate against web companies in pricing or in access to lines. AT&T agreed to offer high-speed Internet for $19.95 a month over the next 30 months without requiring customers to purchase phone service from the company. AT&T also agreed to give up some wireless licenses suitable for high-speed Internet so that other companies could compete. Further, the company had to freeze rates for "special access" lines that served certain large businesses.

Summary of merger benefits

The most immediate and obvious benefit of the merger was the likely impact on wireless customers. Wireless was one of the fastest-growing parts of AT&T, which owned 60 percent of Cingular Wireless. The company expected to use the revenue growth and savings to invest in new technologies and expand its business. Another benefit realized was that the new, simplified ownership and operating structure for Cingular facilitated greater financial exposure to wireless. The merger created a single brand, AT&T, which became more cost-efficient and effective. The merger also helped in accelerating the technology evolution of IP-based services. Cingular Wireless ownership combined with unified wireless and wire line operations became a very important success driver to integrate networks and services faster.

Experts also held the perception that the merger would not impact negatively on consumers as the two companies did not directly compete with each other except in some business accounts.

At the time of the merger, AT&T had 71 million access lines and 9.8 million broadband subscribers, putting it ahead of Comcast's 8.5 million cable modem subscribers. This merger was a strategic attempt by AT&T to seek a real alternative to cable monopolies in the VoIP market and in the "triple play"—broadband voice, data and video service plans. AT&T estimated it would recover some of the market share lost in recent years to IP applications and cellular space, which had cut it out of selling long-distance calls.

There existed opportunities to exploit the alliance in other advanced communication services such as a single voice mail service for wireless and landline phones.

AT&T and BellSouth are also closely aligned when it comes to their wire line broadband strategies, which could mean speedier IP TV deployments for BellSouth customers. The main reason for this is that the companies have built their networks around a similar architecture.

With the acquisition, AT&T brought BellSouth, which had no video strategy, into its broadband services picture.

The merger had put AT&T back on top as the largest telecommunications company in the United States—and, in fact, the world—after it was broken up into eight smaller companies by the Federal Government in 1984.

Operating under the brand AT&T, the company offers one of the world's most advanced and powerful global backbone networks, carrying 23.7 petabytes of data traffic on an average business day to nearly every continent and country, with up to 99.999 percent reliability.

Table 2.7 Financial highlights of AT&T ($ million)

	2006	2007	2008	2009	2010
Revenues	62,518	118,322	123,443	122,513	124,280
Operating income	17,997	29,141	(1690)	21,000	19,573
Net income	12,547	17,228	(2364)	12,447	20,179
Total assets	270,118	274,951	264,700	268,312	268,488

The company offers voice coverage in more than 220 countries, data roaming in more than 200 countries and mobile broadband in more than 130 countries. AT&T is also one of the world's largest providers of IP-based communications services for businesses, with an extensive portfolio of Virtual Private Network (VPN), Voice over IP (VoIP) and other offerings—all backed by innovative security and customer support capabilities. AT&T is also the publisher and distributor of 1250 AT&T real Yellow Pages titles annually. A Fortune 500 company, AT&T is one of the 30 stocks that make up the Dow Jones Industrial Average.

AT&T's acquisition of T-Mobile[3]

T-Mobile

T-Mobile USA is a national provider of wireless voice, messaging and data services. T-Mobile USA is the US operating entity of T-Mobile International AG, the mobile communications subsidiary of Deutsche Telekom AG. Deutsche Telekom is one of the largest global telecommunications companies, with 129 million customers worldwide.

On March 20, 2011, AT&T and Deutsche Telekom entered into a stock purchase agreement under which AT&T agreed to acquire the T-Mobile subsidiary of Deutsche Telekom in exchange for approximately $39 billion. The merger process is expected to be completed within a one-year period.

Mobile data traffic on AT&T's network is expected to increase eight to ten times by 2015 from next-generation bandwidth devices. AT&T's planned merger with T-Mobile was considered to be the most efficient solution for the formidable challenge faced by AT&T in terms of capacity constraints arising from unprecedented demand for mobile data. Statistics show mobile data traffic on the AT&T network grew by 8000 percent from 2007 to 2010. The network synergies of the transaction freed up new capacity—the functional equivalent of new spectrum—in the many urban, suburban and rural wireless markets. It has to be noted that allocation and implementation of new spectrum can take years.

The potential benefits of the combination can be highlighted as follows:

- To improve voice and data network performance across the US, particularly in markets challenged by impending "spectrum exhaust."
- To provide access for 34 million T-Mobile customers to a nationwide, robust LTE network.[4]
- To allow AT&T to expand LTE deployment to more than 97 percent of Americans, reaching approximately 55 million more people.
- AT&T's LTE network will support high-tech industries in the US, making possible a cycle of innovation and growth for device makers, application developers, cloud providers, content providers and customers.
- An estimated 55,000 to 96,000 new direct and indirect jobs will result from AT&T's additional infrastructure investment, according to an analysis by the Economic Policy Institute.[4]

German-owned T-Mobile was the only major foreign-controlled US telecom network that became a part of US-based company.

Fact sheet

	AT&T	**T-Mobile**
Headquarters	Dallas, Texas	Bellevue, Washington
Employees	266,590	37,795
Network	GSM based with HSPA+	GSM based with HSPA+
Wireless subscribers	96 million	34 million
Total wireless revenues	$58.5 billion	$21.3 billion
Wireless Service EBITDA margin	40.7%	29.2%

Transaction terms

The deal amount of $39 billion consisted of $25 billion in cash and up to $14 billion of AT&T common stock. The amount of stock will depend on AT&T's trading price for the 30 trading days ending three business days prior to closing and will be subject to reduction for closing indebtedness, certain divestiture and regulatory costs and any pre-closing distributions in excess of pre-closing cash flow. Assuming no reduction in shares issuable, Deutsche Telekom will receive an approximate 8 percent interest in AT&T. The AT&T stock price used to determine the number of shares to be issued at closing will not be less than $26.0165 nor more than $30.2354. Deutsche Telekom will have the right to appoint one representative to the AT&T board of directors.

Merger synergies

Pro-forma for 2010 results, AT&T's total wireless revenues were expected to increase from $58.5 billion to nearly $80 billion. The scale and combination of assets provided a path to industry-leading margins. The merger will contribute to an improved business mix. Pro forma for 2010, mobile broadband, wired data and managed services comprised 80 percent of total revenues.

M&As by Vodafone Group

Vodafone Group Plc is the world's leading telecommunications company, with a significant presence in Europe, Middle East, Africa, Asia Pacific and the United States through the company's subsidiary undertakings, joint ventures, associated undertakings and investment. The company focuses on three major areas of business solutions, personal solutions and branded phones and devices. The company has more than 371 million customers around the world. Vodafone operate in more than 30 countries and partners with networks in 40 more. Vodafone have one of the largest mobile footprints in the world, with more than 224,000 base station sites. In 2011, Vodafone networks carried around 850 billion minutes of voice traffic (equivalent to 208 minutes per month, per customer) and 161 petabytes of data (equivalent to downloading over 1400 three-minute video clips every second). The company invests around £6 billion a year to maintain its leadership position in networks. In 2011 R&D expenditure amounted to £287 million. The company has identified future areas of growth potential as mobile data, enterprise, emerging markets, total communications and new services.

Table 2.8 Financial highlights of Vodafone, 2008–2010 (£ million)

	2008	2009	2010
Free cash flow	5500	5722	7241
Service revenues	33,042	38,294	41,719
Data revenues	2119	3046	4051
Fixed line revenues	1874	2727	3289

Vodafone's stake in other companies

Business	Country	Ownership
Verizon Wireless	US	45%
SFR	France	44%
Polkomtel	Poland	24.4%
Bharti Airtel	India	4.4%

The Vodafone/AirTouch merger

AirTouch had its origins in the Pacific Telephone & Telegraph Company (PacTel), a product of the 1984 breakup of AT&T. PacTel was spun off a year later in what was then the third largest initial public offering in US history. The new company, known as AirTouch, became America's fifth-largest provider of wireless services. Following the public offering, AirTouch continued to grow rapidly at home and abroad through a series of acquisitions and joint ventures. In 1998, AirTouch became the nation's number two cellular provider when it acquired a major chunk of MediaOne's (formerly US West Media's) cellular business for $5.9 billion.

In January 1999, AirTouch agreed to be acquired by the UK-based Vodafone, in a cash-and-stock transaction valued at $62 billion. Under the terms of the deal, Vodafone provided $9 cash and five of its shares for each AirTouch share, and also assumed $4 billion in AirTouch debt. The resulting company, Vodafone AirTouch Plc, had a market value of $110 billion, and served 23 million customers worldwide. Bell Atlantic had also made a vigorous bid, but its $45 billion offer fell far short of Vodafone's. Vodafone shareholders owned just over 50 percent, and AirTouch shareholders just under 50 percent, of the enlarged equity share capital of Vodafone AirTouch immediately following the merger.

Merger benefits

The combination of Vodafone and AirTouch created the world's largest telecommunications company, which operated either itself or through associates or investments in 23 countries. The two companies shared a common vision of mobile telecommunications as a major platform for voice and data communications, which have replaced fixed line networks. The combined group's operational strength and scale were expected to enhance its ability to develop existing networks.

The completion of the merger created the world's largest mobile telecommunications company, with over 29 million proportionate customers and a combined market capital of approximately £77 billion. On the basis of the combined market values of Vodafone and AirTouch, Vodafone AirTouch Plc became the second largest company in the FTSE-100 Index. The merger doubled the potential for growth in both conventional cellular and new services in the era of the wireless information age. AirTouch was a profitable company, with its cellular and PCS services reaching $149.7 million.

The merger with AirTouch facilitated a major step in Vodafone's strategy to extend the reach, range and penetration of mobile services to the maximum number of customers, in different geographical territories throughout the world, which can sustain viable and profitable operating environments.

In 1999, Vodafone AirTouch announced a $70 billion joint venture with Bell Atlantic called Verizon Wireless, which was composed of the two companies' US wireless assets, Bell Atlantic Mobile (another AMPS spinoff) and AirTouch Cellular. This wireless joint venture received regulatory approval in six months, and began operations as Verizon Wireless on April 4, 2000. On June 30, 2000, the addition of GTE Wireless' assets, in connection with the merger of Bell Atlantic and GTE to form Verizon Communications, made Verizon Wireless the largest wireless communications provider in the US. For the joint venture, Verizon Communications owned 55 percent and Vodafone owned 45 percent. The combined entity was the largest mobile communications business in the US, serving approximately 20 million customers

The Vodafone/Mannesmann merger

Mannesmann was an engineering business with roots going back to 1890. Reconstructed after World War II, it developed from a large steel and coal manufacturer into an increasingly unfocused conglomerate, acquiring businesses in automotive components, measurement and control engineering, information technology and plastics. Its core activities in the telecommunications sector related to mobile and fixed line telephony. It had interests in joint ventures in France, and Austria and owns businesses in Germany, Italy, the UK and the USA.

In 1991, Mannesmann launched Mobilfunk (later 'D2') with technical support from AirTouch. In 1996, the success of this business inspired Mannesmann, in a partnership including Deutsche Bank and AT&T, to acquire the fixed-line subsidiary of DeutscheBahn. This business was named Mannesmann Arcor. Mannesmann later acquired interests in Cegetel France and tele.ring in Austria and, in 1999, majority stakes in the Italian mobile and fixed-line operators Omnitel and Infostrada.

In October 1999, Mannesmann paid Hutchison Whampoa £20 billion for its 44.82 percent stake in Orange, making Mannesmann Europe's largest mobile network operator.

In November 1999, Vodafone AirTouch made a $107 billion bid for German telecom company Mannesmann. Mannesmann turned aside Vodafone's initial friendly offer, leading to an enhanced offer of $120.6 billion—an offer that soon turned hostile with Mannesmann's open rejection of Vodafone's overtures. Mannesmann management finally succumbed to Vodafone's $183 billion deal—the largest takeover deal ever, eclipsing the AOL/Time Warner deal.

On April 12, 2000 the EU Commission gave Phase 1 clearance for Vodafone's acquisition of Mannesmann AG, attaching no burdensome conditions. The EU ruled that Vodafone must immediately sell Orange, and that Vodafone must open its networks to competitors for three years.

The deal was of much significance as the takeover vastly expanded Vodafone's reach in the European market; it was also the first time that a European company had carried off a hostile takeover on such a scale. Mannesmann controlled 49.5 percent of the merged company, which had 42.4 million subscribers in the world.

In May 2000, Vodafone signed an agreement with VivendiNet to develop a multi-access Internet portal in Europe. The company had teamed up with British Telecommunications to acquire shares of the Spanish mobile operator Airtel.

Terms of the merger

The revised offer consisted of 58.9646 Vodafone AirTouch shares for each Mannesmann share. The offer valued each Mannesmann share at €350.50 and Mannesmann's share capital at €181.4 billion based on Vodafone AirTouch's closing price of 368.5 pence on February 3, 2000. Four members of Mannesmann's supervisory board were invited to join the board of Vodafone AirTouch.

Vodafone continued to develop Mannesmann's wireless, wire line and Internet strategy within the combined group. Another strategic objective of the group was to integrate and develop Mannesmann's telecommerce activities. Vodafone AirTouch also pursued the repositioning of Mannesmann's tube businesses.

The new third-generation (3G) rollout was expected in Japan in 2002, and in Europe then in the US by 2003. This was expected to enable a new generation of Internet applications and high bandwidth services and might lead to the convergence of the mobile telecoms, multimedia and Internet sectors. Vodafone and Mannesmann both shared this vision.

Strategic drivers for the acquisition

The mobile phone market was one of the fastest-moving segments in the telecom industry in early 2000. Between 1997 and 1999, the mobile phone market more than doubled from 203 million to 475 million customers. The European market was Vodafone's target for acquisition. Vodafone found a suitable target in Mannesmann of Germany—Germany at the time had the lowest penetration rate in Europe.

European regulation favored convergence—the ability for mobile phone operators to offer the same voice and data services as the fixed line operators—allowing for direct competition between the two. European regulation managed the mobile phone market by requiring licenses for the wireless spectrum. The European licenses were offered under auction, which meant that only the most financially sound mobile phone operators could win the auction. Mannesmann had significant power in certain markets that Vodafone had not yet controlled. The acquisition of Mannesmann tremendously increased Vodafone's market power.

Other mega mergers in the telecom industry

Qwest/US West merger

US West, Inc. was one of seven Regional Bell Operating Companies created in 1983. In 2000, US West merged with Quest Communications International, Inc., and the US West brand was replaced by the Qwest brand. In the 1980s and 1990s, US West became a pioneer in the introduction and rapid system-wide implementation of telephone technologies designed by Telcordia Technologies. Qwest Communications International, Inc. has grown through acquisitions, and offered local and long-distance telephone services, as well as a range of Internet, multimedia, data and voice services in 14 western US States. Qwest operated in three segments: wire line services, wireless services and other services. The wireless services segment was achieved by a partnership with Verizon Wireless. Qwest also partnered with DirecTV to provide digital television service to its customers. Qwest Communications acquired Internet service provider SuperNet in 1997, and LCI and Icon CMT in 1998. Through these acquisitions Qwest spread its network to a residential and business long-distance customer base.

Table 2.9 Financial highlights of Vodafone, 1999–2009 (£ million)

	1999	2000	2001	2002	2003	2004	2005	2006	2007	2008	2009
Sales	3360	7873	15,004	22,845	30,375	33,559	26,678	29,350	31,104	35,478	41,017
Gross profit	1551	3514	6302	9399	12,479	14,098	10,878	12,280	12,379	13,588	15,175
EBIT	1029	1750	–6918	–12,694	–5456	–4333	7871	–14,086	–1560	10,301	5813
Earnings	637	487	–9763	–16,155	–9819	–9015	6410	–21,916	–5426	6660	3078

Qwest/US West merger highlights

In 2000, US West and Qwest Communications International shareholders approved the planned $45.2 billion merger, which resulted in a new company offering local and long-distance telephone and Internet services. Through this merger, US West gave Quest International an additional customer base of 25 million and a 14-state local phone network. The additional local phone network reduced the costs it paid to other local carriers for distance calls. Qwest gave US West a national network that could offer high-speed data services. The merger resulted in a worldwide network of 3 million miles of cable and a 18,000-mile fiber optic domestic backbone. This merger was in line with the strategic pursuits of economies of scale and convergence of technologies undertaken by other telecom companies to provide Internet, communications, content and other value-added services in their own internal network. The merged companies had about 70,000 employees worldwide.

The CenturyLink/Qwest merger

In April 2011, Qwest Communications International merged with CenturyLink. The new brand was named CenturyLink. The transaction was structured as a tax-free stock-for-stock exchange. Under the terms of the merger agreement, Qwest stockholders received 0.1664 shares of CenturyLink common stock for each share of Qwest common stock they owned at closing price plus cash paid in lieu of fractional shares. CenturyLink paid $12.2 billion for Qwest in this all-stock transaction.

CenturyLink is the third largest telecommunications company in the United States. The company provides broadband, voice and wireless services to consumers and businesses across the country. It also offers advanced entertainment services under the CenturyLink™, Prism TV™ and DirecTV brands. In addition the company provides data, voice and managed services to business, government and wholesale customers in local, national and select international markets.

CenturyLink and Qwest have a combined 145,000 miles of local fiber, or more than double the 70,000 miles of fiber that CenturyLink had before the merger. Combining the two companies' network assets will give it a significant presence throughout most of the United States:

- The combination of the two telecom companies would result in a high-capacity 190,000 route-mile fiber network that spans the US from coast to coast, nearly doubling network access points.
- CenturyLink will also benefit from Qwest's investment to upgrade its entire Ethernet backbone to 100Gbps, which will enable the businesses to run high-bandwidth applications.

- The merged company was expected to benefit from the CenturyLink's local operating model.

The France Telecom/Orange deal

France Telecom is the largest telecommunication company in France and the third largest in Europe. It offers services covering fixed and mobile communications, data transmission, the Internet and multimedia, and other value-added services for individuals, businesses and other telecommunications and operators. The four key platforms of France Telecom consist of fixed-line telephony, mainly in France and Poland; broadband access; mobile phone telephony; and IPTV, known as Orange TV.

Orange is the brand used by France Telecom for its mobile network operator and Internet service provider. Orange is one of the main European operators for mobile and broadband Internet services. Under the brand Orange Business Services, the company provides telecom services to multinational companies.

Orange Plc was formed in 1995 as a holding company for the Orange Group. In 2001, France Telecom acquired UK mobile phone company Orange for £25.1 billion ($40.3 billion) from Vodafone, creating Europe's second-largest mobile phone company. France Telecom paid £13.8 billion in cash and £11.3 billion in shares, and took over £1.8 billion in debt of the UK operator. Vodafone had acquired Orange as part of its takeover of German telecoms giant Mannesmann earlier in 2001. This acquisition catapulted France Telecom into becoming the second largest mobile phone company in Europe after Vodafone, with operations in Britain, France, Belgium, Portugal, Germany, Italy and Eastern Europe. The acquisition of Orange was a major step in the international strategy of France Telecom to become a global player. The acquisition was expected to boost earnings by generating savings of €800 million.

France Telecom-Orange became one of the leading telecommunications operators with 170,000 employees worldwide, including 102,000 employees in France. The group has a presence in 35 countries, with a customer base of 221 million customers under the Orange brand, which is the group's single brand for Internet, television and mobile services in a majority of areas of operations in different countries.

The Nortel Network spinoff

Nortel Network was established in 1895 and became a pioneer in communications satellite business by the 1960s. Nortel, based in Canada, was also the second largest telecom equipment supplier. Nortel Networks is a global leader in telephony, data, ebusiness and wireless solutions for the Internet. In the US, it was the first network company to provide an end-to-end VoIP solution.

In 2000, the Canadian Telecommunications giant BCE spun off its stake in Nortel Networks. BCE is the biggest telecom group in Canada, with divisions of telephone and computer services. BCE spun off its 35-per-cent stake in Nortel to its shareholders and retained a 2 percent stake. BCE's shareholders received 0.78 of a Nortel share for every BCE share they held. The market value of the transaction was estimated to be $88 billion. Nortel shareholders received one common share in the new public company for each of their Nortel common shares. BCE wanted to separate its core telecommunications business from Nortel's focus of business.

The creation of the new spun-off company, Netgear, was in line with Nortel Networks' successful strategy of establishing independent businesses for adoption of innovative new technologies. Netgear received US$15 million equity financing investment from Pequot Capital Management to focus on the high-growth home and small business Internet infrastructure market.

The Sprint/Nextel merger

Sprint was established in 1899. It went on to achieve a major milestone in 1986, when the company became the first 100 percent digital fiber optic network in the US. The company was a pioneer in data communications, establishing the world's third largest commercial packet data network in 1980. Sprint is widely known for developing, engineering and deploying innovative technologies, including the first wireless 4G service from a national carrier in the US.

In 1987, Nextel was established as a wireless communications service provider. In 1994, Nextel merged with Dial Call and OneComm. The company also acquired all of Motorola's SMR licenses in the US. By mid-1995, Nextel served all the top 50 markets in US.

In August 2005, Sprint acquired a majority stake in Nextel Communications in a $35 billion stock purchase. The merged company became the third largest US telecommunications provider, behind AT&T and Verizon. The merged company focused on growth by cross-selling their product and service offerings. The blockbuster merger faced high expenses and integration problems. In 2008, the merged entity had to write off about $30 billion as merger cost. Sprint Nextel lost millions of customers owing to competition. By 2011, it had served more than 53 million customers.

Sprint Nextel offers a comprehensive range of wireless and wire line communications services to customers, businesses and government users

Additional References

1. Myeong Cheol Park, Doon Hong Yang and Changi Nam, "Mergers and Acquisitions in the Telecommunications Industry: Myths and Reality," *ETRI Journal*, Vol. 24, No. 1, pp. 56–65, February 2002.
2. http://blog.thomsonreuters.com/index.php/graphic-of-the-day-telecom-ma-volumes-and-top-deals
3. http://www.nytimes.com/2010/03/29/technology/companies/29iht-telco.html
4. http://www.booz.com/media/uploads/BoozCo-Winning-Next-Wave-Telecom-Mergers-Acquisition.pdf
5. http://www.economywatch.com/mergers-acquisitions/international/telecom-sector.html
6. http://www.caslon.com.au/telecomergernote5.htm
7. https://infocus.credit-uisse.com/app/article/index.cfm?fuseaction=openArticle&aoid=275502
8. http://nrri.org/pubs/telecommunications/97-20.pdf
9. http://mcphersongordon.com/mergers-and-acquisitions/mergers-and-acquisitions-intelecom-sector.html
10. "Valuation Drivers in the Telecommunications Industry," E&Y Report 2010, http://www.ey.com/Publications/vwLUAssets/Valuation_drivers_in_the_telecommumications_industry/$FILE/Valuations%20paper.pdf
11. http://blogs.wsj.comdeals/2010/14/dialed-intelecom-ma-volume-bounces-back/
12. http://www.economywatch.com/mergers-acquisitions/international/telecom-sector.html
13. David Lieberman (with Andrew Backover), *USA Today*, "Comcast to Buy AT&T Broadband," http://www.usatoday.com/tech/techinvestor/2001/12/20/att-comcast.htm
14. http://www.3g.co.uk/PR/Nov2005/2135.htm
15. Chris Isidore, "Adelphia Deal to Shuffle Cable," http://money.cnn.com/2005/04/21/technology/adelphia/
16. MCI Inc—SC 13D/A—LCC International Inc. Securities and Exchange Commission. March 14, 2003 (accessed September 25, 2009).
17. http://wayback.archive.org/web/*/http://www.worldcom.com
18. http://www22.verizon.com/about/
19. http://connectedplanetonline.com/finance/news/verizon_mci_acquisition/
20. E. S. Browning, "Is the Praise for WorldCom Too Much?" *The Wall Street Journal*, p. C-24, October 8, 1997. All acquisition amounts are taken from this article.
21. http://www.scu.edu/ethics/dialogue/candc/cases/worldcom.html
22. WorldCom website (www.worldcom.com/global/about/facts/).
23. http://www.ecommercetimes.com/story/45542.html
24. http://www.fundinguniverse.com/company-histories/MCI-WorldCom-Inc-company-History.html
25. http://www.wsws.org/articles/2000/jul2000/bell-j24.shtml
26. http://washingtontechnology.com/articles/2000/06/30/its-official-bell-atlantic-gte-merge.aspx
27. http://news.cnet.com/Critics-blast-GTE-Bell-Atlantic-merger/2100-1033_3-218342.html

28. http://www.zdnet.com/news/merger-mania-bell-atlantic-gte-to-combine-in-53b-deal/100123
29. http://www.nytimes.com/2000/06/17/business/fcc-approves-bell-atlantic-gte-merger-creating-no-1-phone-company.html?pagewanted=all&src=pm
30. http://newscenter.verizon.com/press-releases/bell-atlantic/1999/page-29592299.html
31. http://newscenter.verizon.com/kit/vcorp/factsheet.html#Fast_Facts
32. http://money.cnn.com/2000/06/16/deals/gte/
33. http://www.businessweek.com/bwdaily/dnflash/may2000/nf00511i.htm
34. http://www.thehistoryofcorporate.com/companies-by-industry/information-industry/verizon-communications/
35. http://www.fundinguniverse.com/company-histories/gte-corporation-company-history.html
36. www.advfn.com
37. http://www.fundinguniverse.com/company-histories/Bell-Atlantic-Corporation-company-History.html
38. Stephen Labaton, "FCC Approves Bell Atlantic GTE Merger, Creating No. 1 Phone Company," *The New York Times*, June 17, 2000.
39. http://www.fundinguniverse.com/company-histories/Ameritech-Corporation-company-History.html
40. AT&T website.
41. http://www.networkworld.com/news/0511sbc8.html
42. http://findarticles.com/p/articles/mi_m0UNZ/is_1999_May_3/ai_54528470/
43. http://people.stern.nyu.edu/igiddy/cases/sbc-att.htm
44. http://www.pbs.org/newshour/bb/business/jan-june05/merger_1-31.html
45. http://knowledge.wharton.upenn.edu/article.cfm?articleid=1134.
46. http://news.cnet.com/SBC-closes-AT38T-acquisition/2100-1036_3-5961206.html
47. http://www.celtnet.org.uk/telecos/cingular.php
48. http://money.cnn.com/2004/02/17/technology/cingular_att/
49. http://blog.tmcnet.com/blog/rich-tehrani/voip/att-bellsouth-merger.html
50. http://www.brookings.edu/opinions/2006/0309corporations_crandall.aspx
51. http://seekingalpha.com/article/7440-at-t-bellsouth-merger-announcement-conference-call-transcript-t-bls
52. http://money.cnn.com/2006/03/06/technology/business2_att_telecom/
53. http://www.pcworld.com/article/128356/atandt_closes_bellsouth_acquisition.html
54. http://www.washingtonpost.com/wp-dyn/content/article/2006/12/29/AR2006122901048.html
55. http://www.voip-news.com/news/att-bellsouth-merger/
56. http://reason.org/news/show/att-bellsouth-merger-boosts-ca
57. http://www.fundinguniverse.com/company-histories/BellSouth-Corporation-company-History.html
58. http://news.cnet.com/What-does-the-ATT-BellSouth-merger-mean-for-consumers/2100-1033_3-6046436.html
59. http://www.nytimes.com/2006/12/30/business/30tele.html
60. http://www.wirelessindustrynews.org/news-mar-2006/0389-030606-win-news.html
61. http://mobilizeeverything.com/uploaded-files/Deal_Factsheet.pdf

62. www.at&t.com
63. http://www.vodafone.com
64. http://www1.iwon.com/home/careers/company_profile/0,15623,1210,00.html
65. http://findarticles.com/p/articles/mi_m0BFP/is_1999_July_5/ai_55071558/
66. http://ec.europa.eu/competition/mergers/cases/decisions/m1795_en.pdf
67. Chris Higson, "Value Creation at Vodafone," Case study, London Business School, CS-09 009, http://www.cybozone.com/vcu/Vodafone_Air_Touch_-_The_Acquisition_of_Mannesmann.pdf
68. http://www.centurylinkqwestmerger.com/entry.php
69. http://www.zdnetasia.com/shareholders-approve-qwest-us-west-merger-13021213.htm
70. http://www.fool.com/news/1999/foth991008.htm
71. http://www.networkworld.com/news/2011/040111-centurylink-qwest-merger.html
72. http://www.4-traders.com/FRANCE-TELECOM-4649/news/FRANCE-TELECOM-Orange-acquires-a-34-minority-interest-in-Skyrock-s-web-operations-13876435/
73. http://news.bbc.co.uk/2/hi/business/769293.stm
74. http://money.cnn.com/2000/05/30/deals/orange/
75. http://www.cbc.ca/news/business/story/2000/05/01/nortelbce000501.html
76. http://www.nortel.com/corporate/news/newsreleases/2000a/03_13_0000128_netgear_spinoff.html
77. www.sprint.com
78. http://www.investopedia.com/articles/financial-theory/08/merger-acquisition-disasters.asp#ixzz1fIKcBx80

3
Mergers and Acquisitions in the Technology Sector

Introduction

Mergers and acquisitions in the global technology market increased by 44 percent to dollars 127 billion in 2007 from dollar 88 billion in 2006. The recession led to a period of dull activity during the period 2008–2009. M&A in the technology sector witnessed a strong rebound from recession in 2010. According to IDC Report, about 1900 M&As with a value of over $200 billion took place in the information and technology sector in 2010. The total M&A in technology sector was $119 billion in 2010, compared to $94.8 billion in 2009.

During the period January–March 2011, M&A activity in the technology sector witnessed a 124 per jump, which amounted to $27 billion. In 2010, HP, Oracle and Intel were the most active companies. During the past two and a half years Google had acquired 39 companies. In 2011, Microsoft's $9.08 billion acquisition of Skype was the largest single transaction, which represented more than 20 percent of all acquisition spend for the industry. The majority of the M&A deals were concentrated in application-related areas including enterprise applications and Internet applications. In 2011, Intel's $7.7 billion deal for McAfee and SAP's acquisition of Sybase for $5.8 billion were the largest deals in the infrastructure segment. AOL and Facebook had nine deals in 2010. Major IT vendors including Cisco, Dell, HP, IBM, Intel, Oracle and VMware made significant acquisitions. Cisco Systems is known as the "master acquirer," making 140 acquisitions in the past 20 years.

Strategic drivers for M&A in the technology sector

In the technology sector, M&A has become a strategic tool for companies to acquire new products and technologies in order to maintain competitive advantage, growth rate and profitability. Acquisition of knowledge is a main value driver for M&A in the IT sector. Small technical-oriented IT companies with high-quality applications are constrained by an inadequate sales network to promote their product in the market. In this scenario, acquisitions of these niche companies by large companies become an effective strategy for growth.

M&A are also used as a strategic pursuit for gaining market share. Adobe's $1.8 billion acquisition of Omniture was meant for expansion into Web analytics that focuses on programs that monitor website traffic and improve online advertising. Oracle's purchase of Sun Microsystems was basically for entry into the computer hardware market. Cisco's $3 billion bid for Tandberg was aimed at expansion into the videoconferencing market.

M&A in the IT services sector have thrived on account of customer demand for one-stop shopping. The trend has been that IT services companies offer everything from integrating computer systems to IT consulting to overseeing back-office processes that handle accounting and healthcare plans. Specific examples in this context include HP's acquisition of Electronic Data Systems for $13.9 billion; Dell's purchase of Perot Systems for $3.8 billion; and Xerox's offer of $6.4 billion for Affiliated Computer Services.

The pursuit of strategic technologies in support of converging technology industry megatrends is a primary driver for deals. The latest trend indicates that innovations in security, smart mobile technology, cloud computing and social networking have become important strategic drivers facilitating M&A in the global technology sectors. Cloud computing represents a paradigm shift in the delivering of technology in every sector. M&A in the smart mobility industry reflects the demand for mobile infrastructure, with applications, contents and services in the context of a proliferation of smartphones, tablets and other mobile devices. Innovations in the models of social networking have also become a significant factor for stimulating M&A activity.

One of the biggest change factors that have become a strategic imperative for M&A in the technology market has been the blurring of the boundary between the software and hardware sectors. Convergence has emerged as a major theme for facilitating M&A in the global technology industry. The new trend among software companies and corporate clients has been to allocate their IT spend to a smaller number of integrated suppliers. The $7.1 billion acquisition of Sybase, a provider of databases, by German software giant SAP and the $7.6 billion acquisition of McAfee, the maker of antivirus software, by Intel are specific examples of M&A for achieving convergence in the technology market. Similarly, Safran SA bought authentication technology company L-1 Identity Solutions, Inc. for $1.6 billion, and HP bought intrusion detection software company ArcSight, Inc. for $1.5 billion.

Nokia Siemens Networks acquired the majority of the wireless network infrastructure assets of Motorola, Inc. for $1.2 billion in cash to boost its network infrastructure business in the US. HP completed its $1.2 billion acquisition of smart phone maker Palm. The deal revived Palm's innovative WebOS mobile platform in conjunction with the release of new smart phones, net books and tablets.

M&A activity in the technology market is driven by security, storage, ecommerce and business analytics needs along with changes in online and mobile games, advertising and marketing. Information security needs are also driving many deals.

It is quite evident that technology is enabling innovation in all industrial sectors based on the fact that technology-related deals by non-technology companies witnessed an increase in value from $7.5 billion in 2009 to $17.3 billion in 2010.

M&A are also being used as an efficient method of enhancing R&D initiatives. In this context it is worth mentioning that large, cash-rich IT and software companies are making solid strategic acquisitions for their technological prospects.

JDS Uniphase sells technology components to companies that build systems to run fiber-optic networks. In 2000, JDS acquired SDL, a maker of fiber optic network lasers, for $41 billion. The merger agreement provided for the exchange of 3.8 JDS shares, or $441.51, for each SDL share. The growth of the Internet had created huge demand for bandwidth to increase telecommunication network capacity. In this context, the merger of JDS Uniphase and SDL facilitated the creation and deployment of high-capacity flexible optical networks. In June 2000, JDS Uniphase also purchased communications equipment maker E-Tek Dynamics for $17.93 billion. The merger agreement provided for the exchange of 1.1 shares of JDS Uniphase's common stock for each common share of E-Tek. E-Tek became a wholly owned subsidiary of JDS Uniphase. Synergistic benefits were expected from the combination of E-Tek's packaging technology and capacity with JDS Uniphase's optical capability.

In 2007, Kohlberg Kravis Roberts (KKR) bought First Data Corp., the credit-card processing firm, for $27.7 billion. First Data was split off from American Express Co. in 1992 as an information-processing company that would handle billions of credit card and other transactions for

Table 3.1 Biggest technology deals

Year	Acquirer	Target	Value in $ billions
2000	JDS Uniphase	SDL	41
2007	KKR	First Data	27.7
2001	Hewlett Packard	Compaq	25
1999	Lucent Technology	Ascend Communication	23.9
2000	VeriSign	Network Solutions	20.8
2000	JDS Uniphase	E-Tek	17.93
1998	Veritas	Seagate Software	17.6
2005	Symantec	Veritas	13
2011	Google	Motorola Mobility	12.5
2005	Oracle	People Soft	10.3
1998	Nortel Networks	Bay Networks	9.10
2011	Microsoft	Skype Communications	9.08
2000	Nortel Networks	Alteon Web Systems, Inc.	7.8
2011	Intel	McAfee	7.68
2010	Oracle	Sun Microsystems	7.4
2000	Phone.com	Software.com	6.4
2006	AMD, Inc.	ATI Technologies	5.4
2006	Cisco Systems	Scientific Atlanta	6.5
2011	Texas Instrument	National Semi Conductor	6.5
	Applied Materials	Varian	4.9
2011	Consortium of Sony, Microsoft, Apple, RIM	Nortel Networks (patents)	4.5

third parties. It became the fifth-largest LBO on record, behind KKR's $31.3 billion acquisition of RJR Nabisco, Inc. in 1988.

In 1999, Lucent Technologies, Inc., the top maker of phone equipment, bought Ascend Communications for $23.9 billion in stock to expand into the fast-growing Internet equipment industry. Lucent required Ascend's powerful switches that direct Internet traffic to compete with top networking companies like Nortel Networks and Cisco Systems. After Lucent Technologies was spun off from AT&T in 1996, Lucent spent more than $32 billion on some 30 acquisitions during the period 1997–1999.

In 2000, VeriSign acquired Network Solutions, Inc. for $21 billion in stock. The merger combined the world's leading provider of Internet domain name registrations and network solutions with one of the leading providers of ecommerce and email security, with more than 12 million worldwide subscribers. VeriSign gained access to Network Solutions' 8.1 million-member subscriber base. With one of the largest subscriber bases on the Internet, the combination of VeriSign and Network Solutions was meant to take ecommerce to the next level.

In a complex $17.6 billion deal in 1998, Seagate Technology, the world's largest disk drive company, was taken over by an investor group led by Silver Lake Partners. The non-operating assets of Seagate, primarily one-third stakes in Veritas Software, was acquired by Veritas and redistributed to Seagate's shareholders.

In 2005, Security firm Symantec and Veritas merged. The all-stock transaction was valued at approximately $13.5 billion based on Symantec's stock price of $27.38 on the day before the announcement. Veritas stock was converted into Symantec stock at a fixed exchange ratio of 1.1242 shares of Symantec stock for each Veritas share. Upon closing, Symantec shareholders owned approximately 60 percent and Veritas shareholders approximately 40 percent of the combined company. Symantec specializes in anti-virus and network security applications, while Veritas is a major player in the data backup and storage software markets. The combined firm became the topmost firm in the data protection segment.

Nortel Networks was formerly known as Northern Telecom Ltd. In 1998, with the acquisition of Bay Networks, the company's name was changed to Nortel Networks to emphasize its ability to provide complete solutions over the Internet and other communications networks. In 2000 Nortel Networks acquired Alteon Web Systems, Inc., the equipment maker for Internet servers, for $7.8 billion in stock. The acquisition was expected to enable Nortel Networks to build the next-generation Internet data center—capable of delivering content at unprecedented levels of speed, efficiency and reliability. In 2009, Nortel filed for protection from creditors in the US, Canada and the UK in order to restructure its debt and financial obligations. By June 2009 Nortel had ceased operations and sold off all its businesses.

The HP/Compaq merger

Hewlett Packard

Two Stanford graduates, Bill Hewlett and David Packard, founded HP in 1939. The company, which originally produced audio oscillators, introduced its first computer in 1966. HP is the world's largest technology company, with a portfolio spanning printing, personal computing, software, services and IT infrastructure. Hewlett Packard introduced its first personal computer in 1980. Five years later, HP introduced the LaserJet printer, which would become the company's most successful product ever. HP serves more than one billion customers in more than 170 countries on six continents. It has approximately 324,600 employees worldwide. HP support 200 top banks and more than 130 of the

Table 3.2 Financial highlights of HP ($ million)

	2006	2007	2008	2009	2010
Net revenues	118,364	104,286	118,364	114,552	126,033
Earnings from operations	6560	8719	10,473	10,136	11,479
Net earnings	6198	7264	8329	7660	8761
Assets	81,981	88,699	113,331	114,799	124,503

world's major stock exchanges. HP acquired 53 companies during the period 2000–2011.

Compaq

Compaq Computer Corporation is a leading global provider of enterprise technology and solutions. Compaq designs, develops, manufactures and markets hardware, software, solutions and services, including industry-leading enterprise storage and computing solutions, fault-tolerant business-critical solutions, communication products, and desktop and portable personal computers that are sold in more than 200 countries.

Merger highlights

In 2001, Hewlett Packard and Compaq Computer Corporation merged to create an $87 billion global technology leader. The merged company offered a complete set of IT products and services for both businesses and consumers, with the focus on open systems and architectures. The new company had worldwide revenue positions in servers, access devices, imaging and printing as well as leading revenue positions in IT services, storage and management software. The merged company had operations in more than 160 countries and over 145,000 employees. Under the terms of the agreement, Compaq shareholders received 0.6325 of the newly issued HP share for each share of Compaq, giving the merger a value of approximately $25 billion. HP shareowners owned approximately 64 percent and Compaq Shareowners 36 percent of the merged company.

The merger consolidated HP's and Compaq's product lines into four major operating groups: services, imaging and printing, access devices and IT infrastructure. Though the merged company remained competitive in individual product segments, the merger created a full-service technology firm along all lines of value creation. The merger was aimed at integrating hardware and software into solutions while providing services at the same time.

Table 3.3 Financial highlights of HP/Compaq in the year of their merger

	HP	Compaq	Pro forma combined
Total revenues	$47 billion	$40.4 billion	$87.4 billion
Assets	$32.4 billion	$23.9 billion	$56.4 billion
Operating earnings	$2.1 billion	$1.9 billion	$3.9 billion

The companies expected annual cost synergies of approximately $2.5 billion by mid-2004. These anticipated synergies resulted from product rationalization; efficiencies in administration, procurement, manufacturing and marketing; and savings from improved direct distribution of PCs and servers.

Significance of the merger

The merger created an $87 billion global technology leader with a complete set of IT products and services. The new HP added substantial shareowner value through significant cost structure improvements and opportunities for growth. The transaction was substantially accretive to pro forma EPS in the first full year of combined operations.

The merger was often seen as a failed attempt as the synergies identified prior to the merger did not materialize. Initially the sons of the cofounders of HP had publicly opposed the deal when the Chief Executive, Carly Fiorina, pitched for the deal.

Major acquisitions by Google

Google, the top online computer software and web search engine company, was founded by Larry Page and Sergey Brin in 1998. Google is the leading property in all major global markets and has been the world's largest search engine. Starting from offering searches in a single language, the company now has dozens of products and services, including various forms of advertising and web applications in scores of languages. Google also provides a variety of services for advertisers of all sizes.

Over the last decade, Google has emerged as the one of the biggest and most successful acquirers in the technology industry. Its core search advertising platform and biggest new businesses, like Android and YouTube, and display advertising have all resulted from acquisitions.

Google has acquired over 150 companies, the largest acquisition being the purchase of Motorola Mobility, a mobile device-manufacturing

Table 3.4 Financial highlights of Google ($ million)

	2007	2008	2009	2010
Revenues	16,594	21,796	23,651	29,321
Cash flow from operations	5775	7853	9316	11,081
Net income	4204	4227	6520	8505
EPS ($)	13.53	13.46	20.62	26.69
Total assets	25,336	31,768	40,497	57,851

Table 3.5 Financial highlights of Motorola Mobility in 2010

Revenues	$114.60 million
Net income	$79 million
Total assets	$620 million

subsidiary of Motorola. This acquisition was nearly four times larger than the previous largest purchase of online advertising company DoubleClick for $3.2 billion. It can be said that Google on average had acquired more than one company per week since 2010.

Biggest deals of Google

Google's acquisition of Motorola Mobility

Motorola Mobility Holdings, Inc., the Mobile Devices division of Motorola, is a communication corporation based in the US. Its portfolio includes converged mobile devices such as smartphones and tablets, wireless accessories, end-to-end video and data delivery, and management solutions, including set tops and data access devices. Motorola has a history of over eight decades in communications technology and products. Its major milestones include the introduction of the world's first portable cell phone and the StarTAC, the smallest and lightest phone.

In the 1990s, Motorola had a leading position in the analog cellphone market, but was unable to capture the digital technology market, making way for global rivals such as Nokia and Samsung. Motorola had shifted its operating system from their proprietary software to Google's Android operating system in 2009.

Merger highlights

In August 2011, Google, Inc. and Motorola Mobility Holdings, Inc. entered into a definitive agreement under which Google would acquire Motorola Mobility for $40.00 per share in cash, or a total of about

$12.5 billion, which represented a premium of 63 percent to the closing price of Motorola Mobility shares on August 12, 2011. The acquisition included a sizeable portfolio of patents owned by Motorola. As of January 2011, Motorola Mobility held approximately 14,600 granted patents and 6700 pending applications worldwide.

The acquisition of Motorola enabled Google to supercharge the Android ecosystem, which would enhance competition in mobile computing. Google expected to add to its competitive advantage as Motorola Mobility had formidable strength in Android smartphones and devices, along with market leadership position in the home devices and video solutions business. Google's strategy for the acquisition rationale was to build up the company's patent portfolio in order to protect Android from anti-competitive threats from Microsoft, Apple and other companies. The transaction was subject to regulatory approvals from the US, Europe and other jurisdictions. The Android system has been at the center of controversy involving patent infringement in which Android manufacturers HTC, Motorola and Samsung were sued by Microsoft, Oracle and Apple. Presently more than 150 million Android devices have been activated worldwide through a network of about 39 manufacturers and 231 carriers in 123 countries.

Acquisitions by Oracle

Oracle Corporation is the world's largest enterprise software company and a leading provider of computer hardware products and services. Oracle develops, manufactures, markets, distributes and services database and middleware software, applications software, and hardware systems, consisting primarily of computer server and storage products. The company is the world's leading supplier of information management software and the world's second largest independent software company. Oracle technology is present in every industry and in the data centers of 100 Fortune Global companies.

The company is organized into three businesses—software, hardware systems and services—which are further divided into seven operating segments. The software, hardware and services businesses constituted approximately 68 percent, 19 percent, and 13 percent respectively of total revenues in 2011. Oracle serves more than 380,000 customers and has a presence in more than 145 countries around the globe.

Strategic acquisitions by Oracle

Over a period of time, Oracle has used acquisitions as a strategic tool to strengthen its product offerings, accelerate innovation, meet customer

Table 3.6 Other major deals by Google

Year	Target	Value	Details
2007	Doubleclick	$3.1 billion	This acquisition launched Google into the display advertising business. Google bought this online advertising company to provide it more dynamic multimedia advertisements. DoubleClick now supports AdSense.
2006	YouTube	$1.65 billion	Google skillfully negotiated contracts with content owners for this online video sharing site company. Analysts have estimated that YouTube provides more than $1 billion in revenue per year for Google.
2009	Admob	$750 million	Google acquired this mobile advertising company in order to focus on the huge mobile advertising business. This transaction was stock-based.
2010	ITA Software	$700 million	Google acquired ITA's software to optimize its travel and flight searching capacity. ITA compiles flight information for airlines, travel agencies and rival search engines.
2007	Postini	$625 million	Postini has emerged as a critical part of Google's enterprise application business. Google bought this email security company to enhance the security and storage products it offers to businesses. Google integrated its add-on email services such as spam blocking and archiving into Gmail for business users.
2011	Admeld	$400 million	Admeld specialized in optimizing advertisement yield by simplifying advertisement display. This acquisition was meant to boost Google's display advertisement business. Google integrated Admeld with its DoubleClick and Invite Media acquisitions.
2010	Slide.com	$182 million	Slide.com, a web2.0 company founded by Paypalco founder Max Levchin, was the third largest party developer of Facebook applications. The focus of this acquisition was to make Google services socially aware. Slide.com operates as a separate entity within Google.

(*continued*)

Table 3.6 Continued

Year	Target	Value	Details
2010	On2 Video Compression	$133 million	The video codec technology developed by On2 was utilized to optimize Google's WebM video format. The acquisition of this provider of digital video compression technology was aimed to cut the bandwidth costs at YouTube.
2010	Widevine Technologies	$158 million	Google purchased this provider of digital rights management software to secure online video content.
2006	dMarc	$102 million	dMarc broadcasting was acquired and integrated into Google's AdSense application.
2010	Applied Semantics	$102 million	Applied Semantics built AdSense, the paid search advertising platform.
2007	Feedburner RSS	$100 million	Feedburner creates tools for advertisers and users to manage RSS feed.
2010	Like.com	$100 million	Google purchased this visual search company to build a search vertical for women's fashion called boutiques.com.
2010	Invite Media	$81 million	Invite Media is a demand side platform (DSP) that helps advertisement buyers place their wares on an advertisement exchange.
2010	Jambool Social Platform	$70 million	Jambool is a company that specializes in mobile payment platforms.
2010	Aardvark	$50 million	Aardvark is a social search Q&A firm.
2005	Android Platform	$50 million	Within three years of acquisition, this mobile phone platform became the most popular smartphone platform in the world.
2004	Keyhole Corp.	Undisclosed	The purchase of this digital mapping service firm propelled Google's maps into the top spot for finding online directions.
2007	GrandCentral	Undisclosed	This web phone service provider was later rebranded as Google Voice.

Source: Company Websites.

Table 3.7 Financial highlights of Oracle ($ million)

	2007	2008	2009	2010	2011
Total revenues	17,996	22,430	23,252	26,820	35,622
Operating income	5974	7844	8321	9662	12,033
Net income	4274	5521	5593	6135	8547
Total assets	34,572	47,268	47,416	61,578	73,535

demand more rapidly and expand partner opportunities. During the period 2005–2011, Oracle acquired more than 66 companies in sectors including database, middleware, applications, product lines, communications and media, financial services, insurance and utilities.

Major deals by Oracle

The PeopleSoft acquisition

In December 2004, Oracle entered into a definitive agreement to acquire PeopleSoft for $10.3 billion, or $26.50 per share, ending a bitter, 18-month hostile takeover battle. The original offer in June 2003 was for $16 a share or $5.1 billion. Oracle raised its offer several times and even lowered it once during the event of a hostile bid. Oracle's hostile takeover bid was initially rejected by PeopleSoft's management and opposed by US anti-trust regulators, who said it would harm competition and lead to higher prices. PeopleSoft's board of directors continued to resist the offer. Oracle had to spend more than $110 million in pursuit of PeopleSoft, which itself spent around $80 million for its anti-takeover defense mechanism. The final offer represented a 75 percent premium from PeopleSoft's market value before Oracle launched the hostile takeover attempt. The final proposal was approved by the board of directors of both companies just three weeks after PeopleSoft had rejected a $24 per share offer.

The acquisition deal highlighted the conflict of interest among PeopleSoft customers, managers and shareholders. Shareholders went to the extent of tendering their shares to Oracle against the wishes of management. Individual investors held about 20 percent of the PeopleSoft's stocks, PeopleSoft investors held 10 percent, and institutional investors the remaining 70 percent. After accepting the offer, California Employees' Retirement System, the largest pension fund in the US, tendered its 1.5 million shares to Oracle. Los Angeles-based Capital Guardian Trust company and its parent company Capital Group International also tendered their 10.2 percent shares to Oracle. Sixty percent of the shareholders supported the bid. Despite this support, the board of PeopleSoft insisted that the price offered was inadequate. Oracle revised the amount to a $10.3 billion bid for $26.50 per share. The announcement followed a tender offer in which more than 97 percent of PeopleSoft shareholders tendered their stock. In July 2003 PeopleSoft acquired J. D. Edwards.

PeopleSoft provided Oracle an extra incentive to take care of its customers by offering unusual guarantees as it resisted the takeover. The guarantees could force Oracle to refund up to $2.4 billion to PeopleSoft customers if product support diminishes.

Immediately following the announcement of the deal, Oracle saw its stock jump 9.1 percent, while PeopleSoft was up by 10.3 percent.

The merger made Oracle the world's second largest seller of business applications software behind SAP AG. By this time Oracle was already the world's largest supplier of databases. The acquisition gave Oracle the size to compete effectively in the applications market. Oracle estimated its earnings would increase by about $400 million or 8 cents per share as a result of the takeover.

Strategic reasons for the acquisition

The technology boom in the late 1990s led to the rapid growth of the global software industry. But profit margins sank in the recession faced by the industry in the early 2000s.

The acquisition was in line with Oracle's strategy of increasing its customer base and product portfolio. Oracle wanted to tap new-growth business by acquiring PeopleSoft. The acquisition was targeted at PeopleSoft's customers who were using the databases of IBM and Microsoft. The acquisition enabled Oracle to capture the enterprise application software business used by large companies. Through the takeover Oracle doubled its customer base and became the largest application vendor in the US. It strengthened its presence in segments like healthcare and government. The acquisition of PeopleSoft provided Oracle customers with a one-stop global shop for databases, applications and other technologies.

The acquisition elevated Oracle to second position in the enterprise management software behind SAP, the market leader. Oracle had the largest application customer base in North America after the acquisition; its combined application was in open source Java. In contrast, SAP's application was based on a proprietary language, ABAP, and a proprietary set of applications.

The Siebel acquisition

In September 2005, Oracle paid $5.85 billion to acquire Siebel Systems, its largest competitor in the market for sales automation programs.

Siebel specialized in customer relationship management (CRM) software. Under the terms of agreement Oracle paid $10.66 in cash or stock for each Siebel share, which represented a premium of 17 percent over Siebel's stock price of $9.13 the previous trading day before the announcement. Siebel had $2.24 billion in cash on hand, reducing Oracle's net takeover cost to $3.61 billion.

The Siebel acquisition bought Oracle closer to its goal of being the leading company in applications globally and a direct competitor for SAP. A major chunk of Siebel's software ran on Oracle databases. The synergy in the deal was that Siebel's CRM technology and Oracle's applications and middleware shared an architecture favoring industry standards. The acquisition was in line with Oracle's focus on providing CRM software through an on demand subscription service rather than through a discrete product. Through the acquisition, Oracle gained 4000 customers and 3.4 million CRM users. Siebel's technology was also useful for Oracle's Project Fusion, which was designed to produce fully integrated software from PeopleSoft and Oracle.

Siebel Systems faced considerable revenues pressures as its revenue fell to $1.3 billion in 2004 from $2.1 billion in 2001.

The Sun Microsystems acquisition

In 2009, Oracle and Sun Microsystems entered into a definitive agreement under which Oracle acquired Sun Microsystems stocks for $9.50 per share in cash. The entire transaction was valued at approximately $7.4 billion, or $5.6 billion net of Sun Microsystems's cash and debt. The acquisition announcement came just days after IBM reportedly backed off acquisition talks after the two companies had failed to agree on a price.

At the time of the deal Sun's proprietary hardware business was facing tough competition from commodity players such as Intel and Dell, and its software business was finding it difficult to keep pace with the larger players in the software business, such as IBM, Microsoft and Oracle itself.

This acquisition transformed the database and business software giant into a hardware company as well. Oracle gained strategic advantage by controlling two key software assets of Sun: Java and Solaris. Java is the most popular programming technology, which is used to build software for websites and cell phones. It is the most important software Oracle has ever acquired, being one of the computer industry's best-known brands and most widely deployed technologies. Oracle Fusion Middleware, one of the fastest-growing businesses of Oracle, is based on Sun's Java language and software. The Sun Polaris System was the leading platform for the Oracle database, which is the largest business sector for Oracle. The acquisition of these assets enhanced the capability of Oracle to pursue further innovation in these technologies.

Through its Sun acquisition, Oracle became a direct competitor to more companies as it was now positioned in the server, storage and processor domains. With the addition of the Solaris operating system, Java, MySQL, servers, storages and Sparc processors to Oracle's portfolio of database, middleware and business applications, the company gained competitive advantage by becoming the only company offering open and integrated systems from application to disk.

The acquisition was significant in the context that more of Oracle's corporate database software runs on Solaris, a version of Unix, than on any other operating system. The acquisition provided scope for Oracle to offer a more complete set of corporate software, from Sun's operating systems and programming tools to Oracle's database and business applications to automate operations including finance and customer relations management. The combined company was able to integrate its software, resulting in reduced costs and enhanced security.

Acquisitions by Microsoft

Founded in 1975, Microsoft is the worldwide leader in software, services and solutions. The 1980s were an era of new technology for Microsoft. It dominated the home operating systems market with MS DOS in the mid-1980s, followed by the Microsoft Windows line of operating systems. Microsoft has offices in more than 100 countries. Its products include operating systems for personal computers; servers, phones and server applications for distributed computing environments; productivity applications, business solution applications; desktop and server management tools; software development tools; video games; and online advertising. Microsoft also designs and sells hardware, including the Xbox360 gaming and entertainment console. Microsoft has eight divisions: Online Services Division; Server and Tools Business; Microsoft Business Solutions; Microsoft Office Division; Interactive Entertainment Business; Windows Phone Division; Windows & Windows Live Division; and Skype Division.

In the fiscal year 2011, revenues grew by 12 percent to $69.9 billion, and more than 400 million Windows 7 licenses and 100 million Office 2010 licenses had been purchased by businesses and consumers.

Table 3.8 Financial highlights of Microsoft ($ million)

	2007	2008	2009	2010	2011
Revenues	51,122	60,420	58,437	62,484	69,943
Operating income	18,438	22,271	20,363	24,098	27,161
Net income	14,065	17,681	14,569	18,760	23,150
Total assets	63,171	72,793	77,888	86,113	108,704

Table 3.9 Biggest deals by Microsoft

Year	Company	Business	Value in $ billion
2011	Skype Communications	Telecommunications	8.5
2007	aQuantive	Digital marketing	6.3
2000	Visio Corp	Wholesale drawing software	1.375
2002	Navision	Software programs	1.33
2008	Fast Search & Transfer	Enterprise search	1.191
2000	Titus Communications	Cable TV	0.9448
2001	Great Plains Software	Business management software	0.939
1997	Hotmail	Internet software	0.5
2008	Danger	Mobile internet software	0.5

Source: Company Website.

Key acquisitions

Microsoft acquired 148 companies during the period 1987–2011. Its first acquisition in 1987 was that of Forethought, which developed a presentation program later known as Microsoft PowerPoint. In 1997 Microsoft acquired Hotmail for $500 million and integrated it into its MSN group of services. Since 1987, Microsoft has made five acquisitions worth over one billion dollars. These were the acquisition of Skype Communications, aQuantive, Fast Search & Transfer, Navision and Visio Corporation.

The Skype Communications acquisition

In October 2011, Microsoft acquired the Internet communications company Skype for $8.5 billion. Skype is the world's leading provider of real time Internet video and video communications services and technology, and became a new division of Microsoft. Skype was founded in 2003. eBayInc bought Skype in 2005 for around $3.1 billion, but took a $1.4 billion charge for the transaction in 2007 when the acquisition failed to realize the expected synergy from the deal. Later in 2009 eBay sold a 70 percent stake in Skype to a group of investors led by private equity firm Silver Lake Partners for $2.75 billion.

This deal was the most expensive acquisition yet made by Microsoft. But Skype was not yet profitable. Despite its widespread use, it has been slow to convert users into paying customers and generate profits. It had a net loss of $7 million in 2010. Skype lets people make free phone calls between computers or pay pennies-a-minute to make overseas calls from traditional phones. Increasingly it is being used in the form of an application on smart phones to avoid paying higher fees to wireless carriers for phone calls.

In 2010, Skype had 170 million connected users and over 207 billion minutes of voice and video conversations.

Microsoft management believes that the Skype acquisition is a perfect fit for Microsoft's strategic vision to connect millions of people and provide them with innovative ways to communicate through PCs, phones, the Xbox and applications such as Office and Lync. Microsoft estimated it would accelerate Skype's reach to one billion users daily. The combination of Microsoft and Skype was expected to extend Skype's world-class brand and networked platform, thereby adding value to Microsoft's existing portfolio of real time communications products and services. Plans were in place to integrate Skype into Microsoft devices and systems such as Xbox and Kinect, Xbox Live, the Windows Phone, Lync, Outlook, Hotmail and Messenger.

Microsoft also expected to turn around its fortunes in the mobile phone market with the Skype acquisition. Phones running Microsoft software were just 7.5 percent of the smartphone market, lagging far behind Apple and Google. This acquisition came at a time when technological growth is facilitated by the exponential growth of social network sites like Facebook and innovative devices such devices as Apple's iPad and iPhone that are reshaping the cell phone and computer markets.

One interesting fact to be highlighted in this acquisition is that Microsoft had planned to purchase Skype with cash held overseas, money that it could not otherwise bring back to the US without paying repatriation taxes of more than 30 percent. The majority of Microsoft's roughly $50 billion in cash is held overseas.

The aQuantive acquisition

In 2007, Microsoft acquired online advertising agency aQuantive for $6 billion in a cash deal. Microsoft paid $66.50 a share, which represented an 85 percent premium over the previous-day share price of aQuantive on the announcement.

The acquisition was a strategic move by Microsoft to strengthen its position against Google and Yahoo! in the online advertising sector. The acquisition came after Google had bought Doubleclick for $3.1 billion and Yahoo! had acquired competitor RightMedia for $680 million. The deal was significant as many of the online services that Microsoft offers from software to video games were increasingly dependent on online advertising revenues. Through the acquisition, Microsoft would be able to better monetize inventory and sell display advertisements on third party sites. The acquisition was made with the strategic aim of providing the advertising industry with a world-class advertising platform across devices and media. This becomes more relevant in the context that the advertisement market is increasingly being shifted to the world of online and IP-served platforms.

The Visio Corporation acquisition

In 2000, Microsoft acquired Visio Corp, the leading supplier of enterprise-wide business diagramming and technical drawing software, with an installed base of more than three million users worldwide. Visio's product lines have become the worldwide standard for graphical solutions in business. The products are available in 12 language versions and sold in more than 45 countries. The merger was structured as an exchange of common stock whereby each share of Visio was exchanged for 0.45 shares of Microsoft. The deal was valued at approximately $1.3 billion. Visio and Microsoft had long-term partnership relationship with respect to both Windows and Office products. The Visio products were rebranded as MS Vision and consist of Microsoft office applications such as the Microsoft Project.

The Navision acquisition

In 2002, Microsoft acquired Navision, the Danish mid-market business applications vendor. The acquisition created a global business application team that focused on the mid-market sector of businesses with annual revenues between $1 million and $800 million. Navision was absorbed into the Microsoft Business Solutions division.

The Navision transaction was structured as a hybrid of cash and stock based on an offer of $37.1 per share, with an estimated transaction value of $1.3 billion. One of the major motives for the acquisition was to gain a strong hold in the business applications market, especially in Europe. Approximately 86 percent of Navision's revenue came from

Europe, so through Navision Microsoft gained access to an extensive network of European partnerships. Partners are considered to be a critical factor in selling to the SME sector. With its 2400 Navision Solutions Centers Navision had a proven network in more than 94 countries.

The Fast Search & Transfer acquisition

In 2008, Microsoft acquired Fast Search & Transfer, a Norwegian-based enterprise search and business intelligence provider. The deal was made at $3.54 per share, which totaled $1.2 billion in value. Enterprise search software and applications help employees locate documents and other data often hidden deep inside corporate networks and databases. The acquisition was aimed to facilitate the growth of Microsoft in the high-end search development platform.

The Titus Communications acquisition

In 2010, Microsoft acquired MediaOne International's stake in Titus Communications, the second largest broadband provider in Japan. This acquisition was in tune with Microsoft's vision for broadband deployment and voice, data, video convergence through a leading Japanese broadband provider.

The Great Plains Software acquisition

In 2000, Microsoft acquired Great Plains Software in order to enhance its entry into the small and medium business application market. This acquisition was also an important part of Microsoft's strategy to deliver the power of the .NET platform to small and medium companies. The acquisition gave Microsoft the ability to give medium to large enterprise customers "one-stop shopping" under the Microsoft brand, with the combination of Windows 2000, Microsoft Exchange, Microsoft SQL Server and Great Plains business functions.

The Hotmail acquisition

In 1998, Microsoft bought Hotmail, the web mail pioneer, for approximately $500 million. This acquisition completed the lineup for Microsoft as the company was missing a search engine and free email on the MS Network portal. The acquisition facilitated the access of Hotmail users to various sites on Microsoft. Hotmail became an important component of the Microsoft Network of online communication and information services, which Microsoft offers free to all Internet users; it includes sites for news, travel, investment, car buying, games, computing and shopping. With this deal Microsoft Network boosted its traffic substantially once Hotmail members were added to its collective sites, Hotmail's webcentric email services complementing Microsoft's family of email and collaboration clients. Hotmail itself had been in need of new services for its members in the areas of personalized information, ecommerce and multimedia content.

Acquisitions by Intel

Intel, the world leader in innovations for semiconductor chips, develops technologies and products. A world leader in computing innovations, Intel was founded in 1968, and introduced the world's first microprocessor in 1971. Over the years, Intel had grown its employee base to 82,500 in 2010. Over one million PCs with Intel technology are sold worldwide per day. Thousands of other devices are also powered by Intel technology—in cars, homes, hospitals, offices and factories. Intel is being transformed from a company with a primary focus on the design and manufacture of semiconductor chips for PCs and servers to a computing company that delivers complete solutions in the form of hardware and software platforms and supporting services.

During the period 1982–2011, Intel Corporation had made 72 acquisitions while taking stakes in 110 companies. Intel had also divested stakes in 46 companies during the period. Intel's most hectic M&A activity was during the period 1997–2002 when it acquired about 40 companies. Intel has made a series of software acquisitions in sectors such as gaming, visual computing, embedded devices and machine software and security.

The McAfee acquisition

In 2011, Intel acquired the security company McAfee for $7.68 billion, or $48 per share in cash. McAfee, founded in 1987, is the world's largest dedicated security technology company, and had $2 billion in revenues in 2009. It delivers proactive and proven solutions and services to secure systems and networks. McAfee products include McAfee Total Protection, McAfee Antivirus, McAfee Internet Security, McAfee Firewall and McAfee IPS as well as an expanding line of products targeting mobile devices

Table 3.10 Financial highlights of Intel ($ billion)

	2006	2007	2008	2009	2010
Revenues	35.4	38.3	37.6	35.1	43.6
R&D	5.9	5.8	5.7	5.7	6.6
EPS (cents)	0.86	1.18	0.92	0.77	2.05

including smartphones. McAfee was integrated as a wholly owned subsidiary reporting to Intel's Software and Services Group.

In the context of the online environment, the acquisition enabled the combination of security software and hardware from one single company to protect consumers, corporations and governments. The acquisition was in line with Intel's mobile wireless strategy of focusing on consumer security concerns now billions of devices connect. The acquisition highlights the fact that providing protection to a diverse online world requires a fundamentally new approach involving software, hardware and services. This strategic acquisition also reflects the point that Intel has elevated the priority of security on par with its strategic focus areas in energy-efficient performance and Internet connectivity. The cyber threat landscape faces millions of new threats, necessitating a safer and more secure Internet environment. The merger could also lead to synergistic benefits in innovations as both Intel and McAfee had the most innovative laboratories and research capability in the high-tech industry.

Intel had earlier made a number of software-related acquisitions including Wind River and Havok. Wind River was purchased for $884 million as a part of Intel's efforts to expand into the mobile and embedded systems markets. Intel also purchased Rapid Mind, a software maker, in order to exploit Intel's multicore processors.

Intel had also bought Apple's Infineon wireless business for $1.4 billion. Infineon was responsible for the baseband technology powering the iPhone and iPad.

Other major acquisitions by Intel can be listed as follows:

- In 2003, Mobilian, a chipmaker for wireless LANs and Bluetooth connectivity, was acquired.
- In 2001, Xircom, a PC modem and network card maker, was acquired for $748 million.
- In 2000, Voice Technologies, a maker of PBX connectivity technology, was acquired.
- In 1999, XLNT, a Gigabit Ethernet switch maker, was acquired.
- In 1999, iPivot, a maker of traffic management technology, was acquired for $500 million.
- In 1999, Dialogic, a computer telephone technology company, was acquired for $780 million.

Advanced Micro Devices' acquisition of ATI Technologies

Advanced Micro Devices (AMD) is a global semiconductor design company with 47 locations worldwide. AMD offers primarily x86 microprocessors for commercial, commercial client and consumer markets and chipsets for desktops and notebook PCs, professional workstations and servers. AMD also sells graphics, video and multimedia products for desktop and notebook computers, including home media PCs, professional workstations and servers and technology for game consoles.

ATI Technologies (ATI) is a major player in the electronics industry. ATI makes chips that enable integrated digital television and image processors that are used to display video on cell phones or mobile hand-held game machines. In 2005, ATI was ranked 25th in the electronics market, with nearly $2 billion in revenues.

In 2006, AMD acquired ATI for $5.4 billion in a cash-and-stock deal, comprising $4.2 billion in cash and $1.2 billion for outstanding ATI stock. In other terms, AMD paid ATI shareholders the equivalent of $20.47 per share of which $16.40 was cash and rest AMD stock. At the time of the acquisition, AMD and ATI had market capitalizations of $8.84 billion and $4.2 billion respectively.

The acquisition combined the world's second largest chipmaker with the largest graphics chipmaker for laptops and notebooks. The acquisition was expected to drive growth and innovation in the entire industry. The deal also gave AMD an entry into the cell phone and digital TV markets as ATI made chips for these products. The acquisition was done to strategically position AMD with respect to Intel. AMD lacked a complete CPU and chipset solution, which Intel had. MD aimed to exploit the potential in the computational power of the GPGPU graphic chip. The buyout of AMD also freed AMD from its reliance on companies such as VIA for chipsets.

The acquisition of National Semiconductor by Texas Instruments

Texas Instruments Incorporated (TI) is one of the world's largest semiconductor companies. TI boasted landmark inventions such as the first commercial silicon transistors, the first integrated circuits and the first electronic hand-held calculator. TI designs, makes and sells high-technology components like integrated circuits or semiconductor chips to electronics designers and manufacturers. TI's analog, embedded processing and wireless technologies affect daily life in many different ways, from digital communications and entertainment to medical services, automotive systems and wide-ranging applications. TI holds more than 38,000 patents worldwide, and has sales operations in more than 30 countries, serving more than 80,000 customers. The company had revenues of $13.97 billion in 2010.

Since 1996, TI has made 33 acquisitions. It acquired National Semiconductor in an all-cash transaction of $6.5 billion, paying $25 for each National share, which represented a premium of 78 percent over the stock's price on the day before the announcement. National Semiconductor is a semiconductor manufacturer, specializing in analog devices and subsystems. The company's products include power management circuits, display drivers, audio and operational amplifiers, communication interface products and data conversion solutions. The combination of TI's sales team and National's portfolio of analog products was expected to increase the combined company's profitability and expansion into additional markets. The sales of analog semiconductors represented almost 50 percent of TI's revenue.

The acquisition combined two industry leaders in the market for analog semiconductors. National became a strategic part of TI's analog growth engine. The two companies had a combined portfolio of 45,000 analog products and a sales force that was ten times larger than National's previous strength. National bought 12,000 analog products to the joint product portfolio. Both companies had been focusing on analog chips, which are competitive with and offer lower prices compared to digital chips. The acquisition gave TI a broader set of products to sell to existing customers in the medical device, telecommunications and industrial equipment markets. The worldwide sales of analog semiconductors earned about $42 billion in revenue in 2010, with TI's share at 14 percent and National at 3 percent.

The acquisition of Varian by Applied Materials

Applied Materials is the global leader in providing innovative equipment, services and software for manufacturing advanced semiconductor, flat panel display and solar photovoltaic products. The company had revenue of $10,517 million in 2010.

In May 2011, Applied Materials and Varian Semiconductor Equipment Associates entered into a definitive agreement under which Applied acquired Varian for $63 per share in cash for a total value of $4.9 billion. The price paid represented a 38 percent premium to Varian's 30-day average closing price before the announcement.

Varian is the leading supplier of ion implantation equipment used by chip makers. Varian's products are used by chip manufacturers worldwide to produce high-performance semiconductor devices. Varian is the market leader in ion implant by virtue of its architecturally superior products offered at low cost. The acquisition of Varian enhanced

Applied's extensive portfolio with market-leading ion implantation technology at a level of $1.5 billion. The acquisition consolidated Applied's leadership position in wafer fabrication equipment. Varian's ion implant products complements Applied's portfolio of products in the areas of transistor, interconnect and wafer level packaging. Applied also planned to focus on Varian's technology to extend into markets of solar, display and light-emitting diodes. The acquisition was aimed at consolidating the market leadership position of the combined company in transistor technologies.

The company estimated savings from the acquisition at $50 million to $60 million annually, mostly from costs of materials.

Major acquisitions by SAP

Founded in 1972, SAP is the world leader in enterprise applications in terms of software and software-related service revenue. Based on market capitalization, SAP is the world's third largest independent software manufacturer. It has more than 176,000 customers in over 120 countries. The SAP Group includes subsidiaries in every major country and employs more than 54,000 people; it has operations in more than 50 countries.

Unlike Oracle, SAP desisted from acquisitions for a long period. SAP's biggest acquisition to date is its $6.8 billion purchase of Business Objects in 2008. The acquisition was aimed to accelerate SAP's growth in the fast-growing market for business intelligence (BI) software. After the acquisition SAP offered Business Objects' software as a standalone product line.

In 2010, SAP bought US-based business software maker Sybase, Inc. for $5.8 billion, gaining technology that allows it to deliver accounting software and other programs to smartphones. SAP paid $65 per share in cash for Sybase, the fourth-largest maker of database software after Oracle, IBM and Microsoft Corp. Sybase's most valuable asset is its mobile software, which would give SAP an edge over Oracle with respect to business management programs. The acquisition move increased the competition between Oracle and SAP in which Oracle had been the leading database company but number two to SAP in business management software The acquisition was aimed to acquire Mobile "on device" software, which had been one of the three key areas of SAP's growth strategy. SAP focused on a diversification strategy of entry into new areas of mobile software and on-demand software alongside further expansion into the enterprise software market.

Acquisitions by IBM

International Business Machines Corporation (IBM), the multinational technology and consulting giant consulting corporation, was established in 1911. IBM manufactures and sells computer hardware and software, and offers infrastructure, hosting and consulting services in areas ranging from mainframe computers to nanotechnology. IBM was the second largest publicly traded technology company in the world by market capitalization in 2011.

For over a century, IBM has transformed industries and advanced the world's most critical systems. IBM holds the highest number of patents among the US-based technology companies and has nine research laboratories worldwide. It employs more than 425,000 employees in over 200 countries. Since 1915 IBM stocks have increased value by 40,000 times the original value. Among the world-renowned inventions by IBM are the automated teller machine (ATM), the floppy disk, hard disk drive, the magnetic stripe card, relational database, Universal Product Code, financial swap and Watson artificial intelligence.

Major acquisitions by IBM

During the last 100 years, IBM has acquired 242 companies, using strategic acquisitions to increase market share, obtain critical mass, establish new growth platforms, extend geographic coverage, add capabilities and focus on core businesses along with portfolio diversification. The company spent $27 billion net on the acquisition of 116 companies since 2000. Post-2005, IBM has invested more than $14 billion in 24 acquisitions to expand its analytics capabilities. IBM's top 25 acquisitions were aimed at domination in Analytics and Cloud software.

IBM's acquisition of Cognos for $5 billion in 2008 was its biggest to date. Cognos, the biggest software company of Canada, is the world's second largest maker of business intelligence software. The business intelligence program of Cognos helps companies monitor data on budgets and inventory. Cognos software is used by many retailers, including Home Depot,

Table 3.11 Financial highlights of IBM ($ million)

	2008	2009	2010
Total revenues	103,630	95,758	99,870
Assets	81,098	109,022	113,452
Net income	12,334	13,425	14,833
Cash flow from operations	18,812	20,773	19,549

Amazon.com, American Eagle Outfitters and 7-Eleven. The acquisition was aimed at strengthening IBM's Information on Demand strategy, which was part of IBM's initiative to support information integration, content and data management and business consulting services.

IBM paid $58 dollars a share cash, which represented a premium of 9.5 percent over Cognos's closing price before the announcement. IBM's offer was about 23 times Cognos' fiscal 2009 earnings. The acquisition enabled IBM to deliver new business insights to new areas beyond the conventional users of business intelligence. In US, the stricter financial reporting requirements imposed by the Sarbanes–Oxley Act had in one way led to the increased interest in business intelligence software.

In 2002, IBM purchased PricewaterhouseCoopers' (PwC) consulting arm for an estimated $3.5 billion. The purchase price of $3.5 billion was in the form of $2.7 billion dollars in cash, $400 million in a convertible note and $400 million in stock. PwC is the world's largest professional services organization, which specializes in global management consulting and technology services. The acquisition created a 60,000 employee-strong business consulting services organization with operations in more than 160 countries.

This acquisition was a major step for IBM in transforming itself from a hardware-and-software company to a consulting-and-services company. IBM's strategy is to deliver superior business value through the fusion of business and technology. Earlier in 2002, HP had tried to buy PwC Consulting for $1.8 billion, but dropped its bid on the grounds of high price. Under the IBM acquisition terms, PwC Consulting became a part of IBM Global Services Business Innovation Services unit. IBM Business Consulting Services was now the world's largest consulting service organization. The acquisition enabled IBM to provide customers with a full range of business and technology consulting services that could leverage IBM's services, infrastructure, technology and financing resources. After the acquisition, PwC retained only its auditing, tax and legal services along with smaller business advisory services.

In the second quarter of 1995, IBM launched a hostile bid for Lotus with a $60 per share tender offer when Lotus stock was trading at $32. Lotus could not find a potential white knight, and IBM increased its bid to $64.50 per share. In July 1995, IBM bought Lotus for $3.5 billion.

In the 1990s, Lotus had bought products such as Ami Pro (word processor), Approach (database) and Thread (Lotus Organizer) in order to compete with Microsoft's Windows applications. IBM created a special subsidiary, White Acquisition Corp, to handle the transaction. Lotus was most commonly known for the Lotus 1-2-3 spreadsheet application.

IBM purchased Lotus primarily to acquire its Notes technology. In the mid-1990s, with the growing prominence of the Web and increasing competition from players like Microsoft, Note developers were facing strategic impediments to growth. The IBM acquisition provided solid financial support and accessibility to world-class technology, which consisted of the HTTP server that became IBM Lotus Domino. In 2008, approximately 145 million Lotus Notes licenses were sold. The release of Lotus Notes 4.0 in 1996 opened up competition for messaging products for web servers and development systems for these products. Its Lotus acquisition helped IBM to establish a presence in the increasingly important client-server computing segment.

Among other M&A activity, in 1996, IBM purchased Object Technology International (OTI) whose technology formed the basis of Eclipse. In 2001, IBM acquired the database assets of Infomix for $1 billion; this acquisition doubled the size of IBM's distributed database business. In 2004, the buyout of Daksh eServices, an Indian outsourcing company, created a formidable business process outsourcing service portfolio. The acquisition of FileNet in 2006 for $1.6 billion expanded IBM's IOD initiative, which combined IBM's software, services, partners and industry consulting expertise to improve clients' business performance. The purchase of Internet Security Systems (ISS) for $1.3 billion in 2006 consolidated IBM's position in the emerging area of security services. In 2010, IBM acquired Netezza for about $1.7 billion, which expanded IBM's business analytics initiatives. IBM acquired Sterling Commerce in 2010 for about $1.4 billion, which offered cross-channel commerce and integration of customer, partner and supplier networks across a wide range of industries.

In other activity, in December 2010, IBM renamed IBM Daksh as IBM Global Process Services India. In 2003, IBM acquired Rational, which provided open industry standard tools, best practices and services for developing business applications and building software products and systems. In 2009, IBM made a strategic acquisition by acquiring SPSS for $1.2 billion, an acquisition that expanded IBM's Information on Demand software portfolio and business analytics capabilities, providing synergistic value for IBM's Business Analytics and Optimization Consulting organization and network of Analytics Solution Centers. In 2010, IBM acquired Coremetrics to expand its business analytics capabilities by enabling organizations to use a Cloud-based delivery model to gain more targeted marketing campaigns through social media networks. In 2005, IBM purchased SRD, which provided identity resolution software, enhancing IBM's business intelligence platform and strengthening its analytical capabilities. In 1996, IBM bought Tivoli Systems for $743 million, which provided integrated service management software to help manage the business value of enterprises' IT infrastructure. The acquisition of XIV in 2008 strengthened IBM's infrastructure portfolio, and enabled IBM to address emerging storage opportunities such as Web 2.0 applications, digital archives and digital media.

IBM acquired Candle in 2004. This acquisition provided customers with an enhanced set of software solutions for managing an on-demand operating environment and complemented IBM's middleware solutions. In 2005, IBM purchased Data Power to help companies improve the performance, security and management of business processes built of reusable open standards-based software components, popularly called SOA (service-oriented architecture). In 2006, IBM acquired MRO Software for $740 million to leverage business consulting, IT services and software development of repeatable tools. IBM's acquisition of ILOG in 2009 combined IBM's BPM (business process management), business optimization and SOA technologies with ILOG's business rules management systems software.

IBM's Telelogic acquisition for $845 million in 2007 improved the development of software used in complex systems such as aircraft radar or a car's antilock system. Transarc was acquired in 1999 for the DFS distributed file system component of distributed computing environments. In 2010, IBM acquired Cast Iron Systems to broaden the delivery of Cloud computing service for clients. In 2010, IBM acquired Unica for $480 million for its enterprise and Cloud marketing software solutions, which facilitate business streamlining and automated marketing processes. In 2009, IBM bought Lombardi Software, which integrated business processes.

Major acquisitions by Yahoo!

Yahoo!, the computer software and web search engine company, was founded in March 1995. Yahoo! has been one of the most visited websites on the Internet. According to company statistics, the latest version of Yahoo! Mail had surpassed 100 million monthly active users, and Yahoo! Mail was the top email provider in the USA.

Yahoo!'s first acquisition was in 1997 when it purchased NetControls, a web search engine company, for $1.4 million. Most of the companies acquired by Yahoo! are based in the US. As of 2011, Yahoo! had acquired 64 companies, the largest being the purchase of Broadcast.com, an Internet radio company, for $5.7 billion in stock.

Table 3.12 Financial highlights of Yahoo! ($ million)

	2006	2007	2008	2009	2010
Revenues	6425.68	6969.27	7208.5	6460.32	6324.65
Operating income	940.97	695.41	12.9	386.69	772.52
Net income	751.39	639.16	418.92	597.99	1231.66
Total assets	11,513.61	12,229.74	13,689.85	14,936.03	14,928.1

Broadcast.com, which was founded in 1995, is the leading aggregator and broadcaster of streaming media programming on the Web. The company broadcasts audio and video programming from television and radio stations and networks such as the BBC World Service. Yahoo! issued 0.7722 of a share of Yahoo! common stock for each share of Broadcast.com. All the outstanding options of Broadcast.com were converted into Yahoo! options, and the company was renamed Yahoo! Broadcast Solutions.

The acquisition expanded Yahoo!'s rich multimedia content offerings for its users, provided additional distribution for content and services partners and enhanced services for advertisers and businesses. The acquisition combined the Web's leading aggregator and broadcaster of streaming audio and video programming with one of the world's leading Web networks. The acquisition was undertaken to provide a powerful advertising and distribution platform for both companies' content, advertising and business service providers. Yahoo! advertisers and merchants obtained the expanded options to promote their businesses through the company's fusion, marking online integrated marketing programs. As of 2010, Broadcast.com redirects to Yahoo.com.

In January 1999, Yahoo! acquired GeoCities for $3.57 billion in stock. The GeoCities company was founded in 1995, and was a web hosting and development company. GeoCities set up communities of people who share similar interests and allowed customers to create their own home page on the Internet.

Within a span of two years Geocities had become the most popular website behind AOL and Yahoo! Under the terms of the deal, GeoCities shareholders received 0.3384 share of Yahoo! for each share of GeoCities they owned. Based on Yahoo!'s closing stock price of $335.875 on the day before the announcement of the deal, the transaction was valued at $3.57 billion, which was a high premium over GeoCities' market capitalization of $2.3 billion.

Through GeoCities, Yahoo! was able to distribute a range of editing tools and content published through personal homepages in an array of services, such as Yahoo! Clubs, Yahoo! Classifieds, Yahoo! Shopping, Yahoo! Auctions and other areas of the network. One of the reasons attributed for the buyout was that Yahoo was facing stiff competition from Excite, AltaVista and Infoseek Corp. But later in 2009, facing the hazards of competition from up-to-date blogging and social sites, Geocities was completely closed down.

In 2003, Yahoo! acquired Overture Services for $1.63 billion in order to consolidate its position against rivals Google and Microsoft in the booming market for Web search advertising. Overture specializes in selling advertising links that accompany search results on sites such as Yahoo! and MSN. Each share of Overture stock was exchanged for $4.75 in cash and 0.6108 of a Yahoo! share, which valued each share of Overture at $24.63, roughly a 15 percent premium over Overture's closing price before the announcement. It was later renamed Yahoo! Search Marketing.

In 2007, Yahoo! acquired Wholly Right Media for $680 million. Earlier it had a 20 percent stake in the company. This acquisition led to increased competition in online advertising between Yahoo! and Google. The acquisition of Right Media gave a way for Yahoo! to sell and broker advertisement outside its own sites, and a competitive position against Google's famous black-box advertising system. In April 2004, Yahoo! acquired Kelkoo, the online shopping firm, for €450 million; it was later sold to a private equity firm. Kelkoo operated in nine countries across Europe and reached nearly 10 percent of Internet users on the Continent, offering price comparisons on electrical goods, CDs, books and cars. In 2002, Yahoo! acquired HotJobs.com for $436 million; it was sold to Monster.com for $225 million in 2010. eGroups.com was bought by Yahoo! for $413 million in a stock deal in 2000. It is now known as Yahoo! Groups. The acquisition allowed Yahoo! to add eGroups' email services to its existing collection of communications properties, including its online clubs site, free email service and instant messenger. Zimbra, the business, education and service provider, was brought by Yahoo! for $350 million in 2007, and subsequently purchased by VMware in 2010. In 2007, Yahoo! acquired BlueLithium for $300 million, and in 2004, Yahoo! acquired Musicmatch for $160 million.

In 2005, Yahoo! acquired Flickr.com, an image hosting and video hosting website, for $50 million. Yahoo! Also acquired Delicious, a social bookmarking web service firm. Delicious became one of the most popular bookmarking services, with over 5.3 million users and 180 million unique bookmarked URLs. Yahoo! had also acquired MyBlogLog, a blog-based distributed social network platform.

Additional References

1. "Five Blockbuster Business Deals," http://www.cbc.ca/news/business/story/2011/08/15f-big-business-deals.htm
2. Rob D. Young, "Google Acquired 11 Companies in 2011, Microsoft Made Biggest Transaction," July 11, 2011, http://searchenginewatch.com/article/2092684/Google-Acquired-11-Companies-in-2011-Microsoft-Made-Biggest-Transaction
3. "Half Year Mergers and Acquisitions Trends Report July 2011," BerkeryNoyes, Investment Bankers, July 2011.
4. "M&A Insights: Analysis and Opinion on Global M&A Activity," Technology Sector, 2008, PricewaterhouseCoopers.
5. Janet Morrissey, "Tech Mergers and Acquisitions Coming Back," October 7, 2009, http://www.time.com/time/business/article/0,8599,1928931,00.html#ixzz1fJpKTi2M
6. Muazzin Mehrban, "M&A in the Technology Sector," June 2009, http://www.financierworldwide.com/article.php?id=4186&page=2
7. Ed Silverstein, "M&A in Technology Sector has 'Strong Start' during 1Q," http://financial.tmcnet.com//topics/mergers-acquisitions/articles/175788-mergers-acquisitions-technology-sector-has-strong-start-during.htm
8. David Rothnie, "Technology M&A Market Heats Up," http://www.efinancialnews.com/story/2010-10-04/technology-mergers-and-acquisitions-heats-up
9. "M&A in the Information Technology and ICT Sector," http://www.corporatefinanceineurope.eu/mergers-acquisitions-information-technology.htm
10. http://www.information-management.com/news/1900-information-technology-mergers-and-acquisitions-in-2010-idc-10020051-1.html
11. Ben Heskett and Erich Luening, "JDS Uniphase buys SDL for US$41 billion," *CNET News*, July 11, 2000, http://www.zdnetasia.com/jds-uniphase-buys-sdl-for-us41-billion-10029058.htm
12. http://www.jdsu.com/News-and-Events/news-releases/Pages/jds-uniphase-and-sdl-agree-to-41-billion-merger.aspx
13. http://www.dealipedia.com/deal_view_acquisition.php?r=9331
14. http://www.marketwatch.com/story/kkr-to-buy-credit-card-processor-first-data-for-29-billion
15. http://articles.latimes.com/1999/jan/14/business/fi-63310
16. "VeriSign Buys Domain Firm," http://money.cnn.com/2000/03/07/deals/verisign/
17. "John, Symantec Buys VeriSign for $13.5 billion," http://www.theregister.co.uk/2004/12/16/symantec_veritas_merger/
18. http://www.hp.com/hpinfo/newsroom/press/2001/index.html
19. http://investor.hp.com/edgar.cfm, Form 425 filed by HP with the SEC on December 19, 2001.
20. http://www.hp.com/hpinfo/newsroom/press/2001/010904a.html
21. http://investor.google.com/releases/2011/0815.html
22. http://techcrunch.com/2011/08/15/breaking-google-buys-motorola-for-12-5-billion/
23. http://googleblog.blogspot.com/2011/08/supercharging-android-google-to-acquire.html
24. Amir Efrati and Spencer Ante, "Google's $12.5 billion Gamble," http://online.wsj.com/article/SB10001424053111903392904576509953821437960.html

25. http://www.businessinsider.com/googles-16-biggest-acquisitions-so-far-and-what-happened-to-them-2011-8#12
26. http://www.thesciworld.com/2011/08/10-most-expensive-acquisitions-by-google/
27. Robert Macmillan and James Niccolai, "It's Official: Oracle Closes on PeopleSoft Acquisition," http://www.computerworld.com/s/article/98835/It_s_official_Oracle_closes_on_PeopleSoft_acquisition
28. Jim Kerstetter, "Finally Oracle Nails PeopleSoft," http://www.businessweek.com/technology/content/dec2004/tc20041213_8884_tc024.htm
29. http://www.chinadaily.com.cn/english/doc/2004-12/14/content_399969.htm
30. http://www.chillibreeze.com/articles_various/Oracle-and-PeopleSoft.asp
31. Dawn Kawamoto and Margaret Kane, "Oracle to Swallow Siebel for $5.8 billion," September 12, 2005, http://news.cnet.com/Oracle-to-swallow-Siebel-for-5.8-billion/2100-1014_3-5860113.html?tag=txt
32. Laurie J. Flynn, "Oracle to Pay $5.85 billion for Siebel," September 13, 2005, http://www.nytimes.com/2005/09/13/technology/13oracle.html
33. Stephen Shankland, "Oracle Buys Sun, Becomes Hardware Company," http://news.cnet.com/8301-30685_3-20000019-264.html
34. Don Clark and Ben Worthen, "Oracle Snatches Sun, Foiling IBM," http://online.wsj.com/article/SBI24022727265I4434703.html
35. Paul McDougall, "Oracle to Acquire Sun Microsystems for $7.4 billion," http://www.informationweek.com/news/software/soa_webservices/216900073
36. Steve Lohr, "In Sun Oracle Sees a Software Gem," April 21, 2009, http://www.nytimes.com/2009/04/21/technology/companies/21sun.html
37. http://www.oracle.com/us/corporate/press/018363
38. http://news.cnet.com/8301-30685_3-20000019-264.html
39. Company website—Oracle.com
40. "Microsoft Corporation Mergers and Acquisitions." Thomson Financial, http://www.alacrastore.com/mergers-acquisitions/Microsoft_Corporation-1011097 (accessed October 31, 2008).
41. "Microsoft Officially Welcomes Skype," http://www.microsoft.com/Presspass/press/2011/oct11/10–13SkypePR.mspx?rss_fdn=Customwww.microsoft.com
42. "Microsoft to Acquire Skype," http://www.microsoft.com/presspass/press/2011/may11/05-10corpnewspr.mspx
43. Nick Wingfield, "Microsoft Dials Up Change," http://online.wsj.com/article/SB10001424052748703730804576314854222820260.html#ixzz1h0fenB6K
44. Chris Isidore, "Microsoft Buys aQuantive for $6 billion," http://money.cnn.com/2007/05/18/technology/microsoft_aquantive/
45. Redmond Wash, "Microsoft Completes Acquisition of aQuantive," http://www.microsoft.com/presspass/press/2007/aug07/08-13MSaQuantivePR.mspx
46. Michael Arrington, "Microsoft Pays $6 billion for aQuantive," http://techcrunch.com/2007/05/18/microsoft-pays-6-billion-for-aquantive/
47. http://www.microsoft.com/presspass/press/1999/sept99/visiopr.mspx
48. "Microsoft Confirms Navision Acquisition Ticket to Europe," *Computerwire*, http://www.theregister.co.uk/2002/05/14/microsoft_confirms_navision_acquisition/
49. http://searchcontentmanagement.techtarget.com/news/2240033438/Microsoft-to-acquire-Fast-Search-Transfer-for-12b

50. Redmond Wash, http://www.thefreelibrary.com/Microsoft+Acquires+Media One+International's+Stake+in+TITUS...-a061801626
51. http://www.techrepublic.com/article/why-microsoft-bought-great-plains-software/1053825
52. Jeff Pelline, "Microsoft Buys Hotmail," 1998, http://news.cnet.com/2100-1033-206717.html
53. http://news.cnet.com/2100-1033-206717.html
54. http://www.microsoft.com/presspass/press/1997/Dec97/Hotmlpr.mspx
55. Bob Brown, "A Short History of Intel Acquisitions," *Network World*, http://www.networkworld.com/news/2010/081910-intel-acquisitions-history.html
56. Patrick Darling, "Intel to Acquire McAfee," http://newsroom.intel.com/community/intel_newsroom/blog/2010/08/19/intel-to-acquire-mcafee
57. Roy Mark, "AMD Acquires ATI, Plans New Kinds of Processors," http://www.internetnews.com/ent-news/article.php/3621996/AMD+Acquires+ATI+Plans+New+Kinds+of+Processors.htm
58. Fuad Abazovic, "The Three Reasons Why AMD Acquired ATI," http://www.theinquirer.net/inquirer/news/1026310/the-three-reasons-why-amd-acquired-ati
59. Andrew Ross Sorkin, "AMD to Acquire ATI Technologies," http://www.nytimes.com/2006/07/24/technology/24cnd-semi.html
60. Eric Bangeman, "AMD to Buy ATI," http://arstechnica.com/old/content/2006/07/7328.ars
61. www.ti.com/deliveringmoretogether
62. http://techcrunch.com/2011/04/04/texas-instruments-acquires-manufacturer-national-semiconductor-for-6-5-billion-in-cash/
63. Don Clark, "Texas Instrument Buys Age Old Rival," http://online.wsj.com/article/SB10001424052748703712504576243133367045662.html#ixzz1hfhgLQb8
64. http://appliedmaterials.com/news/articles/applied-materials-acquire-varian-semiconductor-equipment-associates
65. http://www.marketwatch.com/story/applied-materials-completes-acquisition-of-varian-semiconductor-equipment-associates-2011-11-10
66. "SAP Buys Sybase for $5.8 billion," http://www.pcmag.com/article2/0,2817,2363746,00.asp
67. http://www.ft.com/cms/s/2/dcfb82e0-5e1b-11df-8153-00144feab49a.html#axzz1i3JDU18b
68. James Niccolai, "SAP Buys Business Objects for $6.8 billion," http://www.pcworld.com/article/138165/sap_buys_business_objects_for_678_billion.html
69. www.ibm.com
70. Darryl K. Taft, "Web 2.0, Web Services: IBM's Top 25 Acquisitions Aim for Analytics, Cloud Software Dominatio," June 6, 2011.
71. http://www.bloomberg.com/apps/news?pid=newsarchive&sid=aTUvC2z6S8MY
72. Stephen Shankland, "IBM Grabs Consulting Giant for $3.5 billion," http://news.cnet.com/2100-1001-947283.html
73. http://www-03.ibm.com/press/us/en/pressrelease/585.wss
74. Richard Richtmyer, "IBM to Buy PwC Consulting," http://money.cnn.com/2002/07/30/technology/ibm_pwc/index.htm

75. Thor Olavsrud, "IBM Completes PwC Acquisition," http://www.internetnews.com/bus-news/article.php/1474661/IBM+Completes+PwC+Acquisition.htm
76. http://docs.yahoo.com/docs/pr/release285.html
77. http://money.cnn.com/1999/01/28/technology/yahoo_a/
78. http://news.cnet.com/2100-1030_3-1025394.html
79. Rob Hof, "Yahoo Buys Right Media," http://blogs.businessweek.com/mt/mt-tb.cgi/ 6328.1438712594
80. http://www.zdnet.co.uk/news/it-strategy/2004/03/26/yahoo-acquires-kelkoo-39149931/
81. http://articles.businessinsider.com/2011-03-14/tech/29990819_1_broadcast-com-bluelithium-geocities#ixzz1hrIHCb6b

4
Mergers and Acquisitions in the Entertainment and Media Sector

Introduction

The media sector has witnessed merger waves during the past two decades in response to deregulation and technological development. The Entertainment and Media (E&M) industry is witnessing a transition to mobile access and content offerings in the midst of a digital environment. The changing nature of the industry, with a strategic shift toward digital media, strong corporate cash reserves and proliferation of private equity firms, has acted as the key catalyst for deal activity in the media sector. According to the PwC publication *Global Entertainment and Media Outlook 2011–2015*, increased activity in the video games and social media sectors will enhance M&A activity in future. Improved economic conditions have played a major role in the recovery of overall E&M spending, which rose by 4.6 percent. PwC estimated that aggregate E&M global spending will rise to $1.9 trillion by 2015.

According to the PwC report for 2011, cross-border deals had been an emerging trend in the E&M sector as companies looked to expand their footprint to shore up additional content. Further consolidation in the video games segment is expected as major publishers are seeking to supplement their portfolios with new hit games across platforms. Media companies are expected to continue to make investments in the fast-growing social media sector.

According to the PwC report for 2010, approximately 804 deals were completed in the E&M sector, comprising areas such as cable, broadcasting, movies, video games, music, advertising, services and publishing. In 2009, the number of deals was 780. The disclosed deal value was $37.2 billion and $33.5 billion for 2009 and 2010 respectively. Berkery Noyes estimated the aggregate transaction value of 493 media deals during the period 2008–2010 to be $67.80 billion. The largest transaction tracked during this period was Comcast Corporation's acquisition of NBC Universal for $13.75 billion.

In 1983, 50 major companies dominated the media segment. By 1987 the figure had shrunk to 29. In the early 1990s, the figure became 23, and by the late 1990s, there were only ten big firms. The top ten media companies are AOL Time Warner, Disney, General Electric, News Corporation, Viacom, Vivendi, Sony, Bertelsmann, AT&T and Liberty Media.

The M&A wave in the E&M sector resulted from old media companies seeking to reinvent themselves in order to exploit the growing market for online media. The previous trend had been for diversified media. Another factor for the increased M&A activity in the sector was the keen interest of cash-rich private equity firms in the steady cash flow generated by media companies. But mega mergers had their own share of problems. CBS and Viacom merged in 1999, only to split in 2006. Vivendi bought Universal Studios parent Seagram in 2000 and USA Networks in 2001, and ultimately sold a majority stake in Universal Studios to GE in 2003. A major change for the E&M sector is that on account of M&A activity the lines separating marketing service providers, content providers, technology companies and media companies are becoming increasingly blurred.

The biggest deals in the media sector during the past two decades include Time merging with Warner, buying Turner Broadcasting, and then selling itself to America Online; Disney buying ABC; Viacom buying CBS; and Vivendi buying Universal. Other major deals were the union of Comcast and AT&T Broadband, EchoStar and DirecTV, Vivendi Universal and USA Networks.

Media mega mergers—historical timeline

January 1986: Capital Cities Communications, Inc. purchases American Broadcasting Co. for $3.5 billion to form Capital Cities/ABC, Inc.
June 1986: General Electric buys RCA Corp., parent company of National Broadcasting Co. and NBC television network, for $6.4 billion.
March 1989: Time, Inc. acquires Warner Communications for $14.9 billion to form Time Warner.
November 1989: Sony Corp. buys film and television producer Columbia Pictures Entertainment, Inc. for $33.4 billion.

January 1991: Matsushita Electric Industrial acquires MCA for $6.9 billion.
September 1993: New York Times Co. takes over Affiliated Publications for $1.1 billion.
March 1994: Viacom acquires Blockbuster Video for $8.4 billion.
July 1994: Viacom, Inc. buys the movie, publishing and sports company Paramount Communications for $10 billion.
June 1995: Seagram Co. buys MCA, Inc. from Matsushita for $5.7 billion and renames it Universal Studios.
November 1995: Westinghouse Electrical Corp. buys CBS, Inc. for $5.4 billion.
February 1996: Walt Disney Co. buys Capital Cities/ABC for $19 billion, creating a media conglomerate in movies, television and publishing.
October 1996: Time Warner and Turner Broadcasting System merge in a deal worth $7.6 billion.
December 1996: Westinghouse Electric Corp's CBS Division acquires Infinity Broadcasting for $4.7 billion.
December 1998: Seagram Co. buys the PolyGram music company for $10.4 billion.
April 1999: CBS Corp. buys King World Productions, Inc. for $2.5 billion.
September 1999: Viacom buys CBS Corp. for $81.5 billion.
October 1999: Clear Channel intends to buy the AMFM radio chain in a $23 billion deal.
January 2000: American Online enters into a merger agreement with Time Warner valued at $135 billion.
March 2000: Chicago Tribune publisher, Tribune Co., buys Times Mirror Co. for $6.5 billion.
November 2000: AOL buys Netscape for $4.2 billion.
June 2000: Vivendi, Seagram and Canal+ merge to form a fully integrated global media and communication company.

November 2000: Viacom buys BET for $3 billion.
December 2001: Vivendi Universal plans to acquire USA Networks for $10.3 billion.
December 2001: Comcast Corp. announces a merger with AT&T Broadband in a deal valued at $52 billion.
April 2003: News Corp. acquired Hughes Electronics for $6.6 billion.
October 2003: Vivendi Universal Studio and GE's NBC Television combine to form NBC Universal.
August 2004: Sony Music Entertainment and Bertelsmann Music Group (BMG) merge to form Sony BMG Music Entertainment.
April 2005: Time Warner and Comcast Corp. buy bankrupt cable operator Adelphia Communications Corp. in a $17.6 billion deal.
July 2005: Media giant News Corp. acquires Intermix Media for $580 million.
September 2005: News Corp. acquires IGN Entertainment for $650 million.
December 2005: Paramount Pictures buys independent film studio DreamWorks SKG for $1.6 billion.
January 2006: Walt Disney buys animation studio Pixar for $7.4 billion.
March 2006: The McClatchy Co. buys 32 Knight Ridder, Inc. newspapers in a $4.5 billion deal.
April 2006: Viacom, Inc. buys Xfire, an online games technology company, for $102 million.
September 2006: Vivendi Universal Music acquires BMG Music Publishing in a $2 billion deal.

Source: Collated from Ball State University, "Foundations of Telecommunications," http://www.commoncause.org/site/pp.asp?c=dkLNK1MQIwG&b=4923181, and other sources.

Table 4.1 Biggest deals in media and entertainment

Acquirer	Target	Value in $ billion	Year
AOL	Time Warner	164	2000
Viacom	CBS	34.9	1999
Vivendi	Seagram	34	2000
Apollo Texas Pacific	Harrah's Entertainment	27.4	2006
Bain Thomas Lee	Clear Channel	25.7	2006
Vivendi Games	Activision (Blizzard)	18.8	2007
Walt Disney	Capital Cities/ABC	18.2	1995
Time, Inc.	Warner Communication	16.1	1989
Comcast	NBC	13.5	2011
Seagram	Polygram	10.6	1998
Vivendi	USA Networks	10.3	2001
Viacom	Paramount	9.47	1993
Gemstar	TV Guide	9.8	1999
Time Warner	Turner Broadcasting	9.1	1995
Viacom	Blockbuster	8.49	1994
Web MD	Healtheon	7.9	1999
GE	RCA/NBC	6.4	1986
Matsushita	MCA	6.10	1990
News Corp.	Dow Jones, IGN, Intermix	5	2007

Mergers by Time Warner

Time Warner, Inc. is a global leader in media and entertainment, with businesses in television networks, filmed entertainment and publishing. The main divisions of Time Warner are Turner Broadcasting System, Warner Bros., Home Box Office and Time, Inc.

Turner owns and operates some of the leading cable television networks and related properties, including CNN, HLN, TNT, TBS, Cartoon Network, Turner Classic Movies, Adult Swim, truTV and Turner Sports targeted at a broad domestic and international audience. In addition to its cable networks, Turner manages CNN.com, CNN Mobile, CNNMoney.com, TCM.com and CartoonNetwork.com, as well as NBA.com, PGATour.com, NCAA.com, PGA.com and NASCAR.com.

Warner Bros. Entertainment is a fully integrated, broad-based entertainment company with businesses ranging from feature film, TV and home entertainment production and worldwide distribution to home video, digital distribution, animation, comic books, licensing and international cinemas and broadcasting. America's most successful premium television company, Home Box Office, delivers two 24-hour pay television services—HBO® and Cinemax®. Time, Inc. is one of the largest branded

Table 4.2 Financial highlights of Time Warner ($ million)

	2008	2009	2010
Total revenues	26,434	25,388	26,888
Operating income	−15,957	4470	5428
Net income	−13,402	2477	2578
Assets		66,059	66,524

media companies in the world. The company's magazines reach more than 110 million Americans each month, and its websites attract nearly 50 million unique visitors each month. Time, Inc. brands include publications such as *Time, People, Sports Illustrated, In Style* and *Real Simple*.

Time Warner, Inc. has engaged in a number of mergers, acquisitions and other corporate actions over the years.

The Time/Warner merger

In 1989, Time, Inc. and Warner Communication merged to create a world power in the field of media and entertainment. The merger created the largest media and entertainment conglomerate in the world. Time is a leading book and magazine publisher with extensive cable television holdings. Warner is a major producer of movies and records and has a large cable television operation. The merger made Time Warner one of the few global media giants that were able to create and distribute information in virtually any medium. The merger positioned Time Warner to compete against major European and Asian companies. The merged entity had a stock market value of $15.2 billion and revenue of $10 billion.

Time brought to the combination *Time* magazine and other publications such as *Life, People, Money* and *Sports Illustrated*. It also controlled the second largest cable system in the United States, American Television and Communications, and Home Box Office, the nation's largest cable programming service, which included HBO and Cinemax. Time also maintained a significant presence in book publishing with its Book-of-the-Month Club, Time-Life Books and Little Brown publishers.

Warner Communications was established in 1971 when Kinney National Company spun off its non-entertainment assets following a financial scandal. This was the parent company for Warner Bros Pictures and Warner Music Group during the 1970s and 1980s. It also owned DC Comics and *Mad Magazine*. In the 1970s, Warner set up a joint venture with credit card company American Express to form Warner Amex Satellite Entertainment, which held cable channels including MTV, Nickelodeon and Showtime. Later in 1984, Warner bought American

Express' stake in the joint venture and sold it to Viacom, which was renamed as MTV Networks. In 1982, Warner purchased Popular Library from CBS Publications. Then, in 1983, Warner itself was a takeover target of the News Corporation, which Warner thwarted by offering a larger stake in Warner to Chris Craft. Warner Communications had also acquired Lorimar Telepictures Corp., a preeminent supplier of television programs such as *Dallas* and *Falcon Crest.*

Deal highlights

The merger in which Time acquired Warner was valued at $18 billion. Time exchanged 12.5 percent of its shares for about 10 percent of Warner shares. Each Warner share was exchanged tax free for a 0.465 share of Time, Inc. common stock, with an indicated market value of $50.74 based on Time's closing stock price of $109.125 a share on the day before the announcement. The combined company had $10.7 billion debt. The merger was billed as a 'merger of equals'.

Merger benefits

The new entity owned the most lucrative recorded music and magazine publishing businesses in the US and the largest television programming operation for both pay cable and prime-time network television. As a result of merger, Time Warner could rival Telecommunications, Inc. as its only true competitor in the cable television industry. Warner had first entered television production in the 1950s. Time, Inc. came to cable TV in the 1960s and became a leader on the strength of its innovation of HBO later. The merger elevated Time Warner to the status of biggest television company in the world. The merger provided the scale for Time Warner to position itself against Japanese conglomerates such as Sony and Matsushita.

This merger was also significant as it underscored the network companies' vulnerability to competition. The network companies are not allowed to own cable television systems. The merger facilitated Time Warner's ability to create television programming, distribute it over its own cable system and syndicate it around the world. For the combined firm, half of its revenues came from television-related subsidiaries. The other half came from movie-making, owning and operating one of the top six major music labels and publishing a string of magazines that included *Time, Fortune* and *Money*. After the merger, Time had packaged advertisements for its newest magazine in Warner videotapes; Warner's Looney Tunes cartoon characters appeared in books published by Time. Time had tapped its customer database to promote Warner's movies by mail. Synergy benefits were realized through Time Warner Direct, which oversees the Book of the Month Club and the Quality Paperback Book club as well as the television offers for parapsychology books that sell by mail or telephone. Access to Time Warner's database of 13 million direct marketing customers enabled Warner Brothers to promote their major movies. Warner also became the source of numerous new products promoted by Time's direct marketing operations, which included videotape series featuring such Warner Brothers' properties as World War II movies, Clint Eastwood films and Looney Tunes cartoons.

Analysts believed that the size of the new entity would enable it to fend off unwelcome takeover bids. In 2009, Time Warner spun off the cable operations, Time Warner Cable, as part of continuing restructuring.

The merger of Time Warner/Turner Broadcasting

In 1995, the merger of Time Warner with Turner Broadcasting boosted Time Warner's position as the world's largest entertainment and media conglomerate. Under the merger agreement, Time Warner purchased 82 percent of Turner Broadcasting, in a deal worth an estimated $7.5 billion. The merger gave Time Warner access to the important brands of Ted Turner, which included the Cable News Network (CNN), the Cartoon Network, the Atlanta Braves baseball team and two movie studios. Ted Turner, the chairman of Ted Turner, became a major shareholder and vice chairman of Time Warner. The merger faced stiff competition from major shareholders of Turner including Comcast Corporation, Continental Cablevision, Inc. and US West, the regional Bell telephone company. US West filed a lawsuit to block the merger. US West's investment in Time Warner consisted of a 25.5 percent stake in the Warner Brothers studio, Time Warner Cable and HBO.

In 1995, Turner posted revenues of $3.4 billion, of which $2 billion was from cable programming. Turner wholly owns a number of cable networks including CNN, Headline News, Turner Network Television (TNT), WTBS, Cartoon Network and Turner Classic Movies.

Under the terms of deal, the combined entity was expected to have annual revenues of about $18.5 billion, surpassing that of Walt Disney Company. The combined company accounted for about 40 percent of all cable programming in the US at the time of merger, with Time Warner ranking as second largest cable distributor behind Tele-Communication, Inc. with 11.5 million cable subscribers, representing 17 percent of all US cable television households.

In this all-stock deal, Turner Broadcasting's shareholders received three-quarters of a Time Warner share for each Turner class A or B share.

Turner, who owned 26 percent of Turner's shares, became the largest Time Warner shareholder with 10 percent of Time Warner's voting stock.

The FTC initially opposed the merger on the grounds of anti-competitiveness in cable TV programming and distribution. Tele-Communication, Inc. (TCI) owned 21 percent of Turner and was expected to own 9 percent of the merged entity. TCI was the largest cable operator in the US and Time Warner ranked second. A direct link between the leading two players was opposed as creating a monopoly in the sector. Objections to the merger were apparently overcome, however, after the companies agreed to three amendments that limited the role of major shareholder TCI in the merged company and a pledge that Time Warner would act in a non-discriminatory way toward rival cable operators and programmers.

The Time Warner/AOL merger

On January 10, 2000, Time Warner announced that it had agreed to be taken over by American Online (AOL) at a 71 percent premium to its share price on the announcement date. AOL had proposed the acquisition in October 1999. The deal, valued at $164 billion, became the largest merger on record up to that time.

The merger was structured as a stock swap. Time Warner shareholders received 1.5 shares of the new company for every share of Time Warner stock they owned. AOL shareholders received one share of the new company for every AOL share they held. The shareholders of AOL and Time Warner held 55 and 45 percent of the new company respectively. The combined entity had a market capitalization of $350 billion.

Founded in 1985, AOL is the world leader in providing interactive services, web brands, Internet technologies and electronic commerce services. AOL operates two subscription-based Internet technologies. At the time of the merger announcement, AOL had 20 million subscribers plus another two million through CompuServe. At this time, AOL had less than one-fifth of the revenue and workforce of Time Warner, but almost twice the market value.

The merger created the world's largest vertically integrated media and entertainment company. Basically there was little overlap between the two businesses. Time Warner was a media and entertainment company whereas AOL was largely an Internet Service Provider offering access to content and commerce. The combination of Time Warner's broadband systems, media content and subscriber base was expected to create significant synergies and strategic advantages with AOL's online brand and Internet infrastructure. AOL had the brand and credibility to capitalize upon the growth of broadband Internet but lacked the infrastructure.

As the leading provider of cable television, Time Warner had the distribution capabilities AOL needed. For Warner, merging with AOL was a more effective way to distribute its content via online channels as opposed to building its own capabilities. The new merged entity was expected to provide an important new broadband distribution platform for AOL's interactive services and drive subscriber growth through cross-marketing with Time Warner's preeminent brands. Through the acquisition, AOL achieved a more direct path into broadband transmission as Time Warner cable systems served 20 percent of the US market at the time of the merger. The cable connection facilitated the introduction of AOL TV, which was designed to deliver access to the Internet through TV transmission. At the time of the acquisition announcement, AOL had 22 million subscribers; Time Warner had 28 million magazine subscribers, 13 million cable subscribers and 35 million HBO subscribers.

AOL's subscriber base and advertising revenues were growing exponentially until the dotcom crash of 2000. As a part of a put option contract with German media giant Bertelsmann, AOL had to borrow $600 million in order to buy AOL Europe. By 2002, the total debt of the combined company reached $28 billion. The total loss, including write-down of goodwill for 2002, reached $100 billion. On the merger announcement date, AOL and Time Warner had market values of $165 billion and $76 billion respectively. By 2004, the combined market value of the firm had fallen to about $78 billion. The downfall of this merger is symbolic for the burst of the Internet bubble. At the time of the merger AOL's stocks were overvalued in the context of the Internet bubble.

The merger faced challenging integration issues as the culture at the two organizations was entirely different. A key part of the merger strategy was to position AOL as the major global provider of high-speed services. Time Warner's cable competitors were reluctant to open up their networks for AOL as they feared that AOL could deliver video over the Internet and take away its core television customers. The cable companies were competing with AOL's dial-up and high-speed services by offering a tiered pricing system giving subscribers more options than AOL. Though it was the global leader in the digital revolution, AOL Time Warner failed to build a business model for Internet telephony or Voice over IP (VoIP), which was the emerging trend. The combined entity was not able to promote their idea of a combined music platform.

In 2003, Time Warner decided to drop AOL from its name. The Time Warner President declared "the death of synergy." In 2006, it announced that it was putting 18 of the 50 magazines in its Time magazine division up for sale. In 2009, AOL has about six million paying subscribers in the

US, down from 13 million at the end of 2006. AOL revenues stood at $4.2 billion in 2009 compared to $9.1 billion in 2002.

In 2008, Time Warner Cable and Time Warner Entertainment decided to split. In 2009, Time Warner completed the separation of AOL from Time Warner through a spin-off involving a pro rata dividend distribution of all the AOL common stock held by Time Warner to Time Warner stockholders. Time Warner stockholders received one share of AOL common stock for every 11 shares of Time Warner common stock they held on the record date of November 27, 2009.

Management believed that the spin-off would streamline Time Warner's portfolio of businesses focused on creating, packaging and distributing branded content.

Mergers by Vivendi Group

France-headquartered Vivendi is a major player in the communications and entertainment network chain from production and publishing of content (video games, music, audiovisual works and films) to its distribution, primarily via digital networks. Vivendi focuses directly on end consumers through its major divisions Activision Blizzard, Universal Music, SFR, Maroc Telecom, GVT and Canal+.

Activision Blizzard is the worldwide leader in video games. Universal Music is the world leader in music, responsible for more than one in four records sold around the world and owning the largest catalogue of music rights. SFR is one of Europe's premier alternative mobile and fixed line operators. Maroc Telecom is the leading fixed-line and mobile operator in Morocco. GVT is the alternative telecom operator in Brazil. Canal+ is the leading French publisher of premium and thematic channels.

Vivendi has recently strengthened the competitive position of its businesses through the purchase of TPS by the Canal+ Group, the purchase of Bertelsmann Music Publishing by Universal Music, the purchase of the fixed-line Internet activities of Télé 2 France and NeufCegetel by SFR, the purchase of four telecommunications operators in Africa by

Table 4.3 Financial highlights of Vivendi Group (in millions of Euros)

	2006	2007	2008	2009	2010
Revenues	20,044	21,657	25,392	27,132	28,878
EBIT	4147	4386	4260	3836	4871
Net profit	4033	2625	2603	830	2198
Total assets	43,048	45,079	56,497	58,125	58,993

Maroc Telecom Group, and the merger between Vivendi Games and Activision that led to the formation of Activision Blizzard. The Vivendi Group is focusing on expanding its position in emerging countries—as witnessed by the acquisition of GVT in Brazil, Canal+ Group operations in Vietnam and Africa, as well as partnerships involving Activision Blizzard and UMG in Asia and the Middle East.

The Seagram/Polygram merger

Seagram was a Canadian company with activities in the beverage and entertainment sectors. The entertainment sector was operated by its subsidiary Universal Studios, Inc., active in film entertainment, music and recreation. Seagram's catalogue of films includes such high-profile successes as *Gladiator* and *Jurassic Park*.

In May 1998, Seagram bought PolyGram from the Dutch electronics giant Philips for $10.6 billion. Seagram acquired Philips' 75 percent ownership position in PolyGram as part of a tender offer for all issued shares. The cash-and-shares deal valued PolyGram at $59 per share. Seagram issued a maximum of approximately 47.9 million common shares. The acquisition of PolyGram made Seagram a global entertainment leader, including the world's largest music company, with a truly impressive roster of musical talent. The newly combined music operation was named Universal Music Group.

PolyGram was the world's largest music company and had numerous subsidiary labels including such well-known names as Motown, Mercury, Def Jam, Verve and Deutsche Grammophon. It was home to rock superstars like Elton John and U2. In 1997, PolyGram had 38 albums selling more than a million copies each. In 1995, Seagram Company acquired 80 percent of MCA from Panasonic, and the following year dropped the MCA name; the company became Universal Studio. Universal owned the MCA and Geffen record labels. PolyGram film's operations included PolyGram Films, PolyGram Television, Propaganda Films and Working Title Films. Seagram has limited market presence in EU member states as most of its labels were sold in North America. Seagram was expected to benefit from Polygram's far superior worldwide distribution network, and was forecast to reap from $275 million to $300 million in annual cost savings by integrating the two record labels.

The Vivendi/Seagram merger

In late 2000, the three-way merger between Vivendi, Canal+ and Seagram in a $34 billion deal created the world's biggest media group, Vivendi Universal. The merger combined the Canada-based Seagram's entertainment interests—which included Universal Pictures and the Universal Music Group—with Vivendi's European telecommunications and Internet infrastructure. Canal+ was partly owned by Vivendi Universal. Vivendi started as a water company and diversified into media in the 1990s. The assets of Seagram, the leading entertainment, music and spirits company, included Universal Studios (film), Universal Music and Polygram (records). Canal+ owns France's leading pay television channel. Seagram's Universal Music Group was a world leader in the industry, with operations in 59 countries and a roster of talent that includes Shania Twain, Dr Dre, Sheryl Crow, Sting and U2. Canal+ had more than 14 million subscribers in 11 countries at the time of the merger.

The new company, Vivendi Universal, was able to control the rights to an unrivaled collection of content: over 9000 movies, 27,000 television episodes and over 750,000 songs, as well as the means to distribute them via television and the Internet. The combined entity's movie content was drawn from the storehouses of Universal Pictures and Canal+. Music came from the Universal Music Company. The new company also had a 42 percent equity stake in USA Networks. The other assets acquired by Vivendi Universal as a result of the merger included Universal's Recreation Group, which operates Universal Studios Hollywood, Universal Studios Orlando and Universal Studios Port Aventura in Barcelona, Spain. Vivendi Universal distributed content via both TV and the Internet.

Seagram shareholders received Vivendi shares equivalent in value to $77.35 for each share of Seagram common stock. This exchange represented a premium price for Seagram based on the closing price on merger announcement day. Canal+ shareholders received two shares of Vivendi stock for each share of Canal+ stock. Vivendi owned 59 percent of the merged entity, while Seagram shareholders held 29 percent and Canal+ 12 percent. The merged company had a stock market value of $100 billion and revenues of $55 billion. The new combined firm was organized into four divisions: pay TV and movie production, music, publishing and telecommunications.

Exponential growth was expected in the global music business as digital delivery acted as a catalyst for the online boom. The merger was intended to transform Vivendi into a new global media player to rival America Online. Through this merger, Vivendi acquired the content for music albums and films. The merger made Vivendi Universal a pioneer in combining premier global and local content with next-generation digital distribution.

The acquisition of Houghton Mifflin Company

In 2001, Vivendi Universal acquired Boston-based Houghton Mifflin Company, a leading US educational publisher. Houghton Mifflin was the fourth-largest US educational publisher, and one of the oldest American publishing houses, being founded in Boston in 1832. In 2001, the company had consolidated sales in excess of $1.0 billion.

Houghton Mifflin shares were tendered and purchased by Vivendi Universal at the $60 per share tender offer price. The total consideration of the transaction was approximately $2.2 billion, which included the assumption of Houghton Mifflin's average net debt of $500 million. This acquisition was aimed to consolidate Vivendi's leadership position in key content segments. The acquisition catapulted Vivendi Universal Publishing (VUP) to second place worldwide in educational publishing, particularly in the US textbook market. After the acquisition, Vivendi Universal focused on three main segments: games, education and literature, and health. Approximately 48 percent of VUP's revenues came from the US and the remainder from Europe and the rest of the world.

The acquisition of USA Network

USA Network is cable television's leading provider of original series and feature movies, sports and entertainment events, off-net television shows and blockbuster theatrical films. In October 1981, USA Network was acquired by Time, Inc., Gulf & Western's Paramount Pictures Corp. and MCA, Inc. (now Universal). In June 1987, Paramount and MCA became equal partners in their ownership of USA Network. Later Viacom acquired Paramount, and USA Network was sold to Seagram. Seagram later sold USA Network to Barry Diller's HSNi.

In 2001, Vivendi Universal acquired the movie and television businesses of USA Network, Inc. in a $10.3 billion cash-and-stock deal. Vivendi Universal acquired 93 percent control of the new company, called Vivendi Universal Entertainment. The acquisition gave the French conglomerate a wider footprint in the US market, for along with control of top-rated USA Network came the Sci Fi Network, Newsworld International and other direct marketing units. The deal facilitated Vivendi's access to approximately 80 million USA Network viewers within America, though it still lagged behind other top media players in distribution power.

The deal involved a complicated financing program in which Vivendi Universal sold the 314 million shares it already owned in USA Network through a limited liability company, accounting for approximately 65 percent of the total consideration. Approximately 20 percent of the transaction was conducted in cash.

The Vivendi Games/Activision merger

In 2007, Vivendi's video game division Blizzard merged with Activision, Inc. in an $18.9 billion deal. The combined video company was named

Activision Blizzard. The merged company became one of the largest video game publishers and online entertainment companies in the world. The deal bought together two top publishers, which have released titles from popular and diverse game franchises such as Call of Duty, Crash Bandicoot, Diablo, Doom, Guitar Hero, Quake, Starcraft and the largest massively multiplayer game World of Warcraft. World of Warcraft has more than 12 million subscribers worldwide. The deal strategically benefitted the merged entity as the Guitar Hero franchise became the only place to "play" songs from the Universal Music Group, the world's largest music publisher and a key part of Vivendi's family of media companies.

Vivendi owned about 68 percent of the new company after the two phases of the merger were completed. In the first step, Vivendi Games shares were converted to Activision shares, giving it a valuation of $8.1 billion; and Vivendi purchased 62.9 million shares of Activision (or 52 percent of the company) for $27.50 per share. This brought Activision Blizzard more than $1.7 billion in cash. In the second phase, Activision Blizzard purchased up to 146.5 million shares of the company in a $4 billion all-cash tender offer.

Key to the deal was the access to Blizzard and its MMO (Massively Multiplayer Online) games, which instantly put Activision at the center of the lucrative online gaming business. As a result of the deal, Activision Blizzard acquired the most diversified and broadest portfolio of interactive entertainment assets in its industry.

The NBC merger with Vivendi Universal

The National Broadcasting Company (NBC) is an American commercial broadcasting television network. Formed in 1926 by the Radio Corporation of America (RCA), NBC was the first major broadcast network in the United States. In 1986, ownership of NBC was passed to General Electric when it purchased RCA for $6.4 billion.

In May 2004, NBC bought the entertainment assets of Vivendi Universal, creating a new company, NBC Universal. General Electric owned 80 percent, with the remaining 20 percent staying with Vivendi Universal. In the deal shareowners of Vivendi Universal Entertainment (VUE) received $3.65 billion of cash consideration, of which Vivendi Universal received $3.4 billion. NBC Universal assumed $1.7 billion of debt, previously included in Vivendi Universal's financial statements.

The new entity became one of the world's leading media companies in the development, production and marketing of entertainment, news and information. NBC Universal possessed some of the most recognized and valuable brands such as television networks NBC, Telemundo, USA

Network, Sci Fi Channel, USA Bravo, Trio, CNBC and MSNBC (jointly owned with Microsoft). The other assets included film studio Universal Pictures, television production studios Universal Television, theme parks etc.

As a result of the merger, the companies expected the realization of approximately $400 million to $500 million in potential synergies through cost savings and revenue growth.

But rapid expansion, based on organic growth and heavy investment in high-growth countries, affected the growth of the company and brought it to the verge of bankruptcy and downgrading by credit agencies. In 2009, Vivendi sold off its remaining stake of 20 percent in NBC Universal to General Electric for $5.8 billion. The deal cleared the way for the $30 billion joint venture between NBC Universal and US cable giant Comcast. NBC's portfolio consisted of its lucrative cable channels—USA Bravo, SyFy, CNBC and MSNBC. Comcast brought its portfolio of channels including Versus, the Golf Channel and E Entertainment to the joint venture. The combined portfolio accounted for 82 percent of the joint venture's cash flow.

In 2011, Comcast acquired a majority stake of 51 percent stake in NBC Universal, with 49 percent remaining with General Electric Co. The merger gave Comcast control over some of NBC Universal's hottest TV properties, which included television networks NBC, USA and SyFy and film entertainment and theme parks. The deal combined the USA's biggest cable and Internet service provider with NBC Universal's library of entertainment. Comcast is the number one cable operator, with almost 23 million video subscribers. The acquisition led the way for a new powerhouse and represented the first time that a cable operator had bought a studio. It was expected that the legendary assets of NBC Universal together with the content assets and technology expertise of Comcast would provide new opportunities for consumers.

Major mergers by Viacom

In June 1971, Viacom was established as a public company as a result of its spin-off from Columbia Broadcasting System, Inc. (CBS). Viacom is home to the world's premier entertainment brands that connect with audiences through content across television, motion picture, online and mobile platforms in more than 160 countries and territories. Viacom's approximately 160 media networks reach some 700 million global subscribers. Viacom's leading brands include MTV, VH1, CMT, Logo, BET, Centric, Nickelodeon, Nick Jr., TeenNick, Nicktoons, Nick at Nite, Comedy

Central, TV Land, Spike TV and Tr3s and Paramount Pictures. Paramount Pictures is America's oldest film studio and major global producer and distributor of filmed entertainment. Viacom operates a large portfolio of branded digital media properties for entertainment, community and casual online gaming.

Viacom had grown over the years through its steady acquisition of media companies with an established brand identity. By 1987 it had acquired assets that included networks such as Showtime/Movie Channel, MTV Networks and Life Time, five television stations, eight radio stations and 18 cable systems. During 2007 the company acquired DreamWorks LLC, Caballero Television, Quizilla.com, Harmonix Music Systems, Inc., Atom Entertainment, Xfire, Inc., Y2M: Youth Media & Marketing Networks, and a controlling interest in Nickelodeon UK Limited.

The company expanded using a two-pronged strategy. Firstly, it strengthened its popular brands by acquiring complementary assets and divesting assets with a low yield. Secondly, it focused on the growth of its online/digital businesses through strategic acquisitions and partnerships.

On December 31, 2005, the former Viacom, Inc. was separated into two publicly traded entities, creating a new company known as "Viacom, Inc." The existing company changed its name to "CBS Corporation."

The acquisition of Paramount Communications

In the early 1990s, Paramount Communications was one of the five major film studios in Hollywood, involved in both television and film production. Paramount produced a large number of successful television series, including *Cheers, Family Ties* and *Star Trek*. In 1993, Paramount Communications witnessed the worst crisis in its history when more than 23 motion pictures produced by the company failed at the box office, plunging the company into a serious debt crisis. The acquisition of Paramount Communications was a good strategic fit for Viacom, which was exploring options to expand into the motion picture field.

Table 4.4 Financial highlights of Viacom ($ million)

	2007	2008	2009	2010	2011
Revenues	13,423	14,625	13,619	13,356	14,914
Operating income	2936	2523	2904	3348	3710
Net income	1630	1233	1591	1899	2146
Assets	22,940	22,487	21,900	22,429	22,801

Viacom paid $9.9 billion or $80.61 a share in cash and stock for Paramount. Viacom paid 0.1 share of its class A voting stock and 0.9 share of its class B non-voting stock, as well as $9 a share in cash, making the cash component roughly $1 billion.

The New York-based entertainment company consisted of Paramount Pictures, Simon & Schuster publishing house, Madison Square Garden, the New York Rangers hockey team and the Knicks basketball team. The combined company had sales of $12 billion, just behind Time Warner's $14 billion in sales. The new company had a market capitalization of roughly $17 billion, with about $2.4 billion in debt.

The acquisition elevated Viacom to fifth largest media company in the world. The acquisition vastly expanded the company's presence in the entertainment business, giving it a motion picture library that included such classics as *The Ten Commandments* and *The Godfather* and an entry into the premier movie market. Moreover, in the Paramount deal Viacom gained ownership of Simon & Schuster, Inc., one of the world's largest book publishers.

The acquisition of Blockbuster

In 1994, Viacom acquired Blockbuster, the owner, operator and franchiser of video and music stores. The acquisition was valued at $8.4 billion. In this stock swap, Blockbuster paid $1.25 billion for 23 million shares of Viacom's class B non-voting stock, at $55 a share. Viacom offered Blockbuster shareholders a combination of Viacom stock and options worth $30.97 for each Blockbuster share.

This acquisition was significant in the context of the emergence of interactive cable television networks, which enabled consumers to order movies through computerized television sets. The union of Blockbuster and Paramount made Viacom the fourth largest media and entertainment company, with combined revenues of $7.3 billion.

Viacom acquired Blockbuster as a part of a long-term strategy to use Blockbuster's healthy cash flow to service the $10 billion debt load that was incurred in the acquisition of Paramount. By 1997, this strategy had failed as Blockbuster sustained a pre-tax loss of $323 million. Through the acquisition of Paramount and Blockbuster, Viacom had acquired new enterprises but also incurred huge debt.

Viacom divested many segments of its business. In 1995, the company sold the operations of Madison Square Garden to a partnership of ITT Corp. and Cablevision Systems Corp. for $1.07 billion. In 1998, Viacom spun off its cable system to TCI. Viacom also divested from the radio broadcasting business by selling its ten radio stations to Evergreen Media Corporation.

By 1998, Viacom was on the path to recovery as revenues were enhanced on the basis of the spectacular success of movies like *Titanic* and the sale of book publishing operations for an amount of $4.6 billion. Viacom undertook a global expansion drive and in the process MTV emerged as an international brand.

The Viacom/CBS merger

In 1995, CBS was acquired by Westinghouse Electric, a major electronic equipment manufacturer and operator of radio stations. Later Westinghouse sold off its manufacturing operations and took CBS as its corporate name to focus exclusively on becoming a media giant. In 1999, Viacom made its biggest acquisition when it merged with its former parent CBS Corporation. The all-stock deal was valued at $35.6 billion. The merger combined the broadcasting strength of CBS with the cable and movie-producing power of Viacom. CBS's cable channels TNN and Country Music Television (CMT) came under Viacom control. Later on TNN and CMT were merged into the MTV Network.

As a result of the merger, Viacom became the second biggest media conglomerate, behind Time Warner. Viacom swapped 1.085 of its class B shares for each share of CBS, or $48.89 a share. The combined company became a leader in the cable industry and one of the largest film and TV sitcom producers. The company also emerged as one of the biggest radio and outdoor advertising companies through ownership of Infinity Broadcasting Corp. With advertising revenues of $5.8 billion, CBS-Viacom accounted for nearly one dollar out of every eight spent by American advertisers. The combined company captured 41 percent of the total national broadcasting market.

The merger allowed CBS to broaden its scope to a more youthful audience, with promotional opportunities for Viacom's more youth-oriented channels such as MTV and H-1 and CBS's traditional broadcast network. The merger made the combined firm the largest US owner of outdoor billboards as well as controlling Blockbuster Video, book publisher Simon & Schuster and five amusement parks.

The acquisition of Black Entertainment Television

Black Entertainment Television (BET) is the biggest African-American entertainment conglomerate in the US. In 2001, Viacom acquired BET for $2.43 billion in stock and $570 million worth of debt. BET's portfolio included BET Jazz Channel, BET International, BET Books, online portal BET.com and BET Pictures, a producer of movies and documentaries aired on BET networks. BET had 63 million subscribers at the time of the acquisition. The BET purchase gave Viacom access to cable holdings, publishing and online divisions targeting the black population, which is growing faster than the general population in the US. Black Americans comprised 13 percent of the population but only one percent of the market targeted this group. In the period of acquisition, advertising spending targeting the black population was growing at 15 percent, faster than for the general market. Viacom's creative and distinctive branded programming was expected to provide impetus for the growth of BET's television and online businesses. Viacom's experience of making MTV a global brand was expected to help BET gain global distribution for its music channel BET on Jazz.

Other major acquisitions in media and entertainment sector

Apollo Management and Texas Pacific Group's acquisition of Harrah's Entertainment

Harrah's Entertainment, Inc. is the world's largest provider of branded casino entertainment through its operating subsidiaries. Established over seven and half decades ago, Harrah's has grown through development of new properties, expansions and acquisitions. The company's properties operate primarily under the Harrah's, Caesars and Horseshoe brand names. Harrah's also owns the London Clubs International family of casinos. Harrah's owns 42 casinos in eight states and operates four US tribal casinos and one Canadian property. Overseas, it owns 11 casinos in Egypt, South Africa, the UK and Uruguay.

Founded in 1990, Apollo is a leading company in private equity, debt and capital market investments. Texas Private Group was founded in 1992 and has rich experience with global public and private investments executed through leveraged buyouts, recapitalizations, spinouts, joint ventures and restructurings.

In 2006, Apollo Management Group and Texas Pacific Group acquired Harrah's Entertainment in an all-cash deal valued at $27.8 billion, with the assumption of approximately $10.7 billion debt. This value represented a premium of approximately 36 percent over Harrah's closing price on the day before the acquisition announcement. Each Harrah investor received $90 per share in cash. At the time of the acquisition, this deal was the fourth biggest private equity buyout, coming after the Blackstone Group LP's $36 billion offer to purchase Equity Office Properties Trust; the $33 billion acquisition of hospital company HCA; and Kohlberg Kravis Roberts & Co.'s $30 billion takeover of RJR Nabisco, Inc. in 1988.

In 2006, Harrah's Casinos revenues doubled to $1.08 billion in cash compared to the previous year. Apollo and Texas were attracted by the huge cash reserves of Harrah's, which were expected to be used for financing the purchase.

The acquisition of Clear Channel Communications

Clear Channel Communications, Inc. is a global media and entertainment company specializing in mobile and on-demand entertainment and information services. Clear Channel specializes in radio broadcasting, concert promotion and hosting and fixed advertising in the United States through its subsidiaries.

In 2006, a group led by Thomas Lee Partners LP and Bain Capital Partners acquired Clear Channel in a transaction with a total value of approximately $26.7 billion. Bain Capital is a global private investment firm that manages several pools of capital including private equity, high-yield assets, mezzanine capital and public equity. Thomas Lee Partners is one of the oldest and most successful private equity investment firms in the US. Under the terms of the agreement, Clear Channel shareholders received $37.60 in cash for each share of Clear Channel common stock. The acquisition came at a time when Clear Channel had put itself for sale following a depressing stock price performance as its radio business struggled to boost advertisement sales owing to competition from Internet and satellite radio stations.

The acquisition of Capital Cities Communications/ABC, Inc. by Walt Disney

Founded in 1923, The Walt Disney Company, together with its subsidiaries and affiliates, is a leading diversified international family entertainment and media enterprise with four business segments: media networks, parks and resorts, studio entertainment and consumer products.

Capital Cities Communications (CapCities) was an American media company that purchased American Broadcasting Company in 1985 for $3.5 billion. At the time of acquisition ABC was four times bigger than CapCities. In 1995, Walt Disney became the world's most powerful Media and Entertainment Company by acquiring CapCities/ABC, Inc. for $19 billion. The acquisition combined one of the premier movie studios with the top-rated television network. The combined company brought together the most profitable television network and its ESPN cable service with Disney's Hollywood film and television studios, the Disney Channel, its theme parks and its repository of well-known cartoon characters. At the time of the acquisition, this blockbuster deal was the second largest merger in US history behind the $30.6 billion buyout of RJR Nabisco by Kohlberg Kravis Roberts & Co.

CapCities/ABC owned eight TV stations and 225 affiliate TV stations, and had the US's largest radio network with 21 stations. In addition CapCities/ABC published newspapers, magazines and books. By the acquisition of Capital Cities, Disney became the first media company with a major presence in four distribution systems, consisting of filmed entertainment, cable television, broadcasting and telephone wires. Through the purchase Disney acquired ABC's broad distribution and programming including leading TV news program *World News Tonight* and the top-rated prime time show *Home Improvement*, which was produced by Disney. The acquisition also combined the strengths of the Disney Channel with CapCities/ABC cable properties, which included 80 percent ownership of ESPN and stakes in A&E Television Network and Life Time Television. The combined company had $16.5 billion in revenues.

Under the terms of the deal, CapCities/ABC shareholders received one share of Disney common stock and $65 in cash for each of their shares. Disney borrowed $10 billion to complete the deal. As a result of the acquisition, Disney became the eleventh-largest American corporation in the Fortune 500 list and the largest media company in terms of market capitalization.

The Gemstar/TV Guide union and acquisition by Macrovision

In 1999, Gemstar International bought TV Guide for about $9.2 billion in stock and debt to consolidate its position in providing electronic program guides. TV Guide shareholders got 45 percent of the newly combined company. The acquisition was strategically important for Gemstar, which was focusing on expansion into new markets. Gemstar technology was licensed to most major TV and VCR makers. TV Guide operated a fast-growing and popular service called TV Guide Interactive, which let viewers check listing by time, channel, category or name. This Electronic Programming Guide (EPG) was emerging as one of the most used applications in the digital set-up boxes developed by cable companies. These guides were considered to be the equivalent of web browsers for cable and satellite TV. At the time of the acquisition, there were about 2.3 million users of TV Guide's EPG along with 73,000 visitors to its online site and 34 million readers of its magazine publication. As a result of the union Gemstar/TV Guide became a global leader in video and entertainment guidance with products and services that delivered rich data and information to consumers over multiple media platforms.

In 2007, Gemstar signed a definitive agreement to be acquired by Macrovision in a cash-and-stock deal valued at approximately $2.8 billion. Macrovision raised $800 million of new debt to finance the acquisition. Macrovision is a global leader in protection, enablement and distribution solutions for digital content. The combination of the solution portfolios of two companies enabled extensive libraries of commercial and personal protected content to be accessible on numerous devices through simple and intuitive guides.

As of May 2008, Gemstar-TV Guide International, Inc. became a wholly owned subsidiary of Macrovision Solutions Corporation, which changed its name to Rovi Corporation in 2009.

The GE acquisition of NBC/RCA

NBC was the first major broadcast network, formed by the Radio Corporation of America in 1926. General Electric had previously owned RCA and NBC until 1930, when it had been forced to sell the company on account of antitrust charges. In 1986, GE reacquired RCA at a price of $6.4 billion.

The Matsushita acquisition of MCA

In 1990, Matsushita Electric Industrial Co. paid $6.5 billion for entertainment giant MCA, Inc., parent of Universal Studios. At that time this deal was the largest takeover of a US company by a Japanese firm. By this acquisition, most of the Hollywood studios were now owned by foreign companies. The deal was for about $6.59 billion in cash and securities. MCA, Inc. was the producer of movies, records and books and the owner of two huge theme parks.

At the time of the acquisition, MCA's portfolio consisted of Universal Pictures, Universal Studios Tour in Universal City, a theme park in Florida, a publishing house, record labels and interests in cable television and movie theaters. At the time of acquisition, Matsushita Electronics was among the world's top corporations. The acquisition was facilitated by the presence of Matsushita's large cash flows, particularly from exporting consumer appliances to North America and the availability of cheap loans as a result of the 1980s Japanese property bubble. Matsushita focused on this acquisition in order to expand downstream into content alongside other hardware manufacturers such as Sony. MCA hoped that the acquisition would expand the company's music and television businesses.

However, the addition of MCA's less predictable movie and record operations to Matsushita's consumer electronics business did not yield the expected results, and finally MCA was sold off to Seagram in 1995.

Acquisitions by News Corporation

News Corporation (News Corp.) is the world's second largest media conglomerate in terms of revenues as of 2011. In 1973, News Corp. made its first acquisition by purchasing *San Antonio Express News*, followed in by the purchase of the *New York Post*. During the period 1981–1984, News Corp. consolidated its stake in 20th Century Fox. In 1985, News Corp. bought the Metromedia group of stations, and in 1993, acquired a 63.6 percent stake in the Hong Kong-based Star TV satellite network for over $500 million, followed by the purchase of the remaining stake of 36.4 percent in 1995. In 2003, News Corp. acquired a 34 percent stake in DirecTV Group from General Motors for $6 billion. DirectTV Group was one of the largest American satellite TV systems. Later in 2008, DirecTV group was sold to Liberty Media in exchange for its holdings in News International.

In 2003, News Corp. acquired IGN Entertainment for about $600 million. The acquisition is in line with News Corp's strategy to further expand into online entertainment and media. This was the third Internet acquisition made by News Corp. Earlier in the same year it had purchased Scout Media, a sports web publisher. Under the terms of agreement, IGN and its network sites, which included Team Xbox, GameSpy, Rotten Tomatoes, AskMen.com, and sites within Vault and Planet networks became the part of News Corp's Fox Interactive media unit. IGN had approximately 28 million unique users. Adding that to News Corp's other sites gave the company US Web traffic of nearly 70 million unique monthly users and more than 12 billion page impressions per month. News Corp. now became the fourth largest network in terms of monthly page impressions.

In 2005, News Corp. acquired Intermix, which operated the popular social networking site MySpace.com, with more than 16 million users. The deal was valued at $580 million in cash. Intermix's other web businesses included sites such as grab.com and flowgo.com. As a result of this buyout, News Corp's Web traffic increased to 45 million unique monthly users.

In 2007, News Corporation purchased Dow Jones for an estimated $5.6 billion. In 2007, News Corp. had also spun off a business news channel called Fox Business Network from Fox News. The Dow Jones acquisition ended the century-old Bancroft family ownership. Dow Jones shareholders received $60 in cash for each share of common stock or class B common stock they owned. The deal gave News Corp. the US's most widely read business newspaper, the *Wall Street Journal*. The newspaper had a daily domestic circulation of over two million, which was second only to *USA Today*. The other assets of Dow Jones included Dow Jones Newswires, the Dow Jones indexes, Barron's, the Factiva information service and Marketwatch.com.

The Lycos acquisition by Terra Networks

In 2000, the Spanish Internet Service Provider Terra Networks acquired Lycos, Inc. Lycos, Inc. is a search engine and web portal that encompasses a network of email, web hosting, social networking and entertainment websites.

Terra offered a stock swap that valued Lycos at around $97.55 a share. The deal was valued at $12.5 billion. The new company, called Terra Lycos, had operations in 37 countries, including high-growth markets in North America, Latin America, Asia and Europe. Terra Lycos also had a 49 percent wireless joint venture partnership with Telefonica, the telecommunication giant, which was also the parent company of Terra Networks.

Then, following the dotcom bust, in 2004, South Korea communications giant Daum acquired Lycos from Terra Networks for $95 million. In 2010, an Indian company, Ybrant Digital, acquired Lycos for $36 million.

The acquisition of Netscape by AOL

In 1998, AOL acquired Netscape Communications in a $4.2 billion stock deal. Netscape shareholders received 0.45 shares of AOL common stock for every share they held. Netscape Communications, owned by Sun Microsystems, had pioneered Web navigation with its Navigator browser. AOL now acquired Netscape's Navigator and Communicator software, its ecommerce software and its Netcenter Internet portal site, which was one of the ten most-visited sites on the Internet.

AOL also entered into a strategic development and marketing alliance with Sun Microsystems. Under the terms of the agreement, AOL and Sun had to develop and market products that helped Internet users access America Online brands. Sun became a lead systems and service provider to AOL, with AOL committed to purchase systems and services worth $500 million. Netscape had to face stiff competition from an aggressive marketing assault by Microsoft Corporation, which offered its own browser for free and included it in Windows. Netscape's share of the browser market had shrunk to less than 45 percent in 1998 from a previous share of more than 80 percent. In 1996, Netscape's business had suffered as AOL made Microsoft's Internet Explorer its default browser, giving Microsoft a huge edge in the battle for browser market share. At the time of the acquisition, AOL's flagship online services had 14 million subscribers while Netscape's Netcenter website had

20 million visitors a month. AOL expected to sell Netscape's business software to business partners seeking online advertisements or open storefronts.

Additional References

1. PwC's *Global Entertainment and Media Outlook: 2010–2014.*
2. PwC's *Global Entertainment and Media Outlook: 2011–2015.*
3. http://berkerynoyes.com/Assets/1stHalfMediaEmailVersion.pdf
4. http://www.billboard.biz/bbbiz/industry/global/entertainment-and-media-deals-lead-2010-1005014972.story
5. Jo Anne, "Shift to Digital by US Entertainment and Media Industry Boosts M&A Activity, According to PwC US," http://www.pwc.com/us/en/press-releases/2011/entertainment-and-media-industry.jhtml
6. Paul R. La Monica, "The Return of Media Merger Madness," http://money.cnn.com/2007/05/14/news/companies/media_mergers/
7. Ben H. Bagdikian, *The Media Monopoly*, 6th edn (Boston, MA: Beacon Press, 2000), pp. xx–xxi.
8. http://www.globalissues.org/article/159/media-conglomerates-mergers-concentration-of-ownershipmedia-conglomerates-mergers-concentration-of-ownership
9. www.timewarner.com
10. Kathryn Harris and Paul Richter, "Time Warner Merger Creates a World Power," http://articles.latimes.com/1989-03-05/news/mn-471_1_time-warner
11. Douglas Gomery, "Time Warner-The museum of broadcast communications," http://www.museum.tv/eotvsection.php?entrycode=time-warner
12. Randall Rothenberg, "The Media Business; Time Warner's Merger Payoff," ahttp://www.nytimes.com/1990/12/31/business/the-media-business-time-warner-s-merger-payoff.html?pagewanted=all&src=pm
13. Floyd Norris, "Time Inc. and Warner to Merge, Creating Largest Media Company," http://www.nytimes.com/1989/03/05/us/time-inc-and-warner-to-merge-creating-largest-media-company.html?pagewanted=all
14. Geraldine Fabrikant, "Holders Back Time Warner Turner Merger," October 11, 1996, http://www.nytimes.com/1996/10/11/business/holders-back-time-warner-turner-merger.html
15. http://archipelle.com/Business/AOLTimeWarner.pdf
16. Knowledge@Wharton. "Giving Up on AOL Time Warner," March 2, 2003, http://news.com.com/2009-1069-990592.html?tag=fd_nc_1
17. www.timewarner.com
18. Shireen Cohen, "Vivendi: A Study of the Media Conglomerate's Mergers and Acquisitions Since 2009," http://globalmediastudies.blogspot.com/2011/05/vivendi-study-of-media-conglomerates.html
19. Vivendi company website.
20. http://www.independent.co.uk/news/business/seagram-buys-polygram-from-philips-for-106bn-1158030.html
21. http://www.businessweek.com/bwdaily/dnflash/may1998/nf80513d.htm
22. http://news.bbc.co.uk/2/hi/business/797146.stm
23. http://www.mondaq.com/article.asp?articleid=4875

24. http://christopher.goodman.net/Papers/PolyGram.html
25. Lori Ernos, "Vivendi, Seagram and Canal+ to Merge," *E commerce Times*, http://www.ecommercetimes.com/story/3601.html
26. http://www.thecanadianencyclopedia.com/articles/macleans/seagramvivendi-deal
27. http://www.vivendi.com/vivendi/Vivendi-Universal-Closes-on-2-2
28. http://articles.cnn.com/2001-12-17/world/vivendi_1_vivendi-universal-entertainment-vivendi-chairman-jean-marie-messier-cash-flow?_s=PM:WORLD
29. http://www.upi.com/Business_News/2001/12/17/Vivendi-buys-assets-of-USA-Networks/UPI-78781008626234/#ixzz1jFBRycRV
30. Dan Gallagher, "Vivendi, Activision to Create Video Game Giant," http://www.marketwatch.com/story/activision-vivendi-games-merge-to-create-video-game-giant
31. Andy Eddy, "Vivendi Games, Activision Merging into Activision Blizzard," http://news.teamxbox.com/xbox/15204/Vivendi-Games-Activision-Merging-into-Activision-Blizzard/
32. http://www.mcvuk.com/news/read/activision-blizzard-activision-and-vivendi-games-to-merge/016978
33. http://www.msnbc.msn.com/id/4960838/ns/business-us_business/t/nbc-closes-merger-universal/
34. http://www.guardian.co.uk/media/2009/dec/01/general-electric-vivendi-nbc-share
35. http://www.nytimes.com/2009/12/04/business/media/04nbc.html
36. Richard A. Gershon and V. Ratnadeep Suri, "Viacom Inc.: A Case Study in Transnational Media Management," *Journal of Media Business Studies*, Vol. 1, No. 1, pp. 47–69, 2004.
37. http://www.sramanamitra.com/2007/04/03/viacom%E2%80%99s-digital-strategy/
38. Marc Gunther, "Behind the Shakeup at Viacom," *Fortune*, June 28, 2004, p. 34.
39. http://www.nytimes.com/1994/01/08/business/blockbuster-s-investing-led-to-merger.html?pagewanted=all&src=pm
40. http://www.answers.com/topic/viacom#ixzz1jN1BSAwM
41. "Viacom Tunes into CBS," http://money.cnn.com/1999/09/07/deals/cbs/
42. Martin McLaughlin, "CBS–Viacom Merger: Monopolies Tighten their Grip on the Media," http://www.wqsws.org/articles/1999/sep1999/merg-s11.shtml
43. Skip Wollenberg, "Viacom Acquires BET," http://abcnews.go.com/Business/story?id=89100&page=1
44. Carol King, "Viacom Acquires BET Holdings," http://www.internetnews.com/bus-news/article.php/502781/Viacom+Acquires+BET+Holdings.htm
45. Oliver Staley and Brett Cole, "Harrah's Agrees to Apollo, Texas Pacific Buyout Offer," December 19, 2006, http://www.bloomberg.com/apps/news?pid=newsarchive&sid=axWLMcDhIq2Y
46. http://multivu.prnewswire.com/mnr/harrahs/26409/
47. http://dealbook.nytimes.com/2007/04/09/harrahs-shareholders-approve-17-billion-buyout/
48. http://www.clearchannel.com/Corporate/PressRelease.aspx?PressReleaseID=2243

49. http://www.marketwatch.com/story/clear-channel-sold-to-buyout-group-for-187-billion
50. Geraldine Fabrikant, "The Media Business: The Merger; Walt Disney to Acquire ABC in $19 billion Deal to Build a Giant for Entertainment," August 1, 1995, http://www.nytimes.com/1995/08/01/business/media-business-merger-walt-disney-acquire-abc-19-billion-deal-build-giant-for.html?pagewanted=all&src=pm
51. David Einstein and Jeff Pelline, "Disney's Stunning Deal to Buy ABC: Biggest Media Firm in World Would Emerge," August 1, 1995, http://articles.sfgate.com/1995-08-01/news/17813145_1_cap-cities-abc-stock-capital-cities
52. Jim Davis, "Gemstar Gets Stronger with TV Guide Buy," http://news.cnet.com/Gemstar-gets-stronger-with-TV-Guide-buy/2100-1040_3-230963.html
53. Brian Stelter, "Macrovision Agrees to Buy Gemstar-TV Guide for $2.8 billion in Stock and Cash," http://www.nytimes.com/2007/12/08/business/media/08gemstar.html
54. Anne Rackham, "Matsuhita Deal to Buy MCA Highlights the booming foreign investment in Hollywood," http://www.allbusiness.com/finance/129645-1.html
55. "The Deal for MCA, Review of Matsushita Debt Rating," http://www.nytimes.com/1990/11/27/business/the-deal-for-mca-review-of-matsushita-debt-rating.html
56. Charles Champlin, http://articles.latimes.com/1990-11-28/entertainment/ca-5051_1_film-industry
57. Rhonda Palmer, "Murdoch Catches Rising Star," *Variety*, July 27, 1993, http://www.variety.com/article/VR108977.html?categoryid=18&cs=1
58. Paul R. La Monica, "News Corp Wins Fight for Dow Jones," http://money.cnn.com/2007/07/31/news/companies/dowjones_newscorp/index.htm
59. Richard Perez Pena, "News Corp Completes Takeover of Dow Jones," http://www.nytimes.com/2007/12/14/business/media/14dow.html
60. "News Corp Acquires IGN for $650 million," http://www.businessweek.com/innovate/content/sep2005/id20050911_550700.htm
61. Richard Siklos, "News Corp to Acquire Owner of myspace.com," July 18, 2005, http://www.nytimes.com/2005/07/18/business/18cnd-newscorp.html
62. Jim Hu, "Lycos Bought in First Foreign Portal Deal," http://news.cnet.com/2100-1023-240509.html
63. David Gardner, "Lycos Acquired by Ybrant Digital for $36 million," 2010, http://www.informationweek.com/news/services/data/226700333
64. Sandeep Junnarkar and Tim Clark, "AOL Buys Netscape for $4.2 billion," http://news.cnet.com/2100-1023-218360.html
65. "AOL Netscape Tie Knot," http://money.cnn.com/1998/11/24/technology/aol/
66. Rajiv Chandarasekaran and Elizabeth Corcoran, "AOL in Talks to Acquire Netscape for $4 billion," http://www.washingtonpost.com/wp-srv/washtech/daily/nov98/aol1123.htm

5
Mergers and Acquisitions in the Electrical and Electronics Sectors

Acquisitions by Siemens

Siemens, established in 1850, is a global powerhouse in electrical engineering and electronics. An integrated technology company, it focuses on the four sectors of Energy, Healthcare, Industry and Infrastructure. These sectors are subdivided into 19 divisions. The company has 360,000 employees and a presence in 190 countries.

Major acquisitions of Siemens

Siemens has a history of acquisitions from as far back as the 1890s. The company has strengthened its portfolio through targeted acquisitions and partnerships. In 1903, Siemens acquired the company Elektrizitäts-Aktiengesellschaftvorm. Schuckert & Co., merging it with its own power engineering unit to form Siemens-Schuckertwerke GmbH. Siemens AG has made 329 acquisitions while taking stakes in 194 companies during the period 1984–2011. Siemens AG made 377 divestitures during the same period.

Siemens' acquisitions in the energy and environmental care sector

In 2005, Siemens Power Transmission and Distribution Group (PTD) acquired the Transmission and Distribution Division (T&D) of the Austrian company VA Tech. The acquisition of VA Tech T&D's Switchgear subdivision consolidated Siemens' leading position on the market for high-voltage products and systems. The takeover also strengthened Siemens as ranking second in the global power transformer market. The acquisition expanded Siemens' knowledge base through the addition of more research, development and manufacturing facilities in the high voltage division. The purchase price was approximately 1 billion euros.

Table 5.1 Financial highlights of Siemens (in millions of Euros)

	2007	2008	2009	2010	2011
Sales	64,238	69,577	70,053	68,978	73,515
Net income	4038	5886	2497	4068	6321
Cash flow	6461	5773	4087	7043	5885
Total assets	91,555	94,463	94,926	102,827	104,243

Siemens Power Generation, a unit of Siemens AG, is one of the premier companies in the international power generation sector. In 2005, Siemens Power acquired Wheelabrator Air Pollution Control, Inc., a leader in the design and supply of air pollution reduction products and solutions for the coal-fired power and industrial markets. This acquisition was aimed at expanding Siemens' suite of market-driven solutions for cleaner, more efficient power generation infrastructure.

In 2006, Siemens Power expanded its power plant business with products and solutions for the conversion of coal to electricity by acquiring the technology and engineering activities of Sustec Group, a Swiss-based company. This acquisition comprised, among others the German firm Future Energy GmbH as well as a 50 percent stake in the Chinese joint venture with Shenhua Ningxia Coal Group. Through this acquisition, Siemens hoped to secure a foothold in the developing integrated gasification combined cycle (IGCC) market through expansion in China.

In 2004, Siemens and Denmark-based Bonus Energy A/S entered into an agreement to acquire Bonus Energy. Bonus, with a market share of 9 percent, was one of the five major suppliers of wind energy systems worldwide. Siemens' Wind Power division was formed as a result of this acquisition. With Bonus' expertise in turbine manufacturing and Siemens' expertise in project management, the acquisition was undertaken to help Siemens compete strongly in Europe.

Acquisitions in automation and control

In 2004, Siemens expanded its activities in the global water supply and treatment industry with its acquisition of US Filter Corporation from the French parent company Veolia Environment for $993 million. In 2005, Siemens expanded its business in industrial drive technology by acquiring Flender Holding GmbH, one of the world's leading suppliers of gear systems. The purchase price amounted to €1.2 billion. The acquisition was carried out to expand Siemens' drive technology portfolio by adding gear systems. The Siemens Automation and Drives (A&D) Group is the world's leading manufacturer in the field of automation and drives. In 2005, Robicon, a leading manufacturer of medium voltage converters for AC motors in the US, was acquired by Siemens. This acquisition gave Siemens its hoped-for strength in drives technology. Robicon was active in particular in the key sectors of oil and gas, water/waste water and energy, whereby Siemens secured additional access to the markets for its own products.

In 2007, Siemens acquired the UGS Corporation for $3.515 billion. The acquisition enabled Siemens and UGS to deliver "totally integrated automation" solutions to the market. By means of combining expertise in the physical world of automation and the virtual world of PLM software, Siemens became the only company that was capable of offering integrated software and hardware solutions to its customers throughout the whole production process.

Acquisitions in industrial and public infrastructure

In 2006, Siemens Energy and Automation completed the acquisition of Berwanger, a market leader in front-end engineering, plant services and software. The acquisition of Berwanger complemented Siemens' know-how in the area of drive configurations, power generation and distribution solutions and water treatment solutions. The acquisition allowed Siemens to expand its international reach in the oil, gas and petrochemical industries.

In 2005, the Siemens A&D Group entered into an agreement for the takeover of Electrium, the leading vendor of electrical installation systems in UK, with long-established access to markets in the Middle East. This acquisition positioned Siemens among the top three vendors in the UK.

Acquisitions in the health sector

In 2005, Siemens acquired the molecular imaging company CTI for approximately $1 billion. The transaction was a cash tender offer at a price of $20.50 per share. The acquisition strengthened Siemens Medical Solution's molecular imaging development and technological innovation.

Through the acquisition of Diagnostic Products Corporation (DPC) in 2006, Siemens Medical Solutions entered the in vitro diagnostics (IVD) market. Combined with DPC, Siemens became the first full-service diagnostics company. DPC focused on developing, manufacturing and distributing automated body fluid analyzers and tests such as those related to cancer and cardiac diseases. The acquisition price was $1.86 billion. Each share of DPC was converted into the right to receive a cash payment of $58.50 per share.

Table 5.2 Other notable acquisitions by Siemens

Year	Acquisitions
1985	Siemens buys a stake in Siemens Allis, which supplied electrical control equipment.
1991	Siemens acquires Nixdorf Computers and renames it Informationssysteme AG.
1991	Siemens acquires the Industrial Systems Division of Texas Instruments, Inc.
2000	Shared Medical Systems Corporation is acquired by Siemens' Medical Engineering Group.
2000	Siemens acquires Atecs Mannesman.
2007	Siemens acquires Vai-Ingdesi Automation and Dade Behring.

In 2006, Siemens entered into an agreement with Bayer to acquire the chemical and pharmaceutical company's Diagnostics Division. This acquisition enabled Siemens Medical Solutions to expand its position in the high-growth molecular diagnostics market. The purchase price was roughly $5.4 billion. The acquisition of Bayer Diagnostics fitted into Siemens' overall strategy of developing integrated clinical workflow-oriented solutions by combining IVDs, in vivo diagnostics and healthcare IT.

Acquisitions by Cisco Systems

Cisco Systems is the world leader in networking, leading the transition to a network-centric technology environment. By combining its core strength (IP) with intelligence, the company is creating a powerful communications platform that will serve as the basis for the convergence of data, voice, video and mobile communications in a secure, integrated architecture. It has about 63,000 employees working in 470 offices in 165 countries. The company has 30 major laboratories worldwide and 8000 patents issued. R&D expenses are some $5.3 billion annually.

Cisco Systems is often known as the master acquirer. Its ability to consistently earn above-average returns and gain strategic competiveness is often attributed to the company's acquisition strategy. The company focuses on growth by acquiring firms with products and technologies the firm cannot or does not want to develop internally. During the period 1993–2011 Cisco acquired 148 companies, with 82 of these acquisitions during the period 2000 to June 2008. The peak period of acquisitions was in 2000, when 22 companies were acquired. The company's largest

Table 5.3 Financial highlights of Cisco Systems ($ billion)

	2007	2008	2009	2010	2011
Net sales	34.9	39.5	36.1	40	43.2
Net income	7.3	8.1	6.1	7.8	6.5
Cash flow from operations	10.1	12.1	9.9	10.2	10.1
EPS (dollars)	1.17	1.31	1.05	1.33	1.17

Table 5.4 Biggest acquisitions by Cisco Systems

Date	Company	Business	Value in $ billion
2005	Scientific Atlanta	Digital cable	6.9
1999	Cerent	Synchronous optical networking	6.9
2000	Arrowpoint Communications	LAN-switching	5.7
1996	StrataCom	LAN-switching	4
2010	Tandberg	Video conferencing	3.3
2007	WebEx	Web conferencing	3.2
2009	Starent Networks	System architecture evolution	2.9
2002	Andiamo Systems	Data storage	2.5
1999	Pirelli Optical System	Fiber optic communication	2.15
1999	GeoTel Communications	Voice over Internet Protocol	2
1999	IBM network hardware division	Computer network	2

acquisition as of 2011 is the purchase of Scientific Atlanta, a manufacturer of cable television, telecommunication and broadband equipment, for $6.9 billion. Most of the acquired companies are related to computer networking, including several LAN-switching and Voice over Internet Protocol companies.

In February 2006, Cisco completed the acquisition of Scientific Atlanta, a leading global provider of cable and IPTV set-tops, data and voice cable modems, end-to-end video distribution networks and video systems integration services. The products from the acquisition became a part of Cisco's Routing and Service Provider Technology Group. The acquisition enabled Cisco to offer a world-class, end-to-end data, voice, video and mobility solution for cable and telecom operators. The addition of Scientific Atlanta products, systems, services and video delivery expertise complemented Cisco IP Next Generation Network architecture. The acquisition extended Cisco's presence in the home networking market and firmly positioned the company in the video market. Scientific Atlanta also helped Cisco to enter the consumer electronics business as the company was the second-largest supplier of set-top boxes to the cable industry in the US. The industry scenario was significant as the cable companies were moving toward a new architecture that allows them to deliver video and voice services over converged networks. The telephone companies were making offerings in the entertainment market. Markets were in demand of integrated solutions from a chosen few vendors.

In 1999, Cisco acquired privately held Cerent, a leading developer of next-generation optical transport products. Under the terms of the agreement, shares of Cisco common stock were exchanged for all outstanding shares, options and warrants of Cerent not already owned by Cisco. Through this acquisition, Cisco entered the optical transport market with next-generation products, which provided customers with a complete infrastructure solution for transitional and new world networks. Cerent provided next-generation SONET ADM (Synchronous Optical Network Add-Drop Multiplexer) equipment, which is the fundamental building block in voice and data networks and used to add and remove lower-speed traffic from higher-speed optical rings.

In 2000, Cisco acquired Arrow Point Communications, Inc. for about $6 billion in stock, in a move to add sophisticated software for routing web-page traffic to its portfolio. Arrow Point Communications was the leading provider of content switches that optimize the delivery of web content.

In 1996, Cisco acquired StrataCom in a stock exchange. The combination with StrataCom enabled Cisco to provide end-to-end solutions across public, private or hybrid networks. The combined entity was capable of delivering integrated scalable multiservice network solutions to public carriers, Internet Service Providers and enterprises.

In 2010, Cisco acquired Tandberg, and its various product lines became part of Cisco's telepresence group. In addition to conferencing units, Tandberg has specialized software for managing videoconferencing systems and for creating connections between systems that rely on different underlying technology. The acquisition suited Cisco's mission of backing products that generate more Internet traffic, which in turn drives demand for networking hardware.

The acquisition of WebEx was completed in May 2007. WebEx is a market leader in on-demand collaboration applications, and its network-based solution for delivering business-to-business collaboration extends Cisco's vision for Unified Communications, particularly within the Small to Medium Business (SMB) segment.

In December 2009, Cisco completed its acquisition of Starent Networks, a leading supplier of IP-based mobile infrastructure solutions for mobile and converged network operators. The acquisition was relevant in the context of the rising popularity of smart phones and wireless data.

With the acquisition of Andiamo Systems, Cisco was able to offer enterprise customers the same level of network scalability, performance and manageability to storage networking that Cisco had pioneered in LAN and IP networking. With the acquisition of Pirelli SpA's optical systems unit, Cisco filled a gap in its line of fiber optic products. The acquisition of GeoTel Communications was meant to create an open data and voice software infrastructure for Cisco Systems. Through the buyout of IBM's network hardware division, Cisco was able to provide a powerful combination of networking solutions, technologies and services to businesses and service providers.

Acquisitions by General Electric

In 1890, Thomas Edison established the Edison General Electric Company by bringing his various businesses together. General Electric (GE) is a global infrastructure, finance and media company. From everyday light bulbs to fuel cell technology and cleaner, more efficient jet engines, GE has shaped the world with groundbreaking innovations for the past 130 and more years. GE power generation equipment and technology is used to generate a quarter of the world's electricity every day. GE has over 36,000 technologists working across various businesses. GE has an established presence in over 100 countries. General Electric was one of the original 12 companies listed on the Dow Jones Industrial Average and still remains on the list. GE's divisions include GE Capital, GE Energy, GE Technology Infrastructure and GE Home & Business Solutions.

During the period 1981–2011, GE made **791** acquisitions, while taking stakes in 261 companies. GE also had 620 divestitures during this period. In 1997, GE made its highest number of acquisition at 58 companies. In 1986, GE purchased RCA, primarily for the NBC television network. Again in 1986, GE acquired Kidder, Peabody & Co., a US-based securities firm, which after heavy losses was sold to Paine Webber in 1994. In 2002, GE bought the wind turbine manufacturing assets of Enron Wind after the Enron scandal. In 2004, GE purchased 80 percent of Universal Pictures from Vivendi. In 2007, GE acquired Smiths' Aerospace for $4.8 billion. This acquisition broadened GE's offerings for aviation customers by adding Smiths' Aerospace innovative flight management systems, electrical power management, mechanical actuation systems and airborne platform computing systems to GE Aviation's growing commercial and military aircraft engines and services. The Smiths' Aerospace business has a significant presence on most commercial aircraft, including the Boeing 737 and Airbus A320, as well as many military aircraft.

In 2010, GE had bought a $1.6 billion portfolio of retail credit cards from Citigroup. In 2010, GE announced its acquisition of data migration and SCADA simulation specialists Opal Software.

In 2011, GE made big-ticket deals like the $3 billion acquisition of Dresser, the global energy infrastructure technology and service provider; a $3.2 billion buyout of Converteam, which specializes in energy from wind turbines; and a buyout of John Wood Group Plc for about $2.8 billion. GE plans to expand Dresser's presence in emerging markets such as Latin America and the Middle East, where the company has limited exposure, but where growth prospects are significant.

Additional References

1. www.siemens.com
2. www.alacrastore.com/mergers-acquisitions/Siemens_AG-1015281
3. http://gfxspeak.com/2011/07/19/2007-major-acquisitions-consolidate-plm-industry/
4. http://www.siemens.com/press/en/pressrelease/?press=/en/pr_cc/2005/07_jul/ptd200507378_(va-tech)_1282303.htm
5. http://www.tmcnet.com/usubmit/2005/oct/1190302.htm
6. http://www.siemens.com.tr/web/1247-11692-1-1/siemens_turkiye_-_en/siemens_turkey/press_releases/acquisition_of_flender_holding_gmbh
7. http://www.nema.org/media/ind/20051207a.cfm
8. http://www.medical.siemens.com/webapp/wcs/stores/servlet/CategoryDisplay~q_catalogId~e_-111~a_categoryId~e_1009304~a_catTree~e_100005,1009304~a_langId~e_-111~a_storeId~e_10001.htm
9. http://www.ivdtechnology.com/article/siemens-purchases-bayer-diagnostics
10. http://www.mtbeurope.info/news/2005/503023.htm
11. Marguerite Reardon, "Cisco Closes Scientific Atlanta Buy," http://news.cnet.com/Cisco-closes-Scientific-Atlanta-buy/2110-1036_3-6043542.html
12. Nancy Gohring, "Cisco Buys Scientific Atlanta for $6.9 billion," *IDG News Service*, http://www.networkworld.com/news/2005/111805-cisco-scientific-atlanta.html
13. www.cisco.com
14. http://newsroom.cisco.com/dlls/1996/corp_042296.html
15. http://www.nytimes.com/2009/10/14/technology/companies/14cisco.html?adxnnl=1&adxnnlx=1325666116-T8j/Z3OhU8O3KUxJZxsPlg
16. www.ge.com
17. http://www.alacrastore.com/mergers-acquisitions/General_Electric_Company-1006912
18. http://www.geaviation.com/aboutgeae/presscenter/other/other_20070504.html

6
Mergers and Acquisitions in the Energy Sector

Introduction

The oil industry, like other industries, has been forced to adjust to the massive change forces of technology, globalization, industry transformations and entrepreneurial innovations over a lengthy period of time.

Mergers and acquisitions in the 1980s and 1990s were basically concentrated in the North American region. The late 1990s witnessed mega mergers when Exxon bought Mobil, BP acquired Amoco and Chevron merged with Texaco. In 1997 and 1998, the value of M&A in the oil sector was approximately $88.99 billion and $66.6 billion respectively.

In 1998, the merger of Exxon and Mobil took place. In August 1998, British Petroleum merged with Amoco to form BP-Amoco, which became the third largest oil company in terms of turnover and hydrocarbon reserves after Exxon Mobil and Dutch Shell. These two mega mergers widened the gap between the top players and the rest of the oil companies in the sector. In December 1998, the French Group Total and Belgian group Petrofina merged to form Total Fina.

In 2007, the total number of deals was 752, valued at $372 billion. In 2008, there were 311 deals compared to 339 in 2009. The total value of oil and gas transactions announced globally reached $270 billion in 2010 compared to $200 billion in 2009, according to E&Y's *Oil and Gas Review Report 2010*. According to the report, 947 M&As were announced in 2010, of which 73 percent took place in the upstream hydrocarbon segment. During 2010, there were 19 transactions that involved refineries of which 13 were based in North America and Europe.

According to Dealogic statistics, 2010 accounted for 1717 M&A deals with a value of approximately $322 billion. In 2011, the sector witnessed 1508 mergers with an approximate value of $211 billion. In 2009,

Table 6.1 Global M&A activity in the energy sector

Year	Value in $ billion	Number of deals
2008	302.8	1161
2009	248.5	847
2010	395.2	817

Source: PwC Report, *Oil & Gas Deals, Q1 2011.*

Exxon Mobil announced plans to acquire XTO Energy for $40 billion. In 2010, Vedanta Group acquired an approximately 60 per stake in Cairn India for a stated $9.8 billion. The big-ticket deals of 2011 included Berkshire Hathway's $8.9 billion acquisition of the petrochemical group Lubrizol; BP's gas asset deal with Reliance India and Petrochina's joint venture with Encana in Canada for the development of gas assets. In 2010, Schlumberger Ltd acquired Smith International, Inc. for $11 billion. Baker Hughes, Inc. bought BJ Services for $5.5 billion. In 2011, Halliburton bought Multi Chem, which provided chemical and services to more than 30,000 wells in North America. Lufkin Industries acquired Quinn's Oilfield Supply and Affiliates. In 2011, Statoil, the Norwegian oil and gas giant, strengthened its position in the US market by acquiring Texas-based Brigham Exploration Co. for $4.4 billion. Kinder Morgan created the largest natural gas pipeline system of about 80,000 miles by acquiring El Paso Corp. for $38 billion.

Big M&A deals include the acquisition of Addax Petroleum Corporation by a Sinopec Group company for $8.8 billion and the merger of Atlas Energy Resources with Atlas America for $1.4 billion. The sector is witnessing forward integration and horizontal mergers as Exploration & Production (E&P) companies are acquiring mid-stream companies and mid-stream companies are acquiring other mid-stream companies.

Emerging trends

In its *2010 World Energy Outlook*, the International Energy Agency estimated that approximately 40 percent of the oil production needed by 2020 had yet to be found or developed. By 2030, the target would be close to 60 percent. Saudi Arabia, Venezuela and Canada were indicated as having the largest oil deposit reserves.

M&A deal activity in the energy sector is concentrated in the Exploration and Production (E&P) segment. Worldwide deepwater assets are the major focus of attraction for multinational and national oil companies. Some of the most active areas for exploration activity in the US are oil shale deposits such as the Marcellus Shale in the Appalachians, the Bossier Shale in Texas and Louisiana and the Eagle Ford Shale in south Texas. The interest in shale gas exploration and attractive prices had spurred merger activity in energy firms.

In the energy market, oil companies are acquiring competent and competitive small and mid-tier players. Some significant features could be observed with respect to M&A activity in the late 2000s: there had been increased M&A activity in the oil field & services sector and upstream sector; there was a greater focus on the exploitation of unconventional hydrocarbon resources such as oil sands and coal bed methane. During the 2008–2010 period, the upstream sector accounted for approximately 70 percent of the number of M&A deals.

Strategic reasons

M&A activity for the E&P sector peaked during 2008 and then fell apart during the global economic recession. Unconventional natural gas resources were the primary target and driver of M&A activity in North America. During the boom period, the high commodity prices boosted the cash flows of major oil companies, which placed them in a position to increase M&A activity. Many independent E&P companies progressed rapidly through the discovery and development of unconventional natural gas basins during this period.

Many companies are focusing on growth options through deals that involve non-operating independent outfits along with concentration on unconventional natural gas basins. Independent E&P companies have been prioritizing the divestment of non-core assets in order to focus their capital on core growth areas. For example, Marathon sold its assets in the Permian Basin to Apache. Some deals have taken place in order to benefit from operating synergies and leading positions in key geographic areas. The merger of Suncor and Petro Canada was expected to save $269 million in annual operating costs.

The integrated oil companies have absorbed many independent players and are focusing on alternative energy sources and diversification as a means of growth.

The Exxon/Mobil merger

This mega merger reunited the major disintegrated divisions of the Standard Oil, which had once controlled almost 90 percent of all oil produced in the US. In 1911, the Supreme Court of the United States broke up Standard Oil into 33 companies of which eight were retained

Table 6.2 Largest M&As in the energy sector[a]

Year	Acquirer	Target	Value in $ billions
1979	Shell Oil Corp.	Belridge Oil Co.	3.65
1981	E.I. DuPont de Nemours Co.	Conoco, Inc.	8.039
1981	US Steel Corp.	Marathon Oil Corp.	6.618
1981	Société Nationale Elf Aquitaine	Texas Gulf, Inc.	4.29
1982	Occidental Petroleum Corp.	Cities Service Corp.	4.11
1984	Chevron Corp.	Gulf Corp.	13.20
1984	Mobil Corp.	Superior Oil Co.	5.72
1984	Texaco, Inc.	Getty Oil Co.	10.1
1985	US Steel Corp.	Texas Oil & Gas Corp.	4.09
1985	Occidental Petroleum Corp.	Mid Con Corp.	3.08
1987	Amoco Corp.	Dome Petroleum Ltd	4.18
1989	Exxon Corp.	Texaco Canada, Inc.	4.15
1991	Ente Nazionale Idrocarbur	Enimont SpA	9.9
1997	Duke Energy	Duke Power	7.6
1998	Exxon	Mobil	78.95
1998	British Petroleum	Amoco	63
1999	Total Fina	Elf Aquitaine	50.7
1999	Total	Petrofina	13
2001	Chevron	Texaco	45
2004	Royal Dutch Petroleum	Shell Transport & Trading	74.35
2005	Endesa	Gas Natural SDG	28.29
2005	Chevron Texaco	Unocal	17.12
2006	Carlyle Group, Riverstone Holdings and Goldman Sachs	Kinder Morgan	21.6
2007	ENEL	Endesa	62.6
2007	KKR	TXV	43.8
2011	Exxon Mobil	XTO Energy	40

Note: [a] The largest acquisition ever in the energy sector would have been the mining giant BHP Billiton's hostile takeover of Rio Tinto for $149 billion in 2008. But the deal was aborted owing to regulatory concerns and the economic slowdown.

under the name Standard Oil. After a series of name changes, Standard Oil of New York became Mobil in 1966. By 1972, the former Standard Oil of New Jersey had evolved into Exxon.

With a history of over 125 years Exxon Mobil had become one of the world's largest publicly traded integrated oil and gas companies. Exxon Mobil is among the top wealth creators in terms of market capitalization, and the largest refiner and marketer of petroleum products. Exxon Mobil consists of ten separate companies, which are made up of Upstream, Downstream and Chemicals businesses. In Upstream activities, Exxon

Table 6.3 Financial highlights of ExxonMobil ($ million)

	2006	2007	2008	2009	2010
Sales	365,467	390,328	459,529	301,500	370,125
Cash flow from operations	52,386	56,206	65,710	29,983	51,674
Net income	39,500	40,610	45,220	19,280	30,460
Total assets	219,015	242,082	228,052	233,323	302,510
EPS ($)	6.64	7.31	8.70	3.99	6.24

Mobil explores, develops and produces crude oil, natural gas and petroleum products. In Downstream activities, the global network of the company's manufacturing plants, transportation systems and distribution centers provide fuels, lubricants and high-value products. The company has interests in 12 lubricant refineries and manufactures three brands of finished lubricants, namely Exxon, Esso and Mobil. The Chemicals division manufactures and sells petrochemicals of olefins, aromatics, fluids, synthetic rubber, polyethylene, polypropylene, oriented polypropylene packaging films and other petrochemical products. Fuel products and services are sold to aviation customers at more than 630 airports and to marine customers at more than 180 ports around the world.

In 1989, Canada-based Imperial Oil Ltd, controlled by Exxon Corp., had acquired a 78 percent stake in Texaco Canada in a transaction valued at $4.15 billion.

Exxon Mobil merger highlights

On November 30, 1999 Exxon and Mobil merged to form Exxon Mobil. The deal saw the world's largest energy company, Exxon, acquiring Mobil, the second biggest US oil gas group. The merger created the largest oil company in the world. At the time of merger the combined Exxon Mobil was the third largest company in the world behind GE and Microsoft in terms of market capitalization.

The merger led to approximately 9000 job losses or 7 percent of the group's workforce around the world.

Strategic reasons for the merger

Consolidation of oil companies was taking place on account of high production costs and weak oil prices. The merger brought together two complementary businesses that fitted well in the exploration and production of petroleum and chemicals. By combining complementary assets, Exxon Mobil was able to expand its presence in regions of high potential for future oil and gas discoveries. The merger facilitated the combination of Exxon's rich experience in deepwater exploration with Mobil's production and exploration acreage in Nigeria and Equatorial Guinea. In the Caspian region, Exxon's presence in Azerbaijan coupled with Mobil's presence in Kazakhstan, particularly in the Tengiz field, was expected to yield merger benefits. Complementary exploration and production operations also existed in South America, Russia and eastern Canada.

Cost synergy resulted from the merger through elimination of duplication facilities and excess capacity. General and administrative costs were also reduced. Moreover synergy benefits were realized from applying each company's best business practices across their worldwide operations. By 2002 Exxon had realized project synergies of $7 billion. The merger resulted in an increase of market share by 23 percent. The merger was expected to achieve savings of about $2.8 billion per year.

Terms of the deal

Exxon exchanged 1.32 shares for each share of Mobil. Since Mobil had 780 million shares outstanding, Exxon paid 1030 million shares times the $72 share price of Exxon for a total of $74.2 billion. This was a 26.4 percent premium over Mobil's $58.7 billion market capitalization at the time of the merger announcement. The new company was owned by 70 percent of Exxon's existing shareholders.

Exxon and Mobil sold off 24,131 gas stations, primarily in the northeastern US, California and Texas as required by the Federal Trade Commission as a condition for approval of the merger.

The acquisition of XTO Energy

In 2009, Exxon Mobil acquired XTO Energy in an all-stock deal valued at $41 billion. Exxon Mobil issued 0.7098 of a share of common stock for each common share of XTO. The deal represented a 25 percent premium to XTO stockholders. This acquisition was the largest acquisition made by Exxon Mobil after the Mobil acquisition. The XTO acquisition was significant in the context of the growing relevance of natural gas as the source for clean energy. XTO Energy had been active in extracting natural gas from shale formations in an area between Pennsylvania, New York and West Virginia and in Texas and North Dakota. The company had proven reserves of 13.9 trillion cubic feet of gas and total reserves of 45 trillion cubic feet.

Consolidation has been active as biggest players in the field were on the lookout for independent producers who had suffered on account of low gas prices. The acquisition was basically meant to enhance Exxon

Mobil's position in the development of unconventional natural gas and oil resources. Earlier, energy companies burned off natural gas as a waste product. With the realization of its value as an energy source aided with new technology, natural gas trapped in vast shale oil fields has been freed with a technique known as fracking. Both Exxon Mobil and XTO have established a presence in the Piceance Basin in Colorado. XTO's resource base consists of 45 trillion cubic feet of gas and includes shale gas, tight gas, coal bed methane and shale oil. These assets are expected to complement the assets of Exxon Mobil's holdings in the US, Canada, Germany, Poland, Hungary and Argentina.

The merger of Royal Dutch Petroleum and the Shell Group

Shell had a complex corporate organization consisting of more than 2000 companies worldwide ultimately controlled by the two parent companies—Royal Dutch Petroleum and British-based Shell Transport and Trading Company. For a century Shell had dual ownership, with 60 percent owned by Royal Dutch and 40 percent by the British parent. In 2004, the companies merged to form Royal Dutch Shell, with Upstream, Downstream and Projects and Technology Divisions. The Upstream Division explores and extracts oil and natural gas, while the Downstream Division refines, supplies, trades and ships crude worldwide and produces petrochemicals for industrial customers. The Project and Technology Division manages delivery of Shell's major projects and research initiatives. Shell produces approximately 3.3 million barrels of gas and oil every day.

The merger came as a response to a scandal over the company's downgrading of oil reserves data. The merger was basically to usher investors into an era of "one company, one board and one chief executive." Management believed that scrapping the twin board structure was the best way to eliminate accounting failures as reflected by its overestimated reserves. The exchange of share was on a one-to-one basis. Royal Dutch Shell held approximately 98.5 percent of the outstanding shares of Royal Dutch and is the sole parent of the Shell Group.

Acquisitions by BP

The BP/Amoco merger

BP (formerly British Petroleum) started its journey in 1908 with oil found in a rugged part of Persia (now Iran) after a long and difficult exploration. Standard Oil of Indiana, later called Amoco, began business in 1899. BP is one of the world's leading international oil and gas companies, with interests in fuel, retail services and petrochemicals products. From the 1920s the brands of BP have become well known for quality gasoline, transport fuels, chemicals and alternative sources of energy such as wind, solar and biofuels.

Amoco produced and marketed crude oil and petroleum products and natural gas worldwide. The company ran operations in approximately 30 countries and had more than $32 billion in gross assets at the time of merger. Amoco served 2 million customers through approximately 9300 retail outlets. Its five refineries process more than one million barrels of crude oil per day. In 1997, Amoco and the Shell Oil Company established Altura Energy to operate their oil and gas properties.

In 1998, BP merged with Amoco to form BP Amoco Plc in a $63 billion deal. Under the terms of the merger, Amoco shareholders received 3.97 BP Amoco Ordinary shares in the form of BP Amoco ADS. BP shareholders held approximately 60 percent and Amoco shareholders held 40 percent of the new company. Amoco shareholders received a 25 percent premium above BP's market value at the time of the merger announcement.

The merger came against a backdrop of depressed world oil prices, which had fallen to their lowest levels in over a decade.

The group had combined reserves of around 14.8 billion barrels of oil and gas, and daily production of 3 million barrels, with a prime presence in all main exploration areas. The merger made BP Amoco the largest producer of oil and gas in the US and UK, and a leader in oil and gas investments in Latin America, the Caspian region and Africa. The reserve base of the merged entity became the second largest of the major oil giants, and comprised 50 percent oil reserves and 42 percent gas reserves. The marketing prowess of the combined group was further consolidated with Amoco's market presence and well-known brand name in US coupled with BP's leading position in Europe.

The merger created one of the world's oil super-majors with a market capitalization of approximately $110 billion based on the respective share prices prior to the announcement of the proposed merger. The

Table 6.4 Financial highlights of BP Amoco ($ million)

	2006	2007	2008	2009	2010
Revenues	274,316	291,438	367,053	246,138	308,928
Profit	22,601	21,169	21,666	16,759	−3324
Assets	217,601	236,076	228,238	235,968	272,262

merger enhanced the investment opportunities for the combined firm through production-sharing agreements in the Caspian region. Through the merger, BP improved its market presence in downstream oil and gas retailing in Europe. The merger facilitated the company's development of technological skills in deepwater drilling and proprietary chemical processing technologies.

The merger gave BP Amoco a consolidated base as the combined asset base of BP and Amoco was located in the OECD countries. The merger was expected to realize cost synergies of $2 billion in pretax cost savings annually. The savings were generated from more focused exploration and the streamlining of business processes. The merger also made BP Amoco the leading company in the areas of chemicals, petrochemicals and solar energy. At the time of merger BP had 17,900 service stations around the world while Amoco had 9300 in the US. The deal was the largest takeover to date of an American company by a foreign company. The merger enhanced the combined company's vertical integration, coupling the strength of BP in oil exploration with the skills of Amoco in the business of refining oil and chemicals. BP Amoco is the world's third-largest publicly traded oil company.

The acquisition of Arco

In 2000, BP acquired Atlantic Richfield Co. (Arco) in a stock swap worth about $27 billion. Through the acquisition BP Amoco gained a leading position in the lucrative California gasoline market. BP also hereby obtained access to the oil fields in Alaska and natural gas fields in Asia. Arco shareholders received BP Amoco ordinary shares as American Depository Shares at 0.82 BP Amoco ADS per Arco share.

The acquisition of Burmah Castrol

In 2000, BP Amoco acquired Burmah Castrol for £3 billion. Castrol was the most well-known lubricants brand in the world. The acquisition was of immense significance for BP Amoco since the company lacked a globally recognized lubricants brand. Burmah Castrol had a turnover of nearly £3 billion in 1999. The deal was expected to yield cost savings of more than £160 million a year from 2003.

The acquisition of Veba Oil

In July 2001, BP acquired a 51 percent stake in German oil and petrochemicals company Veba Oil in a swap deal with owner E.on. In return BP gave E.ON a 51 percent stake in Gelsenberg, which holds BP's 25.5 percent stake in German gas distributor Ruhrgas. Veba Oil also owned

Aral, Germany's biggest fuels retailer oil. Aral's domestic network of 2560 retail sites had daily fuel sales of 170,000 barrels and served 1.7 million customers a day in Germany at the time of the deal. This sell-off by E.ON was to deepen its gas interests and exit downstream. BP consolidated Aral's operations with its own marketing business and retained Aral as BP's sole retail fuels brand in Germany.

Other M&As in the energy sector

Enel's acquisition of Endesa

In 2009, Enel SpA, Italy's largest power company, purchased 25 percent of Endesa, Spain's leading electricity company, from construction group Acciona, bringing its total stake to 92 percent. Enel paid €11.1 billion ($14.2 billion) for Acciona's stake, including $8.2 billion in cash and roughly $2.9 billion in renewable energy assets with a capacity to generate 2104 megawatts of electricity. The acquisition gave Enel 22 million customers and a large number of power plants in Europe and Latin America. Endesa had signed an alliance with Gas Natural SDG SA, the Barcelona-based provider of natural gas distribution services. In 2005, Endesa had also acquired the gas clients portfolio of Gas Natural SDG.

Total Fina's acquisition of Elf Aquitaine

In 1999, French major Total acquired Belgium's Petrofina for $12 billion and became Total Fina. After a two-month battle in 1999, Total Fina acquired Elf Aquitaine, with a sweetened $54.2 billion offer. The merger catapulted the new company, Total Fina Elf SA, to the position of fourth largest oil, natural gas and specialty chemicals company in the world.

Total Fina Elf has a refining capacity of 2.4 million barrels per day equivalent and has more than 22,000 service stations and 29 refineries in 100 countries. Total Fina offered Elf shareholders four Total Fina shares for three Elf shares. The offer represented a 15 percent premium for Elf shareholders. Total Fina and Elf have been under pressure to increase in size amid consolidations in the sector that saw Exxon acquiring Mobil Corp. and BP acquiring Atlantic Richfield Co. The combination enabled the combined entity to emerge as the world's leading downstream company in West Africa. In 2001, Total Fina acquired Spain's Cepsa to expand into the Spanish market.

Acquisitions by Chevron Corporation

Chevron Corporation is one of the largest integrated energy companies in the world, with major operations in the most important oil and gas regions. Chevron is a leader in refining, fuels, lubricants and additives. The company is also the world's largest producer of geothermal energy. In 2010, the company's net oil equivalent production averaged 2.763 million barrels per day. Until 1984, Chevron was known as Standard Oil of California. Chevron had discovered the biggest petroleum reserve in the world.

In 1984, Gulf Oil brought in Chevron as a white knight to ward off a hostile takeover attempt by the investor group T, Boone Pickens Jr. The deal was valued at some $13.2 billion. Through the merger with Gulf Oil, Chevron became the leading refiner and marketer in the US. Chevron also became the market leader of gas liquids in the US. The merger consolidated Chevron's presence in regions like the Gulf of Mexico, Canada and the North Sea. The combination gave Chevron access to important assets of Gulf Corp., including the Pittsburg & Midway Coal Mining Co. Gulf Corp. also had a solid marketing and refining system. To comply with federal antitrust provisions, Chevron sold a number of Gulf stations to Cumberland Farms in 1985. In 1988, Chevron acquired $2.5 billion in properties from Tenneco.

In 1984, Texaco, Inc. took over Getty Oil. The acquisition helped to increase Texaco's assets by 37 percent and double its crude oil reserves. In 2001, Chevron Co. acquired Texaco for a deal valued at $36 billion in stock. As a result of the acquisition, Chevron became the world's fifth biggest oil company. At the time Chevron was the second largest oil company in the US and Texaco the third largest. The merger resulted in a company, ChevronTexaco, with a market value of $90 billion. The combined company operated nearly 50,000 gas stations worldwide.

Texaco shareholders were offered 0.77 Chevron shares for each Texaco share, valuing each share at $64.87—a premium of 18 percent. Chevron also took over approximately $7 billion of Texaco's debt. Chevron shareholders owned approximately 61 percent of the combined company while Texaco shareholders held a 39 percent equity stake. The combined company was able to produce about 2.7 million barrels of oil a day, with combined reserves of 11 billion barrels. This buyout took place during a time of high price volatility. Both Chevron and Texaco had strong exploration and production position in West Africa, the former USSR and Latin America. The combined entity realized cost savings of approximately $1.2 billion within nine months of the deal. The new company had a market capitalization of approximately $95 billion.

In 2005, ChevronTexaco acquired Unocal in a stock-and-cash deal valued at approximately $18 billion. Chevron issued 210 million shares of ChevronTexaco stock and paid about $4.4 billion in cash as part of the deal. ChevronTexaco also assumed net debt of $1.6 billion. Energy reserves were a major factor for the acquisition of Unocal.

On addition of Unocal's 1.75 billion barrels of oil-equivalent proved reserves, ChevronTexaco's reserve base increased by 15 percent. The buy-out was a strategic fit for ChevronTexaco as it enabled access to Unocal's operations in the Asia Pacific, the Caspian and the Gulf of Mexico. The merger was expected to save $325 million by getting rid of overlapping operations. At the time of acquisition, Unocal was the ninth largest oil and gas producer, with a market capitalization of $16 billion. ChevronTexaco's acquisition of Unocal was significant in the context of the difficult times companies faced in discovering new oil and natural gas fields.

KKR's leveraged buyout of TXU

In 2007, the investor group led by Kohlberg Kravis Roberts & Co., Texas Pacific Group and Goldman Sachs acquired the utility and power company TXU in a deal valued at $45 billion. With 2.2 million customers TXU was the largest energy provider in Texas. The investor group paid $69.25 for each TXU share, and assumed its debt of $12 billion. This deal was the largest leveraged buyout to date. TXU was facing stiff opposition for its environmental policy with regard to carbon emissions from its coal power plants.

The acquisition of Kinder Morgan

In 2007, an investor group consisting of Goldman Sachs Capital Partners, American International Group, The Carlyle Group and Riverstone Holdings acquired Kinder Morgan in a deal valued at approximately $22 billion, which included the assumption of $7 billion of debt. Kinder Morgan is one of the largest energy transportation, storage and distribution company in North America, with approximately 43,000 miles of pipelines that transport primarily natural gas, crude oil and petroleum products. The company also has more than 165 terminals that store, transfer and handle products like gasoline and coal. Kinder Morgan shareholders received $107.50 in cash for each share of KMI common stock they held.

DuPont's acquisition of Conoco

Established in 1875 as the Continental Oil and Transportation Company, Conoco was one of the first petroleum marketers in the West. Conoco also manufactured commercial petroleum products and coal. By 1981 Conoco had become the ninth biggest American oil company. In 1980, Conoco purchased Globe Petroleum Ltd, with 220 retail outlets in the UK, and entered into an exploration venture with DuPont. In 1981,

Dome Petroleum of Canada bought a 20 percent stake in Conoco. In the same year DuPont became a white knight in view of the threats from Seagram Company and Mobil Corporation for a takeover of Conoco, and finally acquired Conoco for approximately $7.4 billion. The acquisition gave DuPont a secure source of petroleum feedstocks, needed for its fiber and plastics operations, in an era of rapidly rising oil prices and high inflation.

But later in the 1990s, with oil selling at a fraction of the inflation-adjusted price in 1981 and exploration of offshore fields requiring massive capital investments, owning an oil company became no longer attractive to DuPont. In 1999, DuPont sold all of its Conoco shares as a part of its divestment strategy. In August 2002, Conoco merged with Philips Co. to form the sixth largest publicly traded oil company in the world and third largest in the US.

Other major acquisitions

In 1979, Shell Oil Corporation purchased Belridge Oil for $3.65 billion. In 1981, Elf Aquitaine acquired ownership of Texas Gulf in a $5 billion deal. In 1982, Occidental Petroleum Corporation acquired Cities Service Corporation. In 1986, Occidental Petroleum Corporation purchased Midcon Corporation.

In 1982, US Steel diversified into the energy industry with its acquisition of Marathon Oil Company. Then, in 1985, US Steel acquired its second oil company, the Texas Oil and Gas Corporation. The combined company had assets of $22 billion and revenues of $21 billion. In March 1984, Superior Oil was acquired by Mobil Corporation (now part of Exxon Mobil) for $5.7 billion. In 1987, Amoco Canada bought debt-laden Dome Petroleum for approximately $5 billion. In 1989, Texaco sold off its 78 percent stake in Texaco Canada, Inc. to Imperial Oil Ltd, which was controlled by Exxon Corp. In 1991, Italy-based Ente Nazionale Idrocarburi acquired Enimont SpA for $9.9 billion. In 2011, Duke Energy purchased Progress Energy in a $13.7 billion deal that created the largest power utility in the US. Duke Energy is a leader in developing innovative wind and solar energy solutions for customers.

Additional References

1. "A Flood of Energy M&A: Schlumberger Buys Smith for $11 billion," *24/7 Wall St*, http://247wallst.com/2010/02/21/a-flood-of-energy-ma/#ixzz1klxHaPfs
2. http://www.marketwatch.com/story/oil-gas-sector-ripe-for-picking-as-mergers-surge-2011-10-21

3. http://stocks.investopedia.com/stock-analysis/2010/Energy-Mergers--Acquisitions-In-Comeback-XTO-XOM-CHK-TOT-RRC0217.aspx#ixzz1kltREBD
4. *Oil & Gas Mergers and Acquisitions Report, Midyear 2011*, http://www.deloitte.com/assets/Dcom-UnitedStates/Local%20Assets/Documents/Energy_us_er/us_er_OandGMAMidyear2011Report_080811.pdf
5. http://www.istockanalyst.com/article/viewarticlepaged/articleid/5413350/pageid/2
6. *Oil & Gas Deals, Q1 2011*, a PwC Report.
7. http://www.marketwatch.com/story/kinder-morgan-buying-el-paso-in-38-billion-deal-2011-10-16-163310
8. http://www.marketwatch.com/story/oil-gas-sector-ripe-for-picking-as-mergers-surge-2011-10-21
9. Myra P. Saefong, "Oil, Gas Sector Ripe for Picking as Mergers Surge," *MarketWatch*, http://www.marketwatch.com/story/oil-gas-sector-ripe-for-picking-as-mergers-surge-2011-10-21
10. http://globalenergytalent.com/6/7-inside/171-mergers-and-acquisitions-in-energy-sector.html
11. https://www.deloitte.com/assets/Dcom-India/Local%20Assets/Documents/ER%20publications/M&A%20in%20Global%20Oil%20&%20Gas%20Sector.pdf
12. Christopher Click, Justin Pettit and Andrew Steinhubl, "M&A Strategies in North American Oil and Gas Sector," http://www.booz.com/media/uploads/MA_Strategies_NA_Oil_Gas.pdf
13. http://www.allbusiness.com/mining/oil-gas-extraction-crude-petroleum-natural/335883-1.html#ixzz1kmWooSUU
14. http://www.ey.com/PL/en/Newsroom/News-releases/PR11_Raport---fuel-and-oil-sector
15. Fred Weston, "Exxon Mobil Merger, An Archetype," *Journal of Applied Finance*, 12(1) March 2002. Financial Management Association.
16. Deutsche Bank, "ExxonMobil: The Emperor's New Groove," September 2001.
17. ExxonMobil website.
18. http://news.bbc.co.uk/2/hi/business/222402.stm
19. http://www.pbs.org/newshour/bb/business/july-dec98/oil_12-1.html
20. Mayank Mehta, "Exxon Mobil Acquires XTO Energy for $31 billion," http://www.123jump.com/market-update/Exxon-Mobil-Acquires-XTO-Energy-for-$31-Billion/35661
21. Steve Gelsi, "Exxon Mobil to Buy XTO Energy in $41 billion Deal," http://www.marketwatch.com/story/exxon-mobil-to-buy-xto-energy-in-41-billion-deal-2009-12-14?pagenumber=2
22. Jane Wardell, "Royal Dutch/Shell unveils surprise merger, rise in 3Q," http://www.petroleumnews.com/pntruncate/980696136.shtml
23. http://news.bbc.co.uk/2/hi/149139.stm
24. http://www.bp.com/sectiongenericarticle.do?categoryId=2010203&contentId=2014547
25. http://articles.latimes.com/1999/apr/01/news/mn-23311
26. http://news.bbc.co.uk/2/hi/business/676927.stm
27. http://www.icis.com/Articles/2001/07/16/142791/bp-to-acquire-51-stake-in-germanys-veba-oil-in-swap.html

28. http://www.bp.com/genericarticle.do?categoryId=2012968&contentId=2014392
29. "ENel, Acciona Acquire Endesa with $60 billion," http://www.financialexpress.com/news/enel-acciona-acquire-endesa-with-60-bn-bid/225195/1
30. http://www.fundinguniverse.com/company-histories/Total-Fina-Elf-SA-Company-History.html
31. http://articles.latimes.com/1999/jul/06/business/fi-53297
32. http://www.chevron.com/about/history/1980/
33. http://www.ogj.com/articles/2010/01/partnership-acquires.html
34. Andrew Ross Sorkin and Neela Banerjee, "Chevron Agrees to Buy Texaco for Stock Valued at $36 billion," http://www.nytimes.com/2000/10/16/business/chevron-agrees-to-buy-texaco-for-stock-valued-at-36-billion.html?pagewanted=all&src=pm
35. http://news.bbc.co.uk/2/hi/business/973161.stm
36. Tim Arango, "Chevron Update," http://www.thestreet.com/brknews/energy/1126226.html
37. http://www.thestreet.com/story/10215912/1.html
38. http://www.marketwatch.com/story/chevrontexaco-to-buy-unocal-in-18-billion-deal
39. http://www.sfgate.com/cgi-bin/article.cgi?f=/c/a/2005/04/05/BUGS9C355B1.DTL#ixzz1lrlb2WvD
40. http://dealbook.nytimes.com/2007/02/23/kkr-plans-record-buyout-with-txu-acquisition/
41. http://www.altassets.net/private-equity-news/gs-capital-partners-aig-carlyle-riverstone-to-buy-kinder-morgan-in-22bn-deal.html
42. http://phx.corporate-ir.net/phoenix.zhtml?c=93621&p=irol-newsArticle&ID=899575&highlight
43. http://www2.dupont.com/Heritage/en_US/1981_dupont/1981_overview.html
44. http://www.fundinguniverse.com/company-histories/ConocoPhillips-Company-History.html

7
Mergers and Acquisitions in the Finance Sector

Introduction

The primary motives for mergers for financial consolidation are cost savings and revenue enhancement. Cost savings are attributable to economies of scale, economies of scope and more efficient allocation of resources. Consolidation can lead to increased revenues through its effect on firm size, firm scope or market power. Mergers and acquisitions in the banking sector are basically meant to reap the benefits of economies of scale. Mergers also aim for growth in size.

Synergies in financial sector M&A may arise from client-driven linkages, geographic linkages and product-driven linkages. Client-driven linkages will result when a financial institution serving a particular client or group supplies financial services either to the same or another client in the same group more efficiently. Geographic linkages happen when a financial institution can service a particular client or supply a particular service more efficiently in one geographic area owing to its active presence in another area. Product-driven linkages exist when there is the same or a similar financial service in different client areas.[1]

Economies of scope arises through cross-selling whereby the all-in cost to the buyer of multiple financial services from a single supplier will be less than buying from separate suppliers.

One of the advantages stated for financial sector M&A deals is that the diversification of income from multiple products, client groups and geographies will provide more stability to the financial firms involved.

The major drivers encouraging consolidation are advances in information technology, financial deregulation, globalization of financial markets and real markets, increasing shareholder pressure for financial performance and financial distress. New technological initiatives have led to increased consolidation in the sector to spread the high fixed costs across a large customer base. Technological developments have also made it possible for financial service providers to offer a much broader array of products and services to a larger number of clients across different geographic areas.

Over the past two decades, across the world many governments have removed legal and regulatory barriers to financial industry consolidation. This has facilitated the process of consolidation in the industry, especially cross-border M&A activity. The important characteristics of financial deregulation have been the dismantling of interest rate controls, the removal of barriers between banks and other financial intermediaries and the lowering of entry barriers. This has led to disintermediation, investors demanding higher returns, price competition, reduced margins, falling spreads and competition across geographies, forcing banks to look for new ways to boost revenues.

Technological change has facilitated financial globalization. The advent of the euro accelerated the speed of financial market integration in Europe and promoted cross-border M&A activity. Advances in telecommunications and computing have lowered transaction costs. Factors such as the adoption of monetary union in Europe and international accounting standards have ensured transparency in the pricing of financial services.

In the past M&A in the financial sector was segmented along distinct lines—banking, securities and insurance—in line with official regulation and industry practice. With structural reforms in many countries, the boundaries separating these sectors are becoming increasingly blurred. As a result financial institutions now offer all types of products and services that compete not only against those offered by similar institutions but also against offerings by other categories of service providers. The domestic offshore markets have become competitive with the removal of exchange rate controls and barriers to cross-border capital flows.

In the changed scenario many financial service firms are focusing on M&As for reorienting their product mixes to expand into new profitable areas. Financial services firms with mature products are using M&A to achieve growth and gain complementary skills. M&A are also used to improve market presence in new geographic areas. Many established European banks have acquired smaller UK- and US-based investment firms to become global investment banks. Major banks have also expanded operations in foreign markets, especially in emerging economies, to provide services at local level.

During the 1980s and early 1990s, ownership linkages and alliances were increasingly formed between insurance companies and investment banks. Thus consolidation in the sector was aimed at the concept of "one-stop shopping." There has been considerable restructuring in the insurance sector. Insurance firms merging with banking companies, often termed "bancassurance," have been an important trend in Europe. Through this type of combination, bank acquirers were able to expand their retail banking product lines while insurers gained an established distribution network through the bank branches.

Over 10,000 financial firms were acquired in the industrialized nations during the period 1990–2001.[2] The US banking industry experienced more than 7000 mergers between 1980 and 1998. The 1990s saw some of the largest mergers in banking history in the US. The number of US banks declined by more than a third from 1980 to 1997. Moreover, between 1994 and 2002, more than 1300 new banks were opened in the US in direct response to a perceived decline in service resulting from bank mergers. Simultaneously, the proportion of banking assets accounted for by the 100 largest banking organizations rose from over 50 percent in 1980 to nearly 75 percent in 1997. The reasons for the mergers were a new statutory environment that allowed interstate ownership and branching; banks seeking scale economies; geographical diversification; and increased competitive pressures.[3]

M&A in the financial services sector accelerated in the 1980s and 1990s. In the 1990s, banking mergers dominated M&A activity in the financial sector. Banking firms accounted for 60 percent of all financial mergers and 70 percent of the value of those mergers.

In the US financial mergers were more heavily concentrated in banking during recent decades while in Australia, Netherlands and the UK the trend shows a greater proportion of M&As in the insurance, securities and other segments of financial industry.

M&A within the European financial sector have changed the European banking landscape in the past two decades. The number of European banks decreased from 12,670 in 1985 to 8295 in 1999.[4] This development was mostly driven by M&As among European banks.

The largest European banking groups (BNP Paribas in France, IntesaBsci in Italy, Banco Santander Central Hispano and Banco Bilbao Vizcaya Argentaria in Spain, and NatWest/Royal Bank of Scotland in the UK) were formed as a result of mega deals that happened between 1999 and 2002. The four mega mergers of the US banking industry—Citicorp/Travelers, BankAmerica/NationsBank, Bank One/First Chicago and Norwest/Wells Fargo—took place in the year 1998.

Economic recessions have provided opportunities for financial service firms to launch M&A activity to acquire competitors and portfolios of assets of rival firms In 2008, facing a deep recession, banks and other financial service institutions suffered significant write-downs. Consequently the stock prices of these firms witnessed a drastic decline. As a result more and more financial service firms became candidates for takeovers. During the recession, many companies utilized the opportunity to increase the size of business and enter the "too big to fail" category.

For instance, Barclays acquired assets from Lehman Brothers, Bank of America bought Merrill Lynch, and JPMorgan Chase & Co. acquired Bear Stearns and Washington Mutual. Another example is the Wachovia/ Wells Fargo deal, which took place in 2009. Financial institutions have divested underperforming businesses and implemented cost-efficiency initiatives.

According to the PwC Report 2011, many banks in Europe are looking forward to divest their non-core and capital-intensive assets in order to stabilize their businesses and concentrate resources on fewer stronger sources of value. The report says that a further driver for deal activity is EU state aid requirements, which will force a number of banks to divest significant assets by 2012. In the context of the euro zone crisis, the restructuring of the banking sector remains the central driver of M&A activity in the European financial services industry.

Mergers and acquisitions by Bank of America

Bank of America is one of the four largest banks in the US. In 2008, it was the largest commercial bank in the country by both deposits and market capitalization. In 2010, Bank of America was the fifth largest company in the US in terms of total revenue. According to its own statistics, Bank of America serves one in two households in the US and operates in more than 40 countries. The business segments consist of deposits, global card services, home loans and insurances, global wealth and investment management. Bank of America has 57 million consumers and small business relationships. In 2010, it had 5856 retail branches and 19,700 wealth advisors. The company had $643 billion in loans and $699 billion in deposits. Bank of America provided $92 billion in credit to small and medium-sized businesses in the year 2010.

Mergers by Bank of America

Bank of America's growth strategy has been focused on a series of mergers and acquisitions over a lengthy period of time. In 1960, Security National Bank of Greensboro and American Commercial Bank of Charlotte merged to form North California National Bank (NCNB). In 1981, NCNB

Table 7.1 Biggest finance sector deals

SL	Buyer	Seller	Price in $ billion	Year
1	Royal Bank of Scotland	ABN Amro Holdings	95.6	2007
2	Citicorp	Travelers Group	72.66	1998
3	Nations Bank	Bank of America	61.63	1998
4	J. P. Morgan Chase	Bank One Corp.	58.76	2004
5	Bank of America	Merrill Lynch	50	2008
6	Bank of America	Fleet Boston Fin. Corp.	47	2004
7	Mitsubishi Tokyo	UFJ Holdings	41.43	2005
8	Bank of America	MBNA	35.81	2005
9	CitiGroup	Associates First Capital	31	2000
10	Unicredito Italiano	Capitalia	29.9	2007
11	TPG Capital	ALL TEL	27.9	2007
12	Wachovia	Golden West Financial	25	2006
13	Bank of America	Lasalle Bank	21	2007
14	Bank of New York	Mellon Fin. Corp.	18.30	2007
15	Unicreditano Italiano	Bayerische Hypo/Veriensbank	18.26	2005
16	Wachovia	South Trust	14.30	2004
17	HSBC	Household Finance	14.25	2002
18	Regions Financial Corp.	AmSouth Bancorp.	10	2006
19	Banco Bilbao Vizacaya	Compass Bancshares	9.8	2007
20	Travelers Group	Salomon Brothers	9.3	1997
21	SunTrust	National Commercial Financial	6.9	2004
22	Wachovia	A. G. Edwards	6.8	2007
23	AmSouth Bancorp.	First American National Bank	6.3	1999
24	Regional Financial Corp.	Union Planters	5.9	2004
25	State Street Corp.	Investors Financial Services	4.2	2007
26	Bank of America	Countrywide	4	2008
27	Wachovia	Westcorp Inc.	3.9	2006

Table 7.2 Financial highlights of Bank of America ($ billion)

	2008	2009	2010
Total net revenue	739.76	120.944	111.390
Total assets	1817.943	2230.232	2264.909
Total deposits	882.997	991.611	1010.430
Total loans and leases	931.446	900.128	940.440

acquired First National Bank of Lake City Florida. In the 1980s and 1990s, NCNB grew in size by a series of mergers and acquisitions. In 1986, NCNB acquired Banker's Trust, an acquisition that added about $4 billion in assets to NCNB, with a network of 355 branches in the Carolinas.

In 1988, NCNB acquired the First Republic Bank. By early 1990, NCNB had become the tenth largest bank in US.

In 1991, NCNB acquired the C&S/Sovran of Atlanta and Norfolk, and changed the name to NationsBank. In 1993, NationsBank acquired MNC Financial. This acquisition gave NationsBank a competitive advantage as MNC Financial had a significant presence in the District of Columbia, Maryland and Virginia. In 1997, it acquired Barnett Bank, then the largest financial institution in the State of Florida. In the same year, NationsBank also acquired Boatmen's Bank. By acquiring the fifth largest bank NationsBank now became the leading financial institution in three leading geographic regions and served more than 13 million customers in 16 states.

In 1998, NationsBank acquired California-based BankAmerica Corporation and became Bank of America. With the acquisition of Bank of America, the new financial institution became the first coast-to-coast retail banking franchise in the US.

In 1999, Fleet Financial Corporation had acquired BankBoston Corporation to form the fifth largest bank, named FleetBoston Financial. In 2004, Bank of America acquired FleetBoston Financial. In the same year it acquired National Processing Company, which was engaged in the processing of Visa and MasterCard transactions.

With the acquisition of MBNA in 2006, Bank of America became the leading credit card issuer in the world. In 2007, it acquired US Trust and expanded its services to high net worth individuals. Again in 2007, Bank of America secured a strong foothold in the Midwest region through the acquisition of Chicago-originated LaSalle Bank. With the acquisition of Countrywide Financial Corporation, Bank of America became the largest mortgage lender and loan service provider in the US. In the midst of the economic crisis of 2008, Bank of America acquired Merrill Lynch, extending its reach to retail brokerage and wealth management divisions.

As a result of its mergers and acquisitions, Bank of America became the largest issuer of credit, debit and prepaid cards in the world based on purchase volume. Bank of America has the largest consumer and small business bank in the US.

The formation of Bank of America

In 1998, NationsBank and BankAmerica Corporation merged to form Bank of America. This merger resulted in the union of second largest financial institution based on deposits with the largest bank in the Southeast of the US. NationsBank over the decades had undertaken a series of acquisitions to become the largest and fastest-growing financial institution in North Carolina. In the 1980s, NationsBank acquired First National Bank of Lake City and First Republic Bank of Dallas. The primary focus of the bank was to grow in the Southeastern region. In the 1990s, NationsBank expanded into Georgia, Missouri and Florida by acquiring A+S Sovran Corp., Boatmen's Bank and Barnett Bank.

Regulatory hurdles hindered Bank of America, based in the western region of San Francisco, from expanding. The Banking Holding Company Act 1956 forced Bank of America to split off its insurance program. Bank of America is known for its pioneering technological innovations such as automated check processing, magnetic ink character recognition and the first bank credit card—the Bank Americard, which later became Visa. In 1983, Bank of America acquired SeaFirst Corp. of Seattle. In the early 1990s, the acquisition of Security Pacific Corp., Continental Illinois National Bank and Trust Company of Chicago catapulted Bank of America to the position of second largest deposit-based financial institution behind NationsBank.

The merger between the NationsBank and BankAmerica Corporation established the first coast-to-coast interstate retail and commercial retail lending giant in US history. D. E. Shaw & Co., the hedge fund that ran numerous businesses for Bank of America, was lent $1.4 billion by Bank of America in 1997, but suffered significant losses in Russia's bond default in 1998. Bank of America had already suffered heavy losses in 1986 and 1987 on the placement of a series of bad loans in Latin America.

The company's 1998 losses were followed by the acquisition of Bank of America by NationsBank. Technically the deal was a purchase of BankAmerica Corporation by NationsBank, but the deal was structured as a merger with NationsBank, and the new entity was renamed as Bank of America. The deal was valued at approximately $64.8 billion. The new combined bank had combined assets of approximately $570 billion as well as 4800 branches in 22 states.

The acquisition of FleetBoston

In 1999, Fleet Bank merged with Bank of Boston in a $16 billion deal to form FleetBoston, and FleetBoston merged with Summit Bankcorp in a $7 billion deal in 2000. BankBoston was formed in 1996 from the merger between Bank of Boston and BayBank. FleetBoston was the seventh largest bank in the US, with 20 million customers worldwide and revenues of $12 billion as of 2003. After suffering huge losses in Latin America and loan defaults by Enron and other companies, Fleet was aiming to restructure into a consumer bank.

In 2004, Bank of America acquired FleetBoston for $47 billion in a stock swap deal. Under the terms of the deal Fleet shareholders received 0.5553 share of Bank of America for each one share of Fleet, or $45.46 a share, which represented a premium of 43 percent for the target company.

The acquisition created a bank with 33 million customers. As a result of the deal, Bank of America acquired the largest FDIC-rated deposit market share in the US. With assets worth $933 billion, Bank of America became the second largest bank in the US behind Citigroup and also had the maximum retail outlets in the country. The deal gave Bank of America access to the Northeast region. The strategic motive behind the acquisition was to blend the Bank of America's operations in Southern and Western States with FleetBoston's competitive position in the New England region. The combined bank had 5700 retail banking offices and 16,500 automatic teller machines in 29 states. The cost synergies from the deal were expected to be approximately $1.1 billion, which was equal to 6 percent of Fleet's and Bank of America operating expenses. The deal was the biggest for Bank of America in five years since its merger with NationsBank.

The acquisition of MBNA

MBNA, the credit card company, was the leader is affinity marketing, with an established branding relationship with 350 financial institutions and more than 5000 organizations, including sports organizations like the National Football League and NASCAR. MBNA was facing sluggish top-line growth by mid-2000.

In 2006, Bank of America Corp acquired MBNA in a stock-and-cash deal. The deal was valued at approximately $35 billion. Under the terms of the deal, MBNA shareholders received 0.5009 common shares of Bank of America plus $4.125 in cash for each share. The deal valued MBNA at $27.50 per share, which represented a premium of 31 percent.

The acquisition transformed Bank of America into one of the world's largest credit card issuers. With 40 million credit card accounts, Bank of America became one of the leading worldwide payment service companies and issuer of credit, debit and prepaid cards based on total purchase volume. The combination of the powerful distribution channel of Bank of America with the customer base of MBNA products led to significant synergistic growth opportunities. The acquisition brought to the bank expertise in affinity marketing and electronic transaction processing and provided new opportunities to cross-sell each other's products and services. The acquisition added 20 million customer accounts to the portfolio of Bank of America.

Bank of America became a leader in debt card transactions, with approximately 16 percent of market share. The acquisition facilitated entry for Bank of America's credit card offerings in Canada, the UK, Spain and Ireland.

In 2007, the acquisition achieved cost savings of approximately $850 million. This was partly achieved by Bank of America eliminating 6000 jobs across both companies, by reducing overlapping technology and from vendor leverage.

The acquisition of LaSalle Bank

In 2007, ABN Amro, the parent company of LaSalle Bank, sold it to Bank of America in a deal valued at $21 billion. At the time of acquisition LaSalle was a top-20 US bank holding company, with $113 billion in total assets. The bank had retail and commercial operations in 20 states and 26 cities across the US.

By acquiring LaSalle Bank, Bank of America gained market share in Chicago and Detroit, which were the two of the ten largest metropolitan areas in the US. The purchase gave Bank of America an additional 411 branches, 17,000 commercial banking clients, 1.4 million retail customers and 1500 ATMs in the Chicago, Michigan and Indiana areas. The acquisition of LaSalle placed Bank of America ahead of JPMorgan Chase & Co. in Chicago. The purchase also made Bank of America the biggest bank in Michigan. With the acquisition, Bank of America now had more than 14 percent of the deposit market share in Chicago. Bank of America expected after-tax cost savings of $800 million in 2008.

The acquisition of Countrywide

In the midst of the worst housing slump ever, in 2008, Bank of America bought the largest mortgage lender, Countrywide Financial Corporation, for about $4 billion. Countrywide faced a crisis brought about by rising defaults among subprime borrowers. Shareholders of Countrywide received 0.1822 of a share of Bank of America stock in exchange for each share of Countrywide.

The purchase gave Bank of America about 9 million borrowers to whom the bank could sell other products. With the acquisition, Bank of America had become US's dominant home lender, accounting for one out of every four mortgages. With the addition of Countrywide's $209 billion in assets, Bank of America became the second biggest bank by assets next only to Citigroup. But the deal soon went sour. Bank of America had to write down the value of Countrywide assets by 10 percent owing to lower housing values, and had inherited huge mortgages that resulted in significant losses. Bank of America's mortgage business, which included Countrywide, registered losses of $8.9 billion in 2010 and $3.8 billion in 2009. The bank had racked up nearly $40 billion in losses by 2011.

The acquisition of Merrill Lynch

During the economic crisis of 2008, Bank of America purchased the crisis-affected world's largest retail brokerage firm, Merrill Lynch, in an all-stock deal worth $50 billion. Merrill Lynch & Co., Inc. offered wealth management, investment banking and securities brokerage services. It was the one of the premier wealth management, capital markets and advisory companies in the world. Bank of America exchanged 0.8595 Bank of America shares for each Merrill Lynch common share. The purchase price was $29 per share, representing a 70 percent premium to Merrill Lynch's share price. Merrill Lynch had been battered by $52.2 billion in losses and writedowns from subprime mortgage-contaminated securities and its stock value had plunged more than 80 percent from its peak of $97.53 in 2007. The buyout gave Bank of America a sales force of 16,690 brokers who managed $1.6 trillion assets in value.

RBS Consortium's acquisition of ABN Amro

ABN Amro is a leading commercial bank based in the Netherlands, with a major global presence, serving retail, private and commercial banking customers with a comprehensive range of products and services. The bank had an extensive business network across North America, Latin America, the Caribbean islands, Europe, the Middle East, Africa and the Asia Pacific region. In November 2007, a consortium led by Royal Bank of Scotland (RBS) acquired the Dutch bank in a deal that became the largest financial services merger in history. The consortium consisted of RBS, Fortis Group of Belgium and Santander Central Hispano of Spain. In October 2008, the Dutch Government bought Fortis Bank Nederland, including its interests in ABN Amro, and in December 2008, the Dutch state replaced Fortis as a stakeholder in RFS Holdings. ABN Amro is now owned by RBS, Santander and the Dutch Government. In 2010, ABN Amro and Fortis Bank Nederland merged to form the current ABN Amro Bank N. V.

The offer comprised of €35.6 in cash plus 0.296 new RBS shares for every ABN Amro share. RBS, Fortis and Santander paid respectively 38.3 percent, 33.8 percent and 27.9 percent of the consideration amount. The RBS offer for ABN Amro was roughly €38 a share—equivalent to a premium of more than 70 percent for ABN Amro.

The consortium paid three times the book value for ABN Amro. But by the time the deal was settled, ABN Amro had sold off its Chicago-based subsidiary LaSalle Bank to Bank of America. Thus RBS was left with the London-based investment banking and Asian operations. The Government had to bail out RBS, which was finding it difficult to cope with the costs of its acquisitions. The ABN acquisition was stated to be the major reason for the potential loss by RBS of $41 billion for 2008. RBS also suffered losses through credit impairment charges. Fortis Bank was nationalized by the Dutch Government.

Acquisitions by Citicorp

Citigroup, established in 1812, is a global diversified financial services holding company providing business services to consumers, corporation, governments and institutions. Citigroup consists of two primary business segments: Citicorp and Citi Holdings. The broad divisions of Citicorp are Regional Consumer Banking Business and the Institutional Client Group. Citi Holdings consist of Citi's brokerage and asset management, local consumer lending business and a special asset pool. Citi has more than 200 million customer accounts and a presence in more than 160 countries. Citicorp is the company's global bank for consumers and businesses, and represents Citi's core franchise.

Citigroup made 315 acquisitions and took stakes in 242 companies during the period 1981–2011.[5]

Citicorp's merger with Travelers Group

In 1998, Citicorp and Travelers Group merged together to form the world's biggest financial services company, named Citigroup, offering banking, insurance and investment operations in over 100 countries. Travelers Group was a New York-based financial services firm whose companies included Salomon, brokerage firm Smith Barney, Travelers Life & Annuity and Primerica Financial Services. The merged company

Table 7.3 Citigroup, Inc. and subsidiaries: Financial highlights ($ billion)

	2008	2009	2010
Revenues	106.499	76.635	79.516
Net income	−27.684	−1.606	10.602
Deposits	774.2	835.9	845
Market capitalization	37	94	137
Assets	1938	1856.646	1913.902

retained Travelers familiar red umbrella as a part of its logo. Over the decades, Citicorp had developed a strong global retail franchise along with worldwide corporate banking business. Travelers had evolved as a major investment and insurance conglomerate. Through the merger Citicorp secured access to an expanded client base of investors and insurance customers. Travelers in turn was able to market mutual funds and insurance to Citicorp's retail customers. The merger brought investment products such as stocks and bonds within the reach of middle-class customers throughout the world.

With approximately $698 billion in assets and $135 billion in market capitalization, the new combined group became the largest financial firm in the world, ahead of Tokyo-Mitsubishi Bank Ltd. The combined group had revenues of about $50 billion and operating income of approximately $7.5 billion.

The merger deal was driven by the logic of creating financial services one-stop shopping for customers by offering traditional banking, investment banking, brokerage and insurance services under one umbrella throughout the world. At the time of merger, Citicorp was the largest issuer of credit cards in the world.

Citicorp shareholders received 2.5 shares and Travelers shareholders one share in the new company for each share they held. Each company's shareholders owned 50 percent of the combined company. The deal was valued at $70 billion.

Over a period of years, Citicorp had also acquired stakes in international banks and brokerage firms including Nikko Beans, the Japanese online brokerage firm; Bank Handlowy Warszawie, a leading corporate bank in Poland; Mexico's Banacci; and Diner's Club of Europe. By acquiring the European American Bank in 2001, Citigroup added 97 branches in the New York area. Citicorp also added 352 branches and 1.5 million new customers in the California and Nevada markets by acquiring Golden State Bancorp.

The acquisition of Associates First Capital

Associates First Capital, established in 1918, was a major player in various business activities such as issuing credit cards, providing home equity and mortgage loans, and leasing trucks and heavy equipment. Associates First Capital, which was first owned by Gulf & Western Corporation, was sold to Ford Motor Company, which later spun it off. In 2000, Citigroup bought the Associates First Capital Corporation, the largest American consumer finance company, in a stock deal valued at $31.1 billion. By this acquisition, Citigroup became the fifth biggest consumer finance company in Japan, which was the world's second largest market for consumer lending. The acquisition also improved Citigroup's position in the credit card and commercial leasing business. The combined companies had about 2000 retail branches across the US. Citigroup became the top US provider of credit cards, home equity loans and commercial leasing services. Associates First had more than 700,000 customers and was the fifth largest consumer finance company in Japan. Associates First operated private label credit card programs for several operators of gas station and retailers including Radio Shack. Citicorp had the biggest market share in the credit card business through its Citibank Visa and MasterCard products.

Under the terms of the deal, Citigroup exchanged 0.7334 share of its stock for each share of Associates First Capital. Associates was valued at $42.49 per share, which represented a premium of 52 percent for the company. Associates First shareholders owned about 10 percent of Citigroup shares following the deal. On account of considerable overlap of businesses, duplicated services were eliminated with cost savings to the combined company. The deal was expected to result in cost savings of approximately $400 million and $600 million within two years of the acquisition.

Travelers Group acquisition of Salomon Brothers

In the year before its merger with Citicorp, Travelers Group acquired the investment banking powerhouse Salomon Brothers in a stock deal valued at $9 billion, or $78.46 per Salomon share. Salomon was then absorbed into the Travelers' brokerage firm Smith Barney to form Salomon Smith Barney. Travelers issued 1.13 shares of its stock for each share of Salomon, Inc. The merged entity became the second largest securities firm in the US. Through this acquisition Travelers Group extended its base overseas as established a foothold in investment banking. In the US, the new entity was ranked third in equity underwriting, first in municipal underwriting, fourth in global equity underwriting and second in underwriting of all American and international debt offerings. The merged company had about 10,400 financial consultants in 438 offices and 5 million customers, with operations in 26 countries. The company had approximately $538.1 billion of assets in its client accounts.

Acquisitions by JPMorgan Chase Bank

JPMorgan Chase is one of the oldest and largest financial institutions in the world, with assets worth $2.3 trillion. JPMorgan Chase & Co. is the name of the holding company, and the firm serves its customers and clients under its Chase and JP Morgan brands. The US consumer and commercial banking businesses serve customers under the Chase brand. The businesses under the JP Morgan brand include investment banking, asset management, treasury services, worldwide securities services, private banking and private client services. The bank has a presence in more than 60 countries.

JPMorgan Chase is a product of a series of mergers and acquisitions. All four of JPMorgan Chase's major New York City heritage firms—JP Morgan & Co., The Chase Manhattan Bank, Manufacturers Hanover Trust Co. and Chemical Bank—grew through mergers in the 1950s and 1960s.

Merger highlights: 1990–2010

Year	Deals
1991	Manufacturers Hanover Corp. merges with Chemical Banking Corp., then the second largest banking institution in the US.
1995	First Chicago Corp. merges with NBD Bancorp to form First Chicago NBD.
1996	Chase Manhattan Corp. absorbs Chemical Banking Corp.
1998	Bank One Corp. merges with First Chicago NBD under the name of Bank One Corp.
2000	JP Morgan & Co. merges with Chase Manhattan Corp. to form JPMorgan Chase & Co.
2004	JPMorgan Chase & Co. acquires Bank One Corporation.
2008	JPMorgan Chase & Co. acquires The Bear Stearns Companies, Inc.
2008	JPMorgan Chase & Co. acquires the deposits, assets and certain liabilities of Washington Mutual's banking operations.
2010	JP Morgan acquired full ownership of its UK joint venture, JP Morgan Cazenove.

The JP Morgan and Chase Manhattan merger

In 2000, Chase Manhattan Corp. merged with JP Morgan & Co., Inc., in effect combining four of the largest and oldest money center banking institutions in New York City (Morgan, Chase, Chemical and Manufacturers Hanover) into one firm now known as JPMorgan

Chase & Co. The Chase Bank was the product of the union of three New York banks that had combined in the previous decade—Chemical Bank, which purchased Chase Manhattan in 1996 and Manufacturers Hanover, which Chemical bought in 1991. In this merger deal, Chase bought out its US rival in a $34 billion all-stock deal. The combined bank became the third largest bank holding company in US after Citigroup and Bank of America, with assets of $660 billion. The deal was valued at $207 a share, which represented a 16.7 percent premium over Morgan's closing price before the merger announcement. The merger motive was to satisfy Chase's goal of acquiring a major investment banking firm. The merger resulted in cost savings of approximately $1.5 billion, which came from real estate, systems integration and reduced staffing. The new bank consolidated its ranking position in asset management and wealth management. In 2007, the bank became the largest hedge fund firm in the US.

The merger of Bank One with JPMorgan Chase

In 2004, JPMorgan Chase took over Bank One in a $58 billion deal. Under the terms of the deal, Bank One shareholders received 1.32 JP Morgan shares for each Bank One share, valuing Bank One at $51.77 a share, which represented a premium of 14.5 percent over Bank One's closing price in the period before the merger. The new combined company became the US's second-biggest bank, with $1 trillion of assets and 2300 branches in 17 states, centered in the Midwest and Northeast regions. The deal combined the investment and commercial banking strength of JP Morgan with the consumer banking operations power of Bank One. This model of integration was expected to lead to less volatile earnings and a higher market valuation. JP Morgan was able to consolidate its position in the retail and credit card segment as Bank One was the world's largest Visa Card issuer. The merger also facilitated the cross-selling of each other's products.

Cost-cutting was one of the strategic aims of the deal. The merger eliminated about 10,000 jobs as a part of an effort to attain cost savings of $2.2 billion within a three-year period. Though technically the deal was a takeover of Bank One by JP Morgan the new board consisted of equal numbers of members from each bank. The merger costs were expected to be $3 billion.

Acquisitions by Wachovia

Wachovia Corporation is a diversified financial services company based in the US that provides a broad range of banking, asset management, wealth management and corporate and investment banking products and services. In 2001, First Union Corporation merged into Wachovia Corporation. In the same year Wachovia sold off its $8 billion credit card portfolio to Bank One. In 2003, the Prudential Securities Division of Prudential Financial, Inc. merged with Wachovia Securities to form Wachovia Securities LLC. Again in 2003, Wachovia acquired Metropolitan West Securities, an affiliate company of Metropolitan West Financial.

In 2004, Wachovia Corp. purchased SouthTrust Corporation in a $14.3 billion stock deal that created the largest bank in the Southeast US, with an 18 percent deposit share. It gave Wachovia entry into the fast-growing Texas market. SouthTrust shareholders received 0.89 share of Wachovia for each of their shares, worth about $41.83. The combined company had $464 billion of assets, $267 billion of deposits, 3200 branches, 5300 automated teller machines and 98,000 employees.

In 2006, Wachovia Corp. completed the acquisition of Westcorp for $3.42 billion by which the company expanded its auto finance group into a national business with offices in 47 US states. Westcorp is a financial services holding company whose principal subsidiaries are WFS Financial, Inc. and Western Financial Bank. Wachovia also acquired the 16 percent of Western Financial Bank held by the public. This acquisition made Wachovia the ninth largest auto finance lender in the US auto finance market.

In 2006, Wachovia Corp. acquired Golden West Financial Corp., the parent company of World Savings Bank, in a $25.5 billion stock-and-cash deal valued at $81.07 per share. Shareholders of Golden West received 1.051 shares of Wachovia common stock and $18.65 in cash for each share of Golden West stock owned. The deal gave Wachovia an additional 285 bank branches, with $62 billion in retail deposits in ten states and six new markets. The combined company had assets of $669 billion. Wachovia also gained the mortgage lending operations under the World Savings Bank name in 39 states. Golden West, which operates its branches under the World Savings brand. is one of the US's biggest mortgage lenders.

In 2007, Wachovia purchased A.G. Edwards for $6.8 billion to create the second largest retail brokerage firm in the US. Shareholders of A.G. Edwards received 0.9844 of a Wachovia share and $35.80 in cash for each share. A.G. Edwards was the largest independent US brokerage firm, with 6618 brokers and $374 billion of client assets. Wachovia Securities has 8166 brokers and $773 billion of client assets.

In 2009, Wachovia was purchased by Wells Fargo & Company, the diversified financial services company, for $12.7 billion. Wells Fargo is the second-largest mortgage lender in the US. Wells Fargo had to write down $71.4 billion of Wachovia's $482.4 billion loan portfolio. Wachovia shareholders received 0.1991 of a Wells Fargo share for each of their shares, valuing the bank at $5.87 per share. That was down from $59.39 when the Golden West merger was announced in May 2006. The Wachovia/Wells Fargo deal came in a turbulent period when the banks and financial firms were in the midst of ongoing credit crisis, which had led to the bankruptcy of Lehman Brothers Holding, Inc. and failure of Washington Mutual.

The Mitsubishi/UFJ Financial Group merger

Mitsubishi UFJ Financial Group (MUFG) is among Japan's largest financial groups and one of the world's leading banking institutions. In 2005, UFJ Holdings, Inc., the fourth biggest bank, was acquired by Mitsubishi Tokyo Financial Group, Inc. to create the world's biggest bank. Prior to the merger, the Tokyo-based Mitsubishi Tokyo Financial Group was the second largest banking institution in the country by number of assets.

UFJ Holdings was established in 2001 by the merger between Toyo Trust and Banking (owned by the Toyota Motor Corporation), Tokai Bank and Sanwa Bank. It offered various financial services, including securities, consumer finance, credit cards and asset management. The combined assets were worth $1.74 trillion, which was bigger than Citigroup's assets of $1.094 trillion. The merged bank was renamed the Mitsubishi UFJ Financial Group. The exchange ratio was 0.62 Mitsubishi Tokyo shares to one UFJ share.

UFJ was searching for a strong merger partner as the bank had embattled finances. The merger in fact acted as a rescue plan for UFJ after three years of heavy losses. The combination resulted in the reduction of about 8 percent of the global workforce. In September 2008, MUFG announced its intent to purchase 20 percent of the American financial service provider Morgan Stanley.

Other major acquisitions in the banking industry

The Northwest/Wells Fargo merger

In 1998, Wells Fargo, the diversified financial services company, merged with Northwest Financial, the premier consumer finance company, to form the new Wells Fargo. The combined banking franchise had 2859 stores and covered 21 states from California to Ohio.

Acquisitions by Unicredito Italiano

Unicredito Italiano (UCI) is one of Italy's largest banking groups. It was created by the merger of Credito Italiano and Rolo Banca 1473, an Italian regional bank, in 1999. UCI offers universal banking services, with retail and corporate lending, asset management, private banking and investment banking in Italy, Germany, Austria and Central and Eastern Europe. In 1999, UCI acquired the Polish bank Bank Pekao, and in the following year Bulbank (Bulgaria), Pol'nobanca and Unibanka (Slovakia). In 2000, the group also acquired the US fund manager Pioneer Investment of Boston, which was followed by the creation of Pioneer Global Asset Management. In 2002, UCI acquired banks including Zagrebacka Banka (Croatia), Demirbank Romania—then UniCredit Romania—and Živnostenskå Banka (Czech Republic).

In 2005, UCI acquired the German bank Hypo Vereinsbank (HVB), which was the largest cross-border deal in European banking to date. One HVB share was exchanged for five Unicredito shares.

In 2007, UCI completed the merger with Italy's third largest bank, Capitalia SpA, in a stock swap deal valued at $29.47 billion. This merger consolidated UCI's position as Italy's largest bank by market value, which amounted to approximately $135 billion. With a 16 percent market share UCI inched closer to the market leader Intesa Sanpaolo. UCI paid 1.12 of its share for each Capitalia share. With this acquisition, UCI counted 9200 bank branches globally, with 40 million customers in countries from Italy to Russia. It became the second biggest bank in Germany and the leading bank in Eastern Europe.

Other major acquisitions

In 2007, the telecommunications company Alltel was acquired by TPG Capital, the global buyout firm of TPG and GS Capital Partners (GSCP), a subsidiary of Goldman Sachs. TPG Capital and GSCP acquired all common stock of Alltel for $71.50 per share in cash. The total amount paid was $27.5 billion.

In 2007, The Bank of New York Company, Inc. and Mellon Financial Corporation merged to form a new company named The Bank of New York Mellon Corporation. Under the terms of the merger agreement, each share of The Bank of New York common stock was converted into 0.9434 share of The Bank of New York Mellon common stock, and each share of Mellon Financial Corporation common stock converted into one share of The Bank of New York Mellon common stock. The new combined company had about $12.5 billion of annual revenues. In 2010, Bank of New York Mellon purchased the global investment servicing unit of PNC Financial Services Group, Inc., for $2.31 billion.

HSBC acquired the scandal-plagued subprime lender Household International in 2002 for approximately $14 billion. HSBC's broad spread of business was diversified through the addition of Household's consumer lending portfolios. The acquisition of Household also helped HSBC to maintain a balanced worldwide portfolio consisting of approximately 60 percent of HSBC's assets in the Americas, Asia and the Middle East, and 40 percent in Europe.

In 2006, US-based Regions Financial Corporation acquired its rival AmSouth Bancorporation for approximately $10 billion in stock, including options. Under the terms of the agreement, each share of AmSouth Bancorporation was exchanged for 0.7974 shares of Regions Financial common stock. The combined financial institution had almost $140 billion in assets and $100 billion in deposits throughout its 2000 branches in 16 states.

In 2007, Spain's second largest bank, Banco Bilbao Vizcaya Argentaria SA (BBVA), acquired the US bank Compass Bancshares in a cash-and-stock deal valued at $9.8 billion. Compass shareholders were given the option to receive either 2.8 BBVA American Depository Shares (ADS) or $71.82 in cash per share. BBVA operated in 35 countries and had substantial banking interests in the Americas. The transaction facilitated BBVA's growth in Texas and created the largest regional bank across the Sunbelt region.

In 2004, SunTrust Banks, Inc. acquired National Commerce Financial Corp. for $6.98 billion to create the seventh-largest US bank. First American National Bank was a subsidiary of First American National Corporation. In 2000 it was acquired by AmSouth Bancorporation.

Additional References

1. Stephen Lumbkin, *Mergers and Acquisitions in the Financial Services Sector, 2000: Insurance and Private Pensions Compendium for Emerging Economies*, Book 1 Part 1:5c (Japan: OECD Publications, 2000).
2. Ivan de Souza, Gerald Adolph, Alan Gemes and Roberto Marchi, *Perils of Financial Sector M&A: Seven Steps to Successful Integration*, Booz & Co. report, 2009.
3. Group of Ten, *Report on Consolidation in the Financial Sector*, 2001, www.OECD.org
4. PwC, *Sharing Deal Insight Report, Q1 2011*.

5. http://message.bankofamerica.com/heritage/#/merger-history
6. Annual Report, Bank of America.
7. http://media.corporate-ir.net/media_files/irol/71/71595/reports/2010_AR.pdf
8. http://www.soc.duke.edu/NC_GlobalEconomy/pdfs/banks/BankingCS_BankofAmerica.pdf
9. http://www.bizaims.com/articles/banks%20financial%20activity/bank%20america%20largest%20commercial%20bank%20usa
10. http://www.cbsnews.com/stories/2003/10/27/national/main580134.shtml
11. http://money.cnn.com/2003/10/27/news/companies/ba_fleet/index.htm
12. "Bank of America and FleetBoston: Dud Deal?" December 3, 2003, in Knowledge@Wharton. http://knowledge.wharton.upenn.edu/article.cfm?articleid=889
13. Rebecca Byrne, "Bank of America to Acquire Fleet for $47 billion," http://www.thestreet.com/markets/rebeccabyrne/10122344.html
14. http://www.cbsnews.com/stories/2006/01/01/business/main1172538.shtml
15. http://www.msnbc.msn.com/id/8414809/ns/business-us_business/t/bank-america-buys-credit-card-firm-mbna/
16. http://www.bankofamerica.com/annualreport/2005/how_we_grow/hwg3_opportunities_2.cfm
17. Krysten Crawford, "Bank of America Inks $35B Card Deal," http://money.cnn.com/2005/06/30/news/fortune500/boa/index.htm
18. http://mediaroom.bankofamerica.com/phoenix.zhtml?c=234503&p=irol-newsArticle&ID=1389809&highlight=
19. http://www.bizjournals.com/columbus/stories/2007/10/01/daily1.html
20. http://www.seattlepi.com/business/article/Bank-of-America-to-buy-LaSalle-Bank-in-ABN-1235086.php
21. David Mildenberg, "Bank of America to Acquire Countrywide for $4 billion," http://www.bloomberg.com/apps/news?pid=newsarchive&sid=aqKE9kRcKDEw
22. Shanti Bhardwaj, "Bank of America Will Fix Countrywide: Berkowitz," http://www.thestreet.com/story/11415339/1/bank-of-america-will-fix-countrywide-berkowitz.html?cm_ven=GOOGLEN
23. http://blogs.wsj.com/deals/2011/06/29/bank-of-america-countrywide-worst-deal-in-history
24. http://www.cnbc.com/id/26708319/Bank_of_America_to_Buy_Merrill_Lynch_for_50_Billion
25. http://www.msnbc.msn.com/id/26708958/ns/business-us_business/t/bank-america-purchase-merrill-lynch/
26. David M. and Bradley K. *Bank of America to acquire Merrill as crisis deepens*, Rick Green, ed. http://www.bloomberg.com/apps/news?pid=newsarchive&sid=a9O9JGOLdI_U
27. http://www.allbusiness.com/banking-finance/financial-markets-investing-securities/14745052-1.html#ixzz1mS1fdYA
28. http://www.fasken.com/royal-bank-of-scotland-consortium-acquires-abn-amro-in-largest-financial-services-merger-in-history/
29. http://news.bbc.co.uk/2/hi/business/7033176.stm
30. http://www.independent.co.uk/news/business/analysis-and-features/was-abn-the-worst-takeover-deal-ever-1451520.html
31. http://www.banking-business-review.com/companies/abn_amro_holding_nv

32. Mitchell Martin, "Citicorp and Travelers Plan to Merge in Record $70 billion Deal: A new no. 1: Financial Giants Unite," www.nytimes.com/1998/04/07/news/07iht-citi.t.html
33. http://www.independent.co.uk/news/business/citicorp-and-travelers-in-155bn-merger-1155012.html
34. http://money.cnn.com/1998/04/06/deals/travelers/
35. Patrick McGeehan, "Citigroup to Buy Associates First for $31 billion," http://www.nytimes.com/2000/09/07/business/citigroup-to-buy-associates-first-for-31-billion.html?pagewanted=all&src=pm
36. http://money.cnn.com/2000/09/06/deals/citigroup/index.htm
37. http://amarillo.com/stories/100200/bus_100200-8.shtml
38. Peter Truell, "A Wall Street Behemoth: The Deal; Travelers to buy Salomon, Making a Wall St. Giant," http://www.nytimes.com/1997/09/25/business/a-wall-street-behemoth-the-deal-travelers-to-buy-salomon-making-a-wall-st-giant.html?pagewanted=all&src=pm
39. Thomas S. Mulligan, "Travelers to Buy Salomon Bros. for $9 billion," http://articles.latimes.com/1997/sep/25/news/mn-35937
40. Andrew Garfield, "Chase Acquires JP Morgan for $34bn, but 10,000 Jobs May Go," http://www.independent.co.uk/news/business/news/chase-acquires-jp-morgan-for-34bn-but-10000-jobs-may-go-699819.html
41. http://money.cnn.com/2000/09/13/deals/chase_morgan/
42. Thor Valdmanis, Christine Dugas and Adam Shell, "J. P. Morgan, Bank One to Join," http://www.usatoday.com/money/industries/banking/2004-01-14-jpmorgan-bankone_x.htm
43. http://www.smh.com.au/articles/2004/01/15/1073877965942.html
44. http://money.cnn.com/2004/01/14/news/deals/jpmorgan_bankone/
45. www.wellsfargo.com
46. http://www.bizjournals.com/sanantonio/stories/2006/05/08/daily1.html
47. http://money.cnn.com/2004/06/21/news/fortune500/wachovia_southtrust/
48. http://www.prnewswire.com/news-releases/wachovia-corporation-to-acquire-westcorp-and-wfs-financial-inc-in-391-billion-transaction-54876587.html
49. http://www.msnbc.msn.com/id/12680868/ns/business-us_business/t/wachovia-acquires-golden-west-financial/
50. http://www.reuters.com/article/2007/05/31/us-agedwards-wachovia-idUSWEN848520070531
51. http://www.wa-pedia.com/forum/economy-47/ufj-tokyo-mitsubishi-bank-plan-mega-merger-10030/
52. http://www.msnbc.msn.com/id/6992181/ns/business-world_business/t/tokyo-mitsubishi-ufj-set-merger-terms/
53. http://commercialbanksguide.com/mitsubishi+financial+group/
54. http://www.borsaitaliana.it/mediasource/star/db/pdf/63508.pdf
55. Steve Goldstein, "UniCredit to Buy Capitalia in $29 billion Deal," http://articles.marketwatch.com/2007-05-20/news/30710239_1
56. Paolo Biondi and Alberto Sisto, "UniCredit Agrees to Buy Capitalia in £29bln Deal," http://www.reuters.com/article/2007/05/20/us-capitalia-unicredit-idUSL184229220070520
57. http://www.bankpedia.org/eng/voce.php?VoceID=234
58. http://www.mobiledia.com/news/59365.html

59. http://www.innercitypress.org/hsbc.html
60. http://www.hsbc.com/1/2/newsroom/news/2003/hsbc-completes-the-acquisition-of-household
61. http://phx.corporate-ir.net/phoenix.zhtml?c=65036&p=irol-fundBankingMergersDetailWhole&id=92523&type=WHOLE
62. http://phx.corporate-ir.net/phoenix.zhtml?c=77589&p=irol-newsArticle&ID=964154&highlight=

8
Mergers and Acquisitions in the Metal Sector

Introduction

Consolidation is a structural change that has become an inevitable phenomenon in a world steel industry facing an accumulation of excess capacity. During the past two decades the steel industry has witnessed mergers, concentration of resources and streamlining of operations between steel mills, raw material suppliers, iron and steel manufacturers, equipment manufacturers and traders, particularly in Europe and the US.

The steel industry is a highly fragmented industry with the top five steel companies accounting for 20 percent of market share. The remaining 80 percent is held by small and largely fragmented local steel companies. The top three auto giants have approximately 30 percent of the sales while the world's biggest iron ore producers control about 75 percent of the production of steel. But the top two steel makers have just approximately 13 percent of the steel industry market share. According to a PwC report for 2011, 122 deals worth $455.2 billion took place in 2011 compared to 106 deals of $92.6 billion in 2010.

Consolidation in the industry has been highlighted by the need to reduce the cost of production of steel and to supply steel at low, competitive prices. Major steel producers seek low-cost producers in new markets or aim to consolidate their position in existing markets.

M&A activity in the steel industry is basically conducted to achieve economies of scale, increase negotiating power with customers and vendors and to enter into new geographic areas. China is the world's largest producer and consumer of steel, and also, with India, has the most fragmented steel industry. The largest consumers of steel are the automotive and construction sectors, which together absorb more than 50 percent of total steel production.

Table 8.1 M&A deals in the global steel industry

Year	Volume	Value in $ billion
2005	35	135
2006	67	180
2007	73	203
2008	31	160

Source: Deloitte Report.

In 2006, the first steel mega merger took place when Arcelor and Mittal combined to form the world's largest steel company, Arcelor Mittal. In 2007, Tata Steel acquired the UK's Corus Group to emerge as the fifth largest steel producer in the world.

The Arcelor/Mittal merger

The merger between Mittal Steel and Arcelor in 2006 created the world's largest steelmaker, with annual production capacity of more than 110 million tonnes. Arcelor Mittal is the global leader in major steel markets of automobiles, construction, household appliances and packaging. The company has operations in 20 countries spanning four continents. In 2011, Arcelor Mittal had revenues of $9.4 billion and crude steel production of 91.9 million tonnes, which represented approximately 6 percent of world steel output. At the time of the merger, Arcelor was the second largest steel maker of the world. Mittal steel was the largest producer of steel.

Growth of Mittal Steel

Mittal Steel was established in 1976 by L. N. Mittal. In 2004, two sister companies in the Mittal family, LNM Holding and ISPAT International, were merged into Mittal Steel. Mittal Steel's rapid growth can be attributed to its successful consolidation strategy, focusing on multiple acquisitions of underperforming steel plants in rapidly expanding markets from Trinidad to Kazakhstan. Since 2000, Mittal Steel has acquired more than 20 steel companies worldwide, increasing its capacity tenfold during this period.

In addition, in 2004, Mittal Steel acquired the controlling interest in Companhia Siderurgica Tubarao of Brazil, and in 2005, the controlling interest in Warzawa of Poland and Sonasid of Morocco.

Table 8.2 Significant acquisitions made by Mittal Steel

Year	Company	Country
1989	Iron & Steel Co.	Trinidad and Tobago
1992	Sibalsa Steel	Mexico
1992	Siderurgica del Balsas	Mexico
1994	Sidbec Dosco	Canada
1995	Hamburger Stahlwerke	Germany
1997	Thyssen Duisburg	Germany
1998	Inland Steel	US
1999	Unimetal	France
2001	Sidex	Romania
2001	Annaba	Algeria
2003	NovaHut	Czech Republic
2004	BH Steel	Bosnia
2004	Balkan Steel	Macedonia
2004	PHS	Poland
2004	Iscor	South Africa
2005	ISG	US
2005	Kryvorizhstal	Ukraine
2005	Hunan Valin	China
2006	Stelco Subsidiaries	Canada
2006	Arcelor	Europe
2007	Sicarsta	Mexico

History of Arcelor

Arcelor was formed in 2002, when France's Usinor, Spain's Acerlia and Luxembourg's Arbed merged. The Luxembourg Government owned 5.6 percent of Arcelor. Arcelor was a major player in all its main markets, which included automotive, construction, metal processing, household appliances and packaging. In terms of turnover Arcelor was the second largest global steel manufacturer. In 2006, Arcelor acquired Dofasco, Canada's largest steel producer, for Can$5.6 billion by winning a bidding war against German giant ThyssenKrupp.

Merger highlights

In January 2006, L.N. Mittal made an unexpected €18.6 billion offer for Arcelor. The offer was swiftly and harshly rebuked by Arcelor management and a chorus of European politicians. Political passions were stirred up as the French, Luxembourg and Spanish governments strongly opposed the takeover. The Indian Government also took sides in the geopolitics of the deal.

As a part of a defense strategy against Mittal Steel, Arcelor adopted a "poison pill" involving the Dofasco Group. Arcelor transferred the ownership of Dofasco to a Netherlands-based trust in order to prevent Mittal's planned sale of the firm following any takeover. Arcelor bought in Severstal of Russia as a white knight to prevent the deal. The €13 billion deal envisaged a 32 percent stake in Arcelor for Severstal. Arcelor shareholders, including institutional investors and hedge funds, however, were not happy with the Severstal deal. Investment banks advising Mittal Steel activated shareholders across the region to unleash a shareholder rebellion. The unions too swung behind the deal as Mittal promised to make no job cuts. Mittal also capped its stake at under 45 percent and offered 12 to 18 seats on the board to independent directors, including those from the unions, and agreed to lock in on Mittal shares for five years. By mid-June the board of Arcelor was under pressure to consider the deal. Mittal raised its bid once again, taking it to 40 percent over the original offer price and a premium of 80 percent on the pre-offer price of Arcelor shares.

By June 2006, the Arcelor board had decided to go ahead with the merger with Mittal Steel and scrapped plans for Severstal Steel. Mittal Steel paid €40.37 a share for Arcelor, nearly double what the company was trading at when Mittal first made an offer in January 2006. Arcelor investors owned 50.5 percent of the new company ArcelorMittal while Mittal Steel investors held 49.5 percent. Arcelor shareholders got 13 Mittal Steel shares plus €150.60 in cash for 12 Arcelor shares. The total deal was valued at $33.7 billion. Approximately 43 percent of the shares remained within the Mittal family.

The new company ArcelorMittal had three times the capacity of its nearest rival, Nippon Steel, and a 10 percent global market share. The company was the leading steelmaker in North America, South America, Europe and Africa. The merger gave Arcelor entry into emerging markets and access to raw materials through the low-cost operations of Mittal Steel. The merger gave Mittal Steel a leadership position in the high-end steel sector in Western Europe and access to low-cost manufacturing in Brazil. Arcelor's presence was mostly in West Europe and South America where Mittal did not have a presence. Mittal was not making the kind of high-value steel such as flat products, cold-rolled and stainless steel produced by Arcelor.

Acquisitions by Tata Group

Tata Steel is a part of Tata Group, India's largest industrial conglomerate. Tata Steel was established in 1907. Tata Steel has an annual crude steel capacity of over 28 million tonnes per annum (mtpa) and is one of the world's most geographically diversified steel producers, with operations in 26 countries and a commercial presence in over 50 countries. The steel giant had a turnover of $22.8 billion in 2010.

In 2005, Tata Steel purchased Singapore-based NatSteel Ltd for $286.12 million. Tata Steel also acquired the 26 percent stake owned by NatSteel in Southern Steel Berhad, Malaysia. The NatSteel acquisition gave Tata Steel a manufacturing footprint in seven new countries, namely Singapore, China, Malaysia, Thailand, Australia, Vietnam and the Philippines. This acquisition enabled Tata Steel to enter the high-growth regions of China and South East Asia. Tata Steel was able to lower input steel costs and provide more complete steel solutions.

In the same year Tata Steel acquired Millennium Steel, Thailand for approximately $175 million. Millennium Steel had been formed through a merger of three operating companies—The Siam Iron and Steel Company, The Siam Construction Steel Company and NTS Steel Group–and was the dominant steel producer in Thailand. It had a capacity of 1.7 mtpa, producing long products for construction and engineering steel for the auto industries. This acquisition was also the part of Tata Steel's globalization initiatives to enhance its market position in South East Asia.

Tata Steel's acquisition of Corus

In 2006, Tata Steel bid for UK-based Corus in the face of fierce competition from Brazilian rival Companhia Siderurgica Nacional (CSN), and finally closed the deal by offering 608 pence a share for 1.01 billion outstanding shares. The deal was valued at $12.1 billion.

Corus was four times the size of Tata Steel, and had been established in 1999 by a merger between British Steel and Dutch Koninklige Hoogovens. Corus is primarily engaged in the manufacture of semi-finished and finished carbon steel products. It is UK's largest steel company, but had been facing financial problems with huge debts since 2003.

Tata Steel initially started with a 455 pence all-cash bid per share in October 2006. CSN made a counter-bid of 475 pence per share. Tata Steel upped its offer to value Corus at £4.7 billion, which was answered by a CSN offer of 515 pence per share. The deal was sealed when Tata Steel bid 608 pence per share, which was higher than the last bid put down by CSN by 5 pence.

Tata Steel believed that long-term synergies in manufacturing, access to global customers and R&D would result from the Corus acquisition. The deal was expected to increase Tata Steel's capacity exponentially and give it a wider customer base along with an enhanced product portfolio. The acquisition also anticipated cost savings of $350 million per year, partly through exporting cheaper inputs (slabs) from India that would be processed in Corus plants. The export of low-cost slabs from India was regarded as the key to improve Corus profitability. This acquisition was a perfect fit for Tata Steel's deintegration production strategy. The strategy was two-pronged with the focus of steel making close to raw materials (iron ore, coal, gas) and production of finished steel in markets with a high rate of GDP growth where demand for finished steel from the construction sector is high. The combination of low-cost upstream production in India with the high-end downstream processing facilities of Corus improved Corus's European operations significantly.

The strategic objective of the deal for Tata Steel was to increase capacity, and the acquisition added 19 million tonnes of capacity to Tata Steel. The acquisition also gave Tata Steel access to the mature and developed markets of Europe. Corus had highly developed R&D capabilities and multi-locational plants. But Corus was not a fully integrated steel company. Unlike Tata Steel, Corus had to source its raw materials from global markets. Corus would be able to add more value-added specialty products to Tata's product range. The merged entity became the second most geographically diversified steel company, and was the fifth largest steel company in the world.

Other major acquisitions in the steel sector

In 2007, United Steel Corporation (USC) acquired Lone Star Technologies, Inc. for $2.1 billion. This acquisition expanded the tubular product offerings and geographic footprint area for USC. USC also bought Canadian steelmaker Stelco, Inc. for about $1.1 billion and consolidated its position as a supplier to the North American automotive industry.

In 2008, Severstal, the Russian steel giant, acquired Esmark, the manufacturer and distributor of flat-rolled steel products. The acquisition was valued at $775 million. Earlier Severstal had made acquisitions in taking a controlling stake in iron ore pellet manufacturer Karelian Pellet, and production and coking plants Vorkutaugol and Kuzbassugol. Severstal had acquired Rouge Steel, an integrated steelmaking facility, in Michigan, USA in 2004. In 2006, Severstal acquired Lucchini Group, an integrated steel making facility based in Italy and France.

Additional References

1. "Forging Ahead: Fourth-quarter 2011 Global Metals Industry Mergers and Acquisitions Analysis," http://www.pwc.com/en_US/us/industrial-products/assets/forging-ahead-q4-2011-new.pdf

2. http://www.deloitte.com/assets/Dcom
3. Global/Local%20Assets/Documents/dtt_getting_back_in_the_water(1).pdf
4. http://www.steelworld.com/analysis007.pdf
5. Shankar Aiyar, "'The Art of the Deal': Cover Story, Arcelor Takeover," *India Today*, July 10, 2006, pp. 36–42.
6. James Kanter, Heather Timmons and Anand Giridharadas, "Arcelor Agrees to Mittal Takeover," www.nytimes.com/2006/06/25/business/.../25iht-steel.html?pagewanted=all
7. D. N. Mukerjea, "Battleground Arcelor," *Business World*, May 15, 2006, pp. 31–42.
8. D. N. Mukerjea, "Special Report: Outmaneuvering Arcelor," *Business World*, July 10, 2006, pp. 39–40.
9. Piya Singh, "Making Corus Work," *Business World*, February 19, 2007, p. 33.
10. Pallavi Roy, "The Man who Bought Corus and the One who Made it Worth the Buy," *Business World*, February 19, 2007, pp. 36–37.
11. Pallavi Roy and Mobis Philipose, "This is Corus," *Business World*, February 19, 2007, pp. 38–39.
12. Daksesh Pareikh, "Tata's Gambit," *Business India*, November 5, 2006, pp. 48–52.

9
Mergers and Acquisitions in the Automobile Sector

Introduction

The 1950s and 1960s were considered the golden era of the automobile, led by Ford, General Motors and Chrysler. Progress in industrialization led to the growth and production of the Japanese and German automotive markets until by the early 1980s Japan had become the world leader in US markets. In the 1990s, the world automobile industry experienced an unprecedented scale of change in the context of economic globalization. Late in the decade, the automobile industry witnessed problems of overcapacity that necessitated M&A and strategic alliances.

Consolidation in the car industry began in the early days when 200 garage-sized firms were merged into General Motors. American Motors and Simca were acquired by Chrysler. In France Citroën was acquired by Peugeot.

Most of the mega deals in the automobile sector took place in the 1990s. Restructuring in the sector has led to major consolidations like the Daimler/Chrysler union and Nissan/Renault.

The strategic drivers for mergers in the auto sector were basically for economies of scale, growth and augmentation of product ranges. There are six major alliances and groups in the automotive sector, namely GM Alliance, Ford Mazda, DCX Alliance, Toyota, VW Group and Renault Nissan. There has been an increasing focus on functional collaborations and technology and platform-sharing agreements for the purpose of reducing product development times and costs. The trend is that automotive companies are investing in strategic deals to broaden their geographic footprint and strengthen their technology portfolio. These companies are particularly expanding operations in the BRIC (Brazil, Russia, China and India) markets to establish a global presence. The leading automobile manufacturers are investing in production facilities in emerging markets like Latin America, China and Malaysia in order to reduce production costs. The trend is also observed in Europe where production centers are being shifted to new countries in Central and Eastern Europe. With respect to the auto sector, North America and Europe are mature markets and potential opportunities for growth exist in the developing markets led by China and India. Automakers from developing markets like China and India are focusing on overseas acquisitions for key technologies in the areas of propulsion, safety, advanced electronics and materials.

In short, the strategic drivers for M&A activity in the auto sector includes the scope for a broadened geographic footprint, increased market share and enhancement of technological capabilities.

The biggest US automakers—GM, Ford and Chrysler—have undertaken M&A activity or entered into commercial strategic partnerships with Japanese and European automakers in the past decade. One of the biggest mergers in the sector was the Daimler and Renault Nissan merger, undertaken as a strategic move to gain global scale and to consolidate the European automaker's position in the US market. In 2010, Daimler exchanged with Renault and Nissan a 3.1 percent stake in each other's business as a part of a global tie-up of the brands.

Ford took over Jaguar, Volvo and Land Rover, which were later sold off to Tata Motors. In 2008, Tata Motors of the Tata Group, one of India's largest conglomerates, bought the Jaguar and Land Rover brands from Ford for $2.3 billion.

In 2008 and 2009, the automobile industry was crippled by the economic recession. Three major US carmakers were bailed out by the government in order to tide them over the crisis. Emerging markets were less affected than their Western counterparts. In 2009, China overtook the US to become the world's biggest car and van market. The three top Chinese car companies in terms of revenues—SAIC GM, Shanghai Volkswagen and Shanghai GM—were all joint ventures with Shanghai Automotive Industry Corporation.

The global deals in automobile sector were valued at $48.1 billion in the year 2000. During the period 2001–2005, the trend reveals that the value of automobile deals was fluctuating. In 2006 and 2007, the value of worldwide automotive deals was $49.1 and $57 billion, respectively.[1]

The Daimler/Benz merger

Daimler AG is one of the world's biggest manufacturer of premium cars and commercial vehicles. Daimler's divisions consist of Mercedes-Benz

Cars, Daimler Trucks, Mercedes-Benz Vans, Daimler Buses and Daimler Financial Services. Its brand portfolio boasts premium automotive brand Mercedes-Benz, the brands Smart, Maybach, Freightliner, Western Star, BharatBenz, Fuso, Setra, Orion and Thomas Built Buses. In 2011, the Daimler Group had sold 2.1 million vehicles with revenues amounting to €106.5 billion.

In 1995, under the leadership of new chairman Jurgen E. Schrempp, Daimler undertook a series of strategic restructurings in order to enhance competiveness. The group divested Fokker, sold off Dornier Luftfahrt GmbH and dissolved AEG.

In 1998, a merger with Chrysler Corporation to form DaimlerChrysler was announced. It was described as a mega merger of "equals", although Daimler controlled 57 percent of the new DaimlerChrysler. Under the terms of the deal, Daimler-Benz shareholders received one share of the new company for every share they currently owned. Chrysler shareholders received 0.547 of the new company's shares for every Chrysler share they owned. The combined company had a market value of $92 billion and an estimated $130 billion in annual revenue. Daimler-Benz paid a premium of roughly $38 billion to Chrysler's shareholders. This stock swap deal was the largest transatlantic merger at that time.

In 1990, Chrysler was on the brink of bankruptcy. But later Chrysler turned itself into the lowest-cost producer in the US, specializing in sports utility vehicles, minivans and low-priced cars. In 1997, Chrysler generated $57 billons of revenue. Other product lines of Chrysler included compact cars, jeeps and commercial vehicles, which were sold under the Chrysler, Plymouth, Jeep and Dodge marques. With its Mercedes subsidiary Daimler-Benz had a major share in high-priced luxury models. Mercedes-Benz is one of the most luxurious cars and a cash cow for Daimler-Benz.

Strategic reasons

For Chrysler the deal meant entry into the European market. For Daimler-Benz the merger paved the way for the German auto giant to expand into the US. Daimler-Benz luxury vehicles had penetrated less than one percent of the American markets. Through the merger Daimler was able to add a second brand of moderately priced cars and trucks into its portfolio.

The merger hoped to achieve various synergies. The merger combined Daimler's expertise in luxury cars with Chrysler's mass market experience. Mercedes-Benz was the world leader in luxury cars with sophisticated electronic systems. But the company was not a volume car producer.

Hence Benz had a higher cost base. Chrysler had low development costs. Therefore the merger was aimed at realizing the benefits of economies of scale. Daimler had a strong global distribution network, which was expected to be leveraged by Chrysler.

Daimler-Benz wanted to broaden its product lines internationally and Chrysler wanted to leverage Daimler-Benz technology. The merger was also expected to generate cost synergy through joint R&D along with combined purchasing and manufacturing processes. The product lines were complementary in nature. Sales revenues for Daimler came mainly from Europe whereas Chrysler's sales were generated mainly in North America. The merger was expected to create cost savings of $1.41 billion in 1999.

Failure of the merger

The merger was termed as a "merger of equals" in order to avoid cultural clashes even though the merger was an acquisition of Chrysler. Though DaimlerChrysler was incorporated in Germany, it had two different headquarters: one in Germany and the other in Michigan. The merger failed to realize the expected synergies. Chrysler sustained huge losses in a slowdown of sales in the US and also as its product line was becoming increasingly outdated. Daimler tried to turn around Chrysler with a $4 billion plan to restructure Chrysler with the closure of many manufacturing facilities and employee downsizing.

One major reason for the failure of the merger was the lack of culture integration between the German Daimler and US Chrysler. Daimler-Benz had a centralized bureaucracy with an authoritative style. Chrysler had a decentralized management style with a quick decision-making process. By 2003, DaimlerChrysler's stock price had dropped by some 63 percent. Chrysler also had stakes in Mitsubishi and Hyundai, which also made heavy losses. Chrysler was carrying a huge debt in its capital structure. Distribution and retail systems remained separate on account of brand bias. It was observed that Mercedes-Benz dealers were reluctant to include Chrysler vehicles in their retail product offerings. Finally, in 2007, Daimler sold off an 80 percent stake in Chrysler to Cerberus Capital Management, a private equity investment company, for $7.4 billion. DaimlerChrysler was again renamed Daimler.

Additional References

1. http://www.reportsure.com/automotive-reports/automotive-mergers-acquisitions.aspx

2. http://articles.economictimes.indiatimes.com/2011-06-21/news/29683666_1_deal-activity-global-footprint-global-trends
3. http://www.qfinance.com/sector-profiles/automobiles
4. "Driving Value: Automotive M&A Insights 2010," http://www.pwc.com/en_GX/gx/automotive/assets/DT-11-0057-Automotive-MA_v11.pdf
5. "Extinction of the Predator: The Global Car Industry," http://www.economist.com/node/4369762
6. "Daimler-Benz AG," Standard & Poor's Stock Reports, New York: Standard & Poor's, Inc., July 21, 1997.
7. http://mba.tuck.dartmouth.edu/pdf/2002-1-0071.pdf
8. http://www.reportsure.com/automotive-reports/automotive-mergers-acquisitions.aspx
9. http: /money.cnn.com/1998/05/07/deals/benz/
10. http:www.theautochannel.com/news/press/date19980507/press012154.html
11. http://www.renault.com/en/groupe/1-alliance-renault-nissan/pages/1-alliance-renault-nissan.aspx.
12. Eugen Bogenschütz, "Daimler–Chrysler Merger," *International Tax Review*, 02/2000, p. 15.
13. "Daimler-Benz and Chrysler Merge," *The Auto Channel*, http://www.theautochannel.com/news/press/date/19980507/press012154.html

10
Mergers and Acquisitions in the Consumer Goods Sector

Introduction

Consumer goods companies are using M&A as a strategy to expand global reach, enter new markets and consolidate the focus on their core brands. Acquisitions are also used to vertically integrate and optimize supply chain operations. Acquisitions in the sector are also meant for securing critical resources or proprietary technologies in certain product categories. In the context of post-economic crisis, companies in the food, drink, consumer goods and retail sectors are actively involved in M&A activity, especially in developing nations. Pepsi and Nestlé have made nine and seven acquisitions respectively in developing nations during the period 2006–2010. In developing markets like India, China and Russia, M&A deals are driven by the consolidation of smaller companies.

After the implementation of the NAFTA and GATT agreements, many companies in the food and beverages industry have focused on M&A. These mergers have been for enhancing the advantage of existing distribution systems or underutilized plant capacity. During the period 2005–2007, approximately 125 mergers and acquisitions took place in the snack food industry.

Post-2008, the sector witnessed increased M&A activity on account of the need to access a broader customer base, leverage economies of scale and create stronger brand awareness. The availability of private equity capital and corporate cash along with the loosening of lending standards are emerging as catalysts for M&A activity. In 2010, the top ten food and beverages companies collectively held $30.1 billion in cash balances which was an increase of 15 percent compared to 2006.

According to the E&Y *Consumer Report 2010*, M&A in the global consumer goods industry stood at $101.6 billion in 2010 compared to $45.7 billion in 2009.

In one of the largest deals, in 2010, KKR/Vestar Capital Group and Centerview Group acquired Del Monte Foods for $53 billion. In 2008, the consumer services industry announced 774 M&A deals. In 2009, the number of deals fell to 582, while in 2010, the number of announced deals was 786. In 2011, Kraft acquired UK confectioner Cadbury for $19.6 billion.

In 2010, both Coca-Cola and PepsiCo. acquired significant portions of their bottling operations in order to reduce their structural costs and enhance the facilities for the testing, launching and scaling of new products. The Coca-Cola Company paid $12.3 billion for Coca-Cola enterprises, while PepsiCo. paid $14.8 billion to acquire Pepsi Bottling Group and Pepsi Americas. In another large deal Kraft acquired Cadbury for $19.6 billion to gain access to new geographic markets and capitalize on synergies associated with complementary product portfolios. The deal

Table 10.1 Major M&As in the consumer goods industry

	Acquirer	Target	Amount in billions
2006	Procter & Gamble	Gillette	$57
2008	InBev	Anheuser Busch	$52
1989	KKR	RJR Nabisco	$25
2007	Groupe Danone	Royal Numico	£12.3
2000	Unilever	Bestfoods	$20.3
2010	Kraft Foods	Cadbury	$19.6
1988	Philip Morris	Kraft	$12.9
2008	Heineken	Scottish & Newcastle (S&N)	$15.3
2006	Cerberus	Albertson	$17.4
2005	Goal Acquisitions	Allied Domecq	$14.4
2010	Coca-Cola	Coca-Cola Enterprises	$12.2
2008	Altria	UST Inc.	$10.4
2000	Diageo Pernod Ricard	Seagram Spirits and Wines	$8.15
2009	PepsiCo Inc.	Pepsi Bottling Group, Pepsi Americas	$7.8
2008	Pernod Ricard	Vin & Spirit (V&S)	£5.7
2007	Kraft Foods	Groupe Danone	$7.6
2007	Nestlé	Gerber (Novartis)	$5.5
2007	Coca-Cola	Energy Brands	$4.10
2002	SAB	Miller	$3.48
2005	SAB Miller	Coors	$3.4
2008	Smucker's	Folgers (Kraft Foods)	$2.95

was expected to realize revenue synergies of $1 billion and cost synergies of $0.75 billion by 2013.

In 2010, the number of private equity activities increased 45 percent relative to 2009. Significant M&A activity resulted in consolidation in consumer sectors such as athletic shoes and apparel, brewing, tobacco, consumer durables and food service distribution.

Globalization, consolidation and changing consumer preferences are shaping the beverage industry. Acquisitions of both mega breweries and microbreweries continue to occur globally.

The growth strategy of Kraft Foods through M&A

Kraft Foods is the world's second largest food company, with annual revenues of $49.2 billion. Krafts has a presence in 170 countries. Its iconic brands include Cadbury, Jacobs, Kraft, LU, Maxwell House, Milka, Nabisco, Oreo, Oscar Mayer, Philadelphia and Trident. These brands generate more than $1 billion in annual revenues.

M&A milestones

Year	Highlights
1928	Kraft Cheese company acquires Phoenix Cheese Corporation, maker of Philadelphia brand cream cheese.
1929	Postum Company, maker of Post cereals, changes its name to General Foods after acquiring several brands, including Baker's Maxwell House coffee, Minute tapioca and Jell-O.
1953	General Foods acquires Perkins Products Company, maker of Kool Aid powdered soft drinks.
1981	General Foods acquires Oscar Mayer & Co. Inc.
1985	Philip Morris Co. purchases General Foods for $5.6 billion.
1988	Kraft Inc. becomes a part of Philips Morris Cos, which purchases Kraft for $12.9 billion.
1989	General Foods and Kraft merge to become Kraft General Foods.
1990	Kraft General Foods International acquires Jacobs Suchard AG for $4.2 billion.
2000	Philip Morris Cos acquires Nabisco Holdings for $19.2 billion and integrates it into Kraft Foods.

2003	Kraft acquires the Back to Nature brand cereal and granola business.
2007	Kraft Foods acquires the global biscuit business of Groupe Danone for $7.6 billion.
2007	Kraft Foods is spun off from parent company Altria Group Inc. (Philip Morris renamed) and becomes fully independent.
2008	Kraft Foods divests its Post cereal business for $2.6 billion.
2010	Kraft Foods divests its Pizza business for $3.7 billion.
2010	Kraft Foods acquires Cadbury Plc for $19.6 billion.

Source: Kraft website.

In 1985, Philip Morris the tobacco and consumer products company, acquired General Foods Corp. for an estimated $5.6 billion. The deal made Philip Morris the largest US consumer-products company, with $23 billion in sales. Under the terms of the agreement, Philip Morris acquired 8.5 million shares of General Foods at $120 a share.

In 1988, Philip Morris acquired Krafts for approximately $13 billion. The Kraft acquisitions gave Morris a huge dairy presence along with well-known brands such as Breyer's, Sealtest, Breakstone and Miracle Whip. At the time of the acquisition, the combined company became the world's largest consumer goods company, displacing Unilever. In 1989, Krafts and General Foods were merged to form Kraft General Foods. The merged firm had a powerful distribution network, particularly for fresh foods. Kraft had acquired many food service distributors in previous years and made General Foods strong in the dry and frozen and refrigerated parts of the supermarket sector. In 1990, Kraft General Foods acquired Jacobs Suchard AG of Zurich, the world's third largest 3 coffee and chocolate company. Before the acquisition, Philip Morris had been disadvantaged in its competition with Nestlé because of the lack of chocolates in its portfolio of food businesses.

In January 1995, Kraft General Foods became Kraft Foods, Inc. and was reorganized into a single operating company.

In the 1980s, the cigarette maker RJ Reynolds merged with snack company Nabisco Brands, which owned brands like Ritz and Oreo, to form RJR Nabisco. In 1988, after a fierce bidding war, Kohlberg Kravis Robert took over RJR Nabisco for $25 billion. In 2000, Kraft acquired Nabisco Brands, which included some of the best-known cookies and crackers in the world, including Chips, Ahoy! Oreo and Ritz, for $19.2 billion and integrated it into Kraft Foods. In 2007, Kraft Foods acquired French giant Groupe Danone for $7.2 billion in cash. The deal strengthened Kraft's snack business and added new products. Kraft Foods also secured access to a strong manufacturing and distribution center in Europe with the acquisition of 36 factories.

In 2007, Altria spun off its Kraft Foods subsidiary to its shareholders by distributing the remaining stake of 88 percent of the shares to Altria shareholders. In 2010, Kraft Foods bought British confectionery maker Cadbury for about $19.6 billion. Under the terms of the deal, Kraft paid 500 pence in cash and offered 0.184 new Kraft shares for each share of Cadbury, which amounted to $13.80 for each Cadbury share. The deal was the largest European food and beverage deal to date. The combined new company became the world's top sweet maker, unseating Mars Wrigley, and brought under one roof Cadbury's Dairy Milk chocolate and Trident gum along with Kraft's Milka, Toblerone and Terry's chocolate brands. Cadbury offered Kraft greater access to the sharply growing emerging markets like India and Latin America as well as some of the world's leading chocolate, sweets and chewing gum brands. The combined group had more than 40 confectionary brands and became the top player in the chocolate and sugar confectionary segments. The group also positioned itself as number two in the high-growth gum segment.

The acquisition of Gillette by Procter & Gamble

In 2006, Procter & Gamble (P&G) bought Gillette in a $57 billion deal that created the largest consumer goods company in the world. P&G paid 0.975 share of its common stock for each share of Gillette common stock. The deal valued Gillette at about $54 per share, which represented a premium of 18 percent for Gillette shares. The new combined company, with over $60 billion in revenues, overtook Unilever as the global leader in consumer products. The deal added Gillette's Duracell battery, Right Guard deodorant and line of razors to P&G's portfolio of more than 300 brands. With this acquisition, P&G became a powerhouse in male grooming products.

It was hoped that the deal would also counter the downward pressure on margins that firms faced when expanding aggressively into markets in developing countries where they had to launch lower-priced products to gain market share. The deal enabled both Gillette and Procter & Gamble to secure better shelf space and distribute products more cheaply. The acquisition boosted P&G's Crest oral care business, which had earlier seen growth from the acquisition of Spin Brush in

2001. In 2003, P&G had acquired Germany's Wella AG hair care line and Clairol.

Acquisitions by Coca-Cola

Coca-Cola had acquired the beverages company Minute Maid in 1960 and the Indian cola brand Thums Up in 1993. It had also acquired the soft drinks company Barq's in 1995. In 2001, Coca-Cola acquired the Odwalla brand of fruit juices. In 2007, the company acquired Fuze Beverages for an estimated $250 million. In 1982, Coca-Cola made its only non-beverage acquisition by purchasing Columbia Pictures for $692 million, which it sold off to Sony for $1.5 billion in 1989.

In 2007, Coca-Cola acquired Energy Brands (Glaceau) Inc. for $4.1 billion in cash. The acquisition boosted the company's presence in the fast-growing "enhanced water" and energy drink markets. Coca-Cola acquisition gave it the full range of Energy Brands products, which included Vitaminwater, Smart water and Vitaminenergy.

In 2010, Coca-Cola purchased the North American operations of bottler Coca-Cola Enterprises Inc. in a deal valued at $12.3 billion. The shareholders of the target company received $10 and one share in the new bottling company for each share they held. The acquisition was expected to result in cost savings and additional revenue opportunities of $350 million over a four-year period. Cola majors sell beverage concentrate and syrup to licensed bottlers who add water and other ingredients and sell the mixture in bottles and cans.

Acquisitions by PepsiCo

In 1977–1978, PepsiCo acquired Pizza Hut and Taco Bell with the aim of becoming the world's largest fast food vendor. In 1986, PepsiCo acquired Kentucky Fried Chicken (KFC) in order to bring the marketing and new product development expertise of Pepsi to KFC products. But these acquisitions failed for various reasons. Later, in 1997, PepsiCo spun off KFC, Pizza Hut and Taco Bell into a separate corporation known as Tricon Global Restaurants Inc. In 1999, PepsiCo spun off its capital-intensive operations to create Pepsi Bottling Group Inc.

In 2010, Pepsi took control of its two biggest bottlers, Pepsi Bottling Group and Pepsi Americas, for about $7.8 billion. This acquisition was expected to garner about $400 million annually in cost savings.

In 2011, PepsiCo completed the acquisition of the leading Russian branded food and beverage company, Wimm-Bill-Dann, for approximately $3.8 billion.

PepsiCo has made multiple acquisitions during the period 2006–2010. The company had acquired nine target firms in European region and South America. In 2008 and 2010, PepsiCo acquired three firms in Russia with the biggest deal being the Wimm-Bill-Dann Foods' acquisition valued at $3.8 billion. PepsiCo had also acquired companies in Mexico, Ukraine, Serbia, Argentina, Bulgaria and Brazil.

Multiple acquisitions by Nestlé

Nestlé, the largest food company in the world, itself was the product of the merger of the Anglo Swiss Milk Company and Société Farine Lactée Henri Nestlé in the year 1905. During the 1980s, Nestlé undertook a number of acquisitions, including the American food giant Carnation, British confectionery company Rowntree Mackintosh, and the Willy Wonka candy brand. In the 1990s, Nestlé acquired mineral water company San Pellegrino and Spillers Pet Foods. Nestlé acquired the animal feed company Ralston Purina in 2002. In the same year, Nestlé merged its US ice cream business into Dreyers and acquired Chef America, well known for the brand Hot Pockets. In 2005, Nestlé acquired Greek company Delta Ice Cream for €240 million. In 2006, Nestlé became the world's largest ice cream producer by acquiring full ownership of Dreyer. In 2006, Nestlé purchased the Medical Nutrition division of Novartis Pharmaceutical for $2.5 billion.

In 2007, Nestlé acquired the US Gerber baby food business of Swiss drug maker Novartis AG for $5.5 billion in cash. According to a Euro Monitor Report, Gerber had a 75 percent share of the US prepared baby food market in 2005. The acquisition was undertaken to expand Nestlé's nutrition business in the US as Nestlé lacked a baby food brand there, though it had a large portfolio of baby brands. In 2010, Nestlé purchased Kraft's North American frozen pizza business for $3.7 billion. In 2011, Nestlé announced the purchase of a 60 percent stake of the Chinese sweets company Hsu Fu Chi International Ltd for $1.7 billion.

In the year 2010, Nestlé acquired four companies in countries like China, Guatemala, Ukraine and Turkey. Yunnan Dashan Drinks of China was acquired for $10 million. During 2007–2008 Nestlé had acquired three companies in Russia, Israel and South Korea.

Acquisitions by Unilever

Unilever was formed in 1930 by the merger between the Dutch margarine maker Unie and British soap maker Lever Brothers. In the past four decades, Unilever has undertaken a series of acquisitions. In 1984, it acquired Brooke Bond and enhanced the company's tea interests. In 1987, the acquisition of Chesebrough Pond's Inc. strengthened Unilever's position in the world skin care market.

In 2000, Unilever made 19 acquisitions in addition to the purchase of Bestfoods. The total purchase consideration for businesses other than Bestfoods was approximately €4451 million. The acquisition of Bestfoods made Unilever's foods business the world's second largest after Nestlé. The deal was valued at approximately $20.3 billion based on the number of shares.

In 2008, Unilever acquired Inmarko, the leading Russian ice cream company.

In 2009, Unilever acquired the Romanian ice cream brand Napoca. Also in 2009, Unilever acquired the global TIGI professional hair product business and its Advanced Education Academies for €411.5 million, and added a range of established salon brands to the company's consumer hair care portfolio. In the same year, Unilever acquired the sauces business of Baltimor Holding ZAO, the leading ketchup business in Russia.

In 2010, Unilever signed an asset purchase agreement with Norwegian dairy group TINE to acquire the activities of Diplom–Is ice cream operations in Denmark. Other major acquisitions in 2010 included that of EVGA's ice cream brands and distribution network in Greece and the Sara Lee Personal Care and European Laundry business for €1.2 billion.

In 2011, Unilever completed the acquisition of Alberto Culver Company, which distributes and markets leading beauty care and other personal products, primarily in the US. Unilever paid $3.7 billion in cash for the acquisition. With this acquisition, Unilever became the world's leading company in hair conditioning, the second largest in shampoo and the third largest in styling.

Other major acquisitions

In 2008, the Belgium-based brewer InBev completed its $52 billion takeover of US's Anheuser Busch to create the world's largest brewer. Anheuser makes Budweiser, the most popular beer in the US, while InBev produces Stella Artois and Beck's. InBev itself was formed by the merger between Brazil's AmBev and Belgium's Interbrew. The combination created the global leader in beer and one of the top five consumer product companies in the world. The combination was renamed Anheuser Busch InBev to reflect the heritage and traditions of Anheuser Busch. Under the terms of merger agreement, all shares of Anheuser Busch were acquired for $70 per share in cash. The deal was expected to generate annual savings of $1.5 billion. The new company, with a portfolio of over 200 brands, was geographically diversified with its focus in both developed and developing markets.

In 2007, Groupe Danone, the maker of Dannon yogurt and Evian waters, acquired Royal Numico NV for $16.8 billion. The addition of Numico made Danone one of the world's largest players in the fast-growing baby food industry. Numico was the world's third largest seller of baby food, controlling a 10 percent stake in the world market.

In 2008, the UK brewer Scottish & Newcastle was acquired for $15.4 billion by Carlsberg and Heineken joint venture Sunrise Acquisitions Ltd. This takeover gave Sunrise Acquisitions a strategic leadership position in brewing in Europe.

In 2006, Supervalu, CVS/pharmacy and Cerberus Capital Management purchased Albertsons for $17.4 billion. In the deal, Supervalu and Cerberus split Albertsons roughly 50/50, with Supervalu's batch being spun off as New Albertsons Inc. and Cerberus' as Albertsons LLC.

In 2005, the beverages major Pernod Ricard acquired Allied Domecq in a friendly takeover. The transaction was made through wholly owned subsidiary Goal Acquisitions Ltd. With this acquisition Pernod Ricard became the second largest spirits and wines company worldwide behind Diageo. In 2008, Pernod Ricard acquired Vin & Sprit, and became the co-leader of the global wine and spirits industry. Vin & Sprit was the owner of the Absolut brand, the global leader in the premium vodka category.

In 2008, the Altria Group purchased UST Inc. for $10.3 billion, with brands like Copenhagen and Skoal snuff, and emerged as the biggest seller of smokeless tobacco ahead of Reynolds American Inc.

In 2000, Pernod Ricard jointly with Diageo acquired Seagram Spirits and Wine from Vivendi Universal for approximately $8.15 billion in cash, on a debt-free basis. Pernod Ricard contributed approximately $3.15 billion or 38.6 percent of the purchase price. Through this acquisition Pernod Ricard added brands like Chivas Regal, Glen Grant, Royal Salute and Extra Dry Gin to its portfolio.

In 2002, South African Breweries (SAB) acquired Miller Brewing from Philip Morris for $5.6 billion, comprising $3.6 billion in stock and Miller's debt of $2 billion. The acquisition positioned the newly formed SABMiller as the world's second largest brewer behind Anheuser Busch Co.

In 2007, SAB Miller and Molson Coors Brewing, the US's second and third ranked brewers, merged their operations in the US and Puerto Rico. The joint venture, called MillerCoors, was expected to result in annual cost savings of approximately $500 million.

Additional References

1. "M&A Deals in Global Consumer Goods Sector to Pick Up: KPMG," *Press Trust of India*, September 19, 2010, http://business-standard.com/india/news/ma-deals-in-global-consumer-goods-sector-to-pick-up-kpmg/109102/on
2. http://www.finance-ol.com/2011/02/mergers-and-acquisitions-last-year-double-the-global-consumer-goods-industry/
3. http://www.grantthornton.com/portal/site/gtcom/menuitem.91c078ed5c0ef4ca80cd8710033841ca/?vgnextoid=cfca69397b602310VgnVCM1000003a8314acRCRD&vgnextfmt=default
4. Intellinet One Source Report, February 28, 2011.
5. Mergermarket Report, February 24, 2011.
6. "M&A in Consumer Business: Challenging Times, Emerging Opportunities," http://www.deloitte.com/assets/Dcom-Philippines/Local%20Assets/Documents/us_ma_challenging_times_cppov_051411.pdf
7. David Jones and Brad Dorfman, "Kraft Snares Cadbury for $19.6 billion," http://www.reuters.com/article/2010/01/19/us-cadbury-idUSTRE60H1N020100119
8. "Kraft Buys Cadbury for £11.9bn," http://www.telegraph.co.uk/finance/newsbysector/retailandconsumer/7027042/Kraft-buys-Cadbury-for-11.9bn-a-QandA.html
9. http://www.tompkinsinc.com/industries/mergers-acquisitions/mergers-acquisitions-consumer-products.asp
10. "Philip Morris Agrees to Buy General Foods," http://articles.chicagotribune.com/1985-09-28/business/8503060172_1_hamish-maxwell-philip-morris-headquarters-in-rye-brook
11. Claudia H. Deutsch, "Case Study: The Philip Morris–Kraft merger; Why Bigness May Not Matter," http://www.nytimes.com/1988/10/23/business/case-study-the-philip-morris-kraft-merger-why-bigness-may-not-matter.html?pagewanted=all&src=pm
12. Chris Isidore, "P&G to Buy Gillette for $57B," http://money.cnn.com/2005/01/28/news/fortune500/pg_gillette/
13. http://www.msnbc.msn.com/id/6878219/ns/business-us_business/t/procter-gamble-buy-gillette-billion/
14. http://www.cbsnews.com/2100-201_162-669959.html
15. http://articles.marketwatch.com/2007-05-25/news/30784675_1_muhtar-kent-chief-executive-neville-isdell-glaceau
16. Chris Burritt and Duane D. Stanford, "Coca-Cola to Purchase Bottler in $12.3 billion Deal," February 25, 2010, http://www.bloomberg.com/apps/news?pid=newsarchive&sid=ayIm0dQClBNA
17. www.pepsico.com
18. http://en.wikipedia.org/wiki/Nestl%C3%A9
19. http://articles.marketwatch.com/2007-04-12/news/30779502_1_nestle-shares-nestle-sa-nescafe
20. http://www.unilever.com/mediacentre/pressreleases/2011/UnilevercompletesAlbertoculveracquisition.aspz
21. http://www.corporatewatch.org/?lid=257
22. http://findarticles.com/p/articles/mi_m3374/is_9_22/ai_63609885/

23. http://news.bbc.co.uk/2/hi/7735953.stm
24. http://www.ab-inbev.com/documents/press_release.pdf
25. http://www.msnbc.msn.com/id/19681627/ns/business-world_business/t/danone-offers-dutch-baby-food-maker/
26. http://www.bloomberg.com/apps/news?pid=newsarchive&sid=ab6rmcKnyrK8
27. http://money.cnn.com/2002/05/30/news/deals/miller_sab/index.htm

11
Mergers and Acquisitions in the Airline Industry

Introduction

Airline industry mergers happen in line with changes in the dynamic economic conditions of the aviation industry. The nature of international aviation has changed dramatically as international markets have been gradually deregulated. Mergers are considered to be an efficient response to deregulation. Deregulation of the airline industry has also led to the rise of low-cost airlines. The airline industry is a cyclical industry. Airline mergers take place basically for financial survival and to reduce overcapacity.

The airline industry is historically a low profit margin industry that is very sensitive to the global economy. The airline industry as a whole has made cumulative losses in its 120 years of existence. More than 100 airlines have filed for bankruptcy since 1979. The profits in the good years are generally low, in the range of 2 to 3 percent, while in times of recession profitability is severely affected. Airline mergers also take place for market accessibility and profitability. Hampered by overcapacity, price competition and economic recession, several top airline carriers, particularly in the US, filed for bankruptcy protection early in the past decade.

There are basically two types of models in the industry. The classical network carriers have a complex hub-and-spoke network (large airports with connections with many destinations), while the low-cost carriers only have a point-to-point network (from airport to airport and no transfers). These airlines are basically smaller companies and focus on specific profitable routes. Major examples of network carriers are British Airways (UK), Lufthansa (GER) and Air France-KLM etc. Southwest Airlines is the pioneer among the low-cost airlines. The low-cost carriers have been successful in capturing market share from the network carriers. A trend observed is that classical network carriers have acquired low-cost carriers in order to adapt the low-cost business model. So Lufthansa has an investment stake in US low-cost carrier JetBlue Airways. Another example is Air France KLM acquiring low-cost airline VLM for short-haul routes to London.

One of the strategic motives for M&As is to gain market power on a particular hub and spoke that could become a profit driver. Domestic airline mergers are considered as a means to create significant domestic route networks and cut costs. Global airline mergers could result in matching international routes with domestic route networks and creating a global hub and spoke system that can lead to lowering the cost of providing international flight services.

The merger of two overlapping networks has immense potential for anti-competitive effects, especially on overlapping non-stop (hub–hub) routes and overlapping connecting routes.

Strategic alliances have also emerged as an alternative to mergers and acquisitions in the industry. Bilateral airline partnerships and strategic alliances have been able to overcome regulatory restrictions to some extent. Three major alliances—Star Alliance, Oneworld and SkyTeam—represent 70 percent of international scheduled traffic, according to *IATA Report 2010*.

Mega mergers in the airline industry

The Delta Airlines/Northwest Airlines merger

In 2008, Delta Airlines and Northwest Airlines merged to create the world's largest airline, named Delta Airlines at the time of the merger. Prior to the merger, Delta was the world's third largest carrier and Northwest the fifth largest, but the combined company was bigger than American Airlines, the previous largest carrier. The new global giant had more than 800 jets, 6400 daily flights and nearly $32 billion in annual revenue. The combined airlines were valued at $17.7 billion. Northwest shareholders received 1.25 new Delta shares for each Northwest share.

The deal combined two big airlines with complementary routes, especially in the Northeast, South and West of the US. Delta customers benefitted from Northwest's greater service to Asian markets. Northwest's customers benefitted from Delta's strengths across the Caribbean, Latin America, Europe, the Middle East and Africa. Delta and Northwest's complementary networks and common membership in the Sky Team helped the integration of the merger. The merger created a global US carrier that could compete with foreign airlines. The merger led to more destinations being available for customers.

The new combined airline had major hubs in Atlanta, Detroit, Minneapolis/St Paul, New York, Amsterdam and Tokyo. Delta Airlines inherited numerous Airbus aircraft as a result of the merger. Delta had the largest fleets of Boeing 757s and Boeing 767s, and had been the largest US operator of the Airbus A330. In 2005, both Delta and Northwest had filed for bankruptcy protection owing to mounting losses and emerged as leaner carriers following cost control measures. While in the period of bankruptcy, Delta had fended off a hostile takeover bid by US Airways.

The Air France/KLM merger

Air France was created by a merger of several French airline companies in 1933. In 2004, Air France and Dutch KLM merged to create Europe's leading airline group, serving a total of 326 destinations worldwide. Air France-KLM Airlines became the holding company for Air France and KLM Royal Dutch Airlines. Both KLM and Air France continued to operate as separate operating companies with their own brand identities. They followed a two-hub strategy based around Paris Charles de Gaulle (CDG) and Amsterdam Schiphol. Air France was the dominant partner in the deal. Both Air France and KLM were members of the Sky Team airline alliance.

The merger was expected to result in cost savings of €220 million ($265 million) to €260 million per year after three years and €385–495 million by the fifth year after the merger. The deal involved a share swap valuing KLM at €784 million ($900 million), which was a premium of 77 percent to its average market value over the three-month period prior to the merger announcement. KLM and Air France were placed under a new common holding company. The combined airlines had revenues of €19 billion. The merger strengthened the Sky Team Alliance, which lagged behind One World.

The United Airlines/Continental merger

United Airlines was founded as a mail carrier in 1926, while Continental was established in 1934. The merger created the world's biggest airline based on the number of passenger miles flown. Both United Airlines and Continental were loss-making airlines. The stock swap deal was valued at $3.2 billion and expected to deliver savings of more than $1 billion a year. Together the combined airlines flew to 370 destinations worldwide, flying more than 144 million passengers a year to 59 countries. United is strong in the US West and the Asia Pacific region. Continental had a huge presence in Southern and Eastern states, with a broad network of flights to Latin America. Both airlines had little geographic overlap, and both had transatlantic routes to London.

The Southwest Airlines acquisition of Air Tran Holdings

In 2011, the low-cost carrier Southwest Airlines completed the acquisition of Orlando-based smaller rival Air Tran Airways for $1.4 billion. This acquisition resulted in the creation of the most expansive network of any low-cost carrier in the US. The deal facilitated Southwest's reach beyond the continental US by expansion into the Mexican and Caribbean regions. Southwest was five times larger than Trans. The combined airlines could fly more than 100 million passengers a year out of more than 100 airports in the US, Caribbean and Mexico regions. The acquisition enabled Southwest to gain a foothold in virtually every large and mid-sized US city.

Southwest also bought Muse Air and Morris Air in the 1980s and ATA's assets in the year 2008.

Other major acquisitions

In 2005, US Airways Group merged with America West Holdings Inc., combining an East Coast route network with one in the Western US. The deal was the first merger attempt among the top ten domestic airlines since the September 11, 2001 terrorist attack. Through this acquisition, America West Airlines rescued the beleaguered carrier US Airways from possible bankruptcy liquidation. America West was eighth largest US carrier and US Airways the sixth largest at the time of the merger. America West was valued at $6.12 a share. The airlines had little overlap. America West being centered in the West and US Airways operations based in the East.

In one of the biggest examples of regional integration, the Santiago, Chile-based LAN Airlines acquired Brazil's TAM for $6.5 billion to form the LATAM Airlines Group. This acquisition created the largest airline in Latin America.

The merger between British Airways and Iberia in 2010 created Europe's third largest airline and the sixth largest in the world by revenues. This merger was the first step toward the creation of a multinational, multi-brand airline group. Both airlines retained their strong brands and had complementary networks. The combined group had a network of 204 destinations.

In 2007, Air India, the national flag carrier of India, absorbed the domestic national carrier Indian Airlines. The merged airline became almost three times the size of its nearest domestic rival, Jet Airways. Air India is also a member of Star Alliance.

Additional References

1. Marilyn Adams and Dan Reed, "World's Largest Airline: Delta, Northwest in Merger Deal," http://www.usatoday.com/travel/flights/2008-04-14-delta-northwest-merge_N.htm
2. http://airtravel.about.com/od/airlines/a/dlnwmerge.htm
3. http://www.guardian.co.uk/business/2010/sep/17/united-continental-merger-agreement
4. http://news.bbc.co.uk/2/hi/business/3480173.stm
5. http://www.flightglobal.com/news/articles/air-france-klm-get-merger-approval-182217/
6. http://www.economist.com/node/2098740
7. http://www.economywatch.com/world-industries/airline/mergers.html
8. http://www.guardian.co.uk/business/2010/sep/17/united-continental-merger-agreement
9. http://www.bbc.co.uk/news/10095080
10. http://www.usatoday.com/money/industries/travel/2010-09-27-southwest-airtran-merger_N.htm
11. http://www.usatoday.com/money/biztravel/2005-05-19-merger_x.htm
12. http://latintrade.com/2011/02/mergers-acquisitions-deals-of-the-year-2010
13. http://www.centreforaviation.com/analysis/british-airways-and-iberia-merger-completed-planning-to-add-more-airlines-to-the-group-44282

References

1 Mergers and Acquisitions in the Pharmaceutical Industry

1. It is said that almost 75 percent of all new drugs coming to market are merely imitations of existing medications. Derivative medications—or "me-too" drugs as they have been called—have identical, or only slightly different, chemical compounds as drugs already on the market, and thus have little or no benefits over their predecessors. Yet drug companies spend billions marketing them. This is because "me-too" drugs are invariably for common ailments such as heartburn or arthritis, with a huge potential target market. An extensive, well-executed marketing campaign for a "me-too" drug (think "little purple pill") can mean a windfall for the manufacturer. The first blockbuster drug was Tagamet, an ulcer medication approved by the Food and Drug Administration (FDA) in 1977. A groundbreaking medication, it relieved ulcer pain better than any drug before it. Its successor, on the other hand, Zantac, which came to market in 1983, could be described as the first "me-too" drug. Many of these "me-too" drugs have become blockbusters, for example, AstraZeneca's Nexium, a medication for severe acid reflux disease (heartburn) introduced in 2001.
2. There were two main reasons for motivations for purchasing PBMs. First, pharmaceutical firms thought that owning a PBM could help ensure that their products were on the formulary list—a list of drugs that determined if insurance companies, health maintenance organizations (HMOs) and hospitals would reimburse the patient for the drug. Where comparable drugs existed, PBMs were using formularies to gain price concessions from drug companies The second reason was to acquire the vast information that PBMs collect on pharmaceutical usage and the skills in analyzing these data.
3. http://www.hoganlovells.com
4. GSK website.
5. http://www.nber.org/chapters/c8653.pdf

2 Mergers and Acquisitions in the Telecommunications Industry

1. In 1982, the US Department of Justice concluded a 13-year antitrust suit against the world's largest corporation, American Telephone and Telegraph Company (AT&T).
2. http://www.att.com/gen/investor-relations?pid=5711
3. http://mobilizeeverything.com/news
4. LTE, short for Long Term Evolution, is considered by many to be the obvious successor to the current generation of UMTS 3G technology, which is based upon WCDMA, HSDPA, HSUPA and HSPA. LTE is not a replacement for UMTS in the way that UMTS was a replacement for GSM, but rather an update to the

UMTS technology that will enable it to provide significantly faster data rates for both uploading and downloading.

7 Mergers and Acquisitions in the Finance Sector

1. http://www.simcorp.dk/Home/Journal/No2-Tableofcontents/MA-economics.aspx
2. http://www.federalreserve.gov/pubs/feds/2002/200247/200247pap.pdf
3. L. H. Meyer, "Mergers and Acquisitions in Banking and Other Financial Services," 1998, www.federalreserve.gov/boarddocs/testimony/1998/19980603.htm
4. *European Central Bank Report 2000.*
5. http://www.alacrastore.com/mergers-acquisitions/Citigroup_Inc-1003632

9 Mergers and Acquisitions in the Automobile Sector

1. PwC reports, Thomson Reuters reports.

Index

Druck:
Canon Deutschland Business Services GmbH
im Auftrag der KNV-Gruppe
Ferdinand-Jühlke-Str. 7
99095 Erfurt